B L O O M' S

HOW TO WRITE ABOUT

Homer

JAMEY HECHT

Introduction by Harold Bloom

BLOOM'S
LITERARY CRITICISM
An imprint of Infobase Publishing

Bloom's How to Write about Homer

Bloom's Literary Criticism
An imprint of Infobase Publishing
132 West 31st Street
New York, NY 10001

Library of Congress Cataloging-in-Publication Data
Hecht, Jamey.
    Bloom's how to write about Homer / Jamey Hecht ; introduction by Harold Bloom.
        p. cm. — (Bloom's how to write about literature)
    Includes bibliographical references and index.
    ISBN 978-1-60413-716-3 (hardcover)
    1. Homer—Criticism and interpretation. 2. Epic poetry, Greek—History and criticism.
3. Criticism—Authorship. I. Bloom, Harold. II. Title.
    PA4037.A5H43 2010
    883'.01—dc22   2010015753

Bloom's Literary Criticism books are available at special discounts when purchased in bulk quantities for businesses, associations, institutions, or sales promotions. Please call our Special Sales Department in New York at (212)967-8800 or (800)322-8755.

You can find Bloom's Literary Criticism on the World Wide Web at http://www.chelseahouse.com

Text design by Annie O'Donnell
Cover design by Ben Peterson
Composition by Mary Susan Ryan-Flynn
Cover printed by Art Print Company, Taylor, PA
Book printed and bound by Maple Press, York, PA
Date printed: October 2010
Printed in the United States of America

10 9 8 7 6 5 4 3 2 1

CONTENTS

SERIES
INTRODUCTION

BLOOM's How to Write about Literature series is designed to inspire students to write fine essays on great writers and their works. Each volume in the series begins with an introduction by Harold Bloom, meditating on the challenges and rewards of writing about the volume's subject author. The first chapter then provides detailed instructions on how to write a good essay, including how to find a thesis; how to develop an outline; how to write a good introduction, body text, and conclusions; how to cite sources; and more. The second chapter provides a brief overview of the issues involved in writing about the subject author and then a number of suggestions for paper topics, with accompanying strategies for addressing each topic. Succeeding chapters cover the author's major works.

The paper topics suggested in this book are open ended, and the brief strategies provided are designed to give students a push forward on the writing process rather than a road map to success. The aim of the book is to pose questions, not answer them. Many different kinds of papers could result from each topic. As always, the success of each paper will depend completely on the writer's skill and imagination.

HOW TO WRITE
ABOUT HOMER:
INTRODUCTION

by Harold Bloom

THE POET-REDACTOR who presumably put together the Homeric epics in the eighth century B.C.E. had to be a person of considerable genius, haunted by the poetry of the past. He or she was the peer of the Yahwist, a woman or man who composed two centuries earlier what is now the most vital strand in Genesis, Exodus, Numbers. Together, Homer and the Yahwist are the foundational authors of Western literature, making possible Dante, Cervantes, Shakespeare, and Tolstoy.

Homer defines epic, from Virgil's *Aeneid* through Dante's *The Divine Comedy* and Spenser's *The Faerie Queene* on to Milton's *Paradise Lost*. High Romantic epics are significant departures to the self's interior and yet, ultimately, remain heroic: Melville's *Moby-Dick*, Whitman's *Song of Myself*, Tolstoy's *War and Peace*, Joyce's *Ulysses*, and Hart Crane's *The Bridge*.

For the *Iliad*, the highest good is victory in battle, a legacy that William Blake protested. A contrast between Achilles and the Hebrew hero, King David, is instructive. Achilles fights to be the best among the Greeks. Is that the ambition of David, to be the foremost warrior of the Jews?

More no than yes, because Yahweh is not Zeus. David fights for the Blessing, distinctly not a Greek vision of the good. Zeus and the other gods look on as we combat and die, with a kind of aesthetic interest and considerable pleasure. Yahweh is a man of war and goes into battle on behalf of his covenanted people.

A lifetime's critical meditation persuades me that this gives Homer the aesthetic palm over the Yahwist and the court historian who composed Samuel. David is far more complete than Achilles, yet Odysseus rivals David and the Yahwist's Jacob in comprehensiveness. Of course there can be no Homeric Moses, which defines the eternal strife between Athens and Jerusalem.

How should one write about Homer? The best guide remains Bruno Snell, whose *The Discovery of the Mind* still defines for me what he calls "the Homeric view of man." Snell is out of fashion now among classical scholars, but fashions ebb and flow, and his insights endure. Homer sees men not as spirits locked up in bodies but as drives or forces that perceive, live, and feel. Achilles, Hector, even the crafty Odysseus "consider themselves a battleground of arbitrary forces and uncanny powers."

In book XVIII of the *Iliad*, Achilles returns to the battle:

And forth the wall he stept and stood, nor brake the precept
   given
By his great mother (mixt in fight), but sent abroad his voice,
Which Pallas farre off echoed — who did betwixt them hoise
Shrill Tumult to a toplesse height. And as a voice is heard
With emulous affection, when any towne is spher'd
With siege of such a foe as kils men's minds, and for the
   towne
Makes sound his trumpet: so the voice from Thestis' issue
   throwne
Won emulously th' eares of all. His brazen voice once heard,
The minds of all were startl'd so, they yeelded; and so feard
The faire-man'd horses that they flew backe and their
   chariots turn'd,
Presaging in their augurous hearts the labours that they
   mourn'd

A litle after; and their guides a repercussive dread
Tooke from the horrid radiance of his refulgent head,
Which Pallas set on fire with grace. Thrice great Achilles
    spake,
And thrice (in heate of all the charge) the Troyans started
    backe.
Twelve men, of greatest strength in Troy, left with their lives
    exhald
Their chariots and their darts with his three summons cald.
                                                            (ll. 181–97)

I quote from George Chapman's magnificent Elizabethan version, which so enchanted John Keats. Exalted and burning with the divine flames of Pallas Athena, Achilles seeks to recover his arms and armor and the body of his beloved Patroclus. Totally unarmed as he is, his battle cries terrify the Trojans into a panic, coupled as they are with the answering outcry of Athena.

Yahweh roars in Isaiah and in Joel and shouts "like a man of war," but there is no superb antiphony as between mortal hero and goddess. I am suggesting that one way of writing about Homer is to compare classical and biblical texts, with their sublime contrasts. In old age, I find Homer to be totally antithetical to the Bible, which certainly can dispute his moral vision but not his aesthetic eminence.

HOW TO WRITE
A GOOD ESSAY

By Laurie A. Sterling and Jamey Hecht

WHILE THERE are many ways to write about literature, most assignments for high school and college English classes call for analytical papers. In these assignments, you are presenting your interpretation of a text to your reader. Your objective is to interpret the text's meaning in order to enhance your reader's understanding and enjoyment of the work. Without exception, strong papers about the meaning of a literary work are built upon a careful, close reading of the text or texts. Careful, analytical reading should always be the first step in your writing process. This volume provides models of such close, analytical reading, and these should help you develop your own skills as a reader and as a writer.

As the examples throughout this book demonstrate, attentive reading entails thinking about and evaluating the formal (textual) aspects of the author's works: theme, character, form, and language. In addition, when writing about a work, many readers choose to move beyond the text itself to consider the work's cultural context. In these instances, writers might explore the historical circumstances of the time period in which the work was written. Alternatively, they might examine the philosophies and ideas that a work addresses. Even in cases where writers explore a work's cultural context, though, papers must still address the more formal aspects of the work itself. A good interpretative essay that evaluates Charles Dickens's use of the philosophy of utilitarianism in his novel *Hard Times,* for example, cannot adequately address the author's treatment of the philosophy without firmly grounding this discussion in the book itself. In other words, any ana-

1

lytical paper about a text, even one that seeks to evaluate the work's cultural context, must also have a firm handle on the work's themes, characters, and language. You must look for and evaluate these aspects of a work, then, as you read a text and as you prepare to write about it.

WRITING ABOUT THEMES

Literary themes are more than just topics or subjects treated in a work; they are attitudes or points about these topics that often structure other elements in a work. Writing about theme therefore requires that you not just identify a topic that a literary work addresses but also discuss what that work says about that topic. For example, if you were writing about the culture of the American South in William Faulkner's famous story "A Rose for Emily," you would need to discuss what Faulkner says, argues, or implies about that culture and its passing.

When you prepare to write about thematic concerns in a work of literature, you will probably discover that, like most works of literature, your text touches upon other themes in addition to its central theme. These secondary themes also provide rich ground for paper topics. A thematic paper on "A Rose for Emily" might consider gender or race in the story. While neither of these could be said to be the central theme of the story, they are clearly related to the passing of the "old South" and could provide plenty of good material for papers.

As you prepare to write about themes in literature, you might find a number of strategies helpful. After you identify a theme or themes in the story, you should begin by evaluating how other elements of the story—such as character, point of view, imagery, and symbolism—help develop the theme. You might ask yourself what your own responses are to the author's treatment of the subject matter. Do not neglect the obvious, either: What expectations does the title set up? How does the title help develop thematic concerns? Clearly, the title "A Rose for Emily" says something about the narrator's attitude toward the title character, Emily Grierson, and all she represents.

WRITING ABOUT CHARACTER

Generally, characters are essential components of fiction and drama. (This is not always the case, though; Ray Bradbury's "August 2026: There

Will Come Soft Rains" is technically a story without characters, at least any human characters.) Often, you can discuss character in poetry, as in T. S. Eliot's "The Love Song of J. Alfred Prufrock" or Robert Browning's "My Last Duchess." Many writers find that analyzing character is one of the most interesting and engaging ways to work with a piece of literature and to shape a paper. After all, characters generally are human, and we all know something about being human and living in the world. While it is always important to remember that these figures are not real people but creations of the writer's imagination, it can be fruitful to begin evaluating them as you might evaluate a real person. Often you can start with your own response to a character. Did you like or dislike the character? Did you sympathize with the character? Why or why not?

Keep in mind, though, that emotional responses like these are just starting places. To truly explore and evaluate literary characters, you need to return to the formal aspects of the text and evaluate how the author has drawn these characters. The 20th-century writer E. M. Forster coined the terms *flat* characters and *round* characters. Flat characters are static, one-dimensional characters who frequently represent a particular concept or idea. In contrast, round characters are fully drawn and much more realistic characters who frequently change and develop over the course of a work. Are the characters you are studying flat or round? What elements of the characters lead you to this conclusion? Why might the author have drawn characters like this? How does their development affect the meaning of the work? Similarly, you should explore the techniques the author uses to develop characters. Do we hear a character' own words, or do we hear only other characters's assessments of him or her? Or, does the author use an omniscient or limited omniscient narrator to allow us access to the workings of the characters's minds? If so, how does that help develop the characterization? Often you can even evaluate the narrator as a character. How trustworthy are the opinions and assessments of the narrator? You should also think about characters' names. Do they mean anything? If you encounter a hero named Sophia or Sophie, you should probably think about her wisdom (or lack thereof), since *Sophia* means "wisdom" in Greek. Similarly, since the name *Sylvia* is derived from the word *sylvan,* meaning "of the wood," you might want to evaluate that character's relationship with nature. Once again, you might look to the title of the work. Does Herman Melville's "Bartleby, the Scrivener" signal anything about Bartleby himself? Is Bartleby adequately defined by his job as scrivener? Is this part of Melville's point? Pursuing questions like these can help you develop thorough papers about characters from psychological, sociological, or more formalistic perspectives.

WRITING ABOUT FORM AND GENRE

Genre, a word derived from French, means "type" or "class." Literary genres are distinctive classes or categories of literary composition. On the most general level, literary works can be divided into the genres of drama, poetry, fiction, and essays, yet within those genres there are classifications that are also referred to as genres. Tragedy and comedy, for example, are genres of drama. Epic, lyric, and pastoral are genres of poetry. *Form,* on the other hand, generally refers to the shape or structure of a work. There are many clearly defined forms of poetry that follow specific patterns of meter, rhyme, and stanza. Sonnets, for example, are poems that follow a fixed form of 14 lines. Sonnets generally follow one of two basic sonnet forms, each with its own distinct rhyme scheme. Haiku is another example of poetic form, traditionally consisting of three unrhymed lines of five, seven, and five syllables.

While you might think that writing about form or genre might leave little room for argument, many of these forms and genres are very fluid. Remember that literature is evolving and ever changing, and so are its forms. As you study poetry, you may find that poets, especially more modern poets, play with traditional poetic forms, bringing about new effects. Similarly, dramatic tragedy was once quite narrowly defined, but over the centuries playwrights have broadened and challenged traditional definitions, changing the shape of tragedy. When Arthur Miller wrote *Death of a Salesman,* many critics challenged the idea that tragic drama could encompass a common man like Willy Loman.

Evaluating how a work of literature fits into or challenges the boundaries of its form or genre can provide you with fruitful avenues of investigation. You might find it helpful to ask why the work does or does not fit into traditional categories. Why might Miller have thought it fitting to write a tragedy of the common man? Similarly, you might compare the content or theme of a work with its form. How well do they work together? Many of Emily Dickinson's poems, for instance, follow the meter of traditional hymns. While some of her poems seem to express traditional religious doctrines, many seem to challenge or strain against traditional conceptions of God and theology. What is the effect, then, of her use of traditional hymn meter?

WRITING ABOUT LANGUAGE, SYMBOLS, AND IMAGERY

No matter what the genre, writers use words as their most basic tool. Language is the most fundamental building block of literature. It is essential that you pay careful attention to the author's language and word choice as you read, reread, and analyze a text. Imagery is language that appeals to the senses. Most commonly, imagery appeals to our sense of vision, creating a mental picture, but authors also use language that appeals to our other senses. Images can be literal or figurative. Literal images use sensory language to describe an actual thing. In the broadest terms, figurative language uses one thing to speak about something else. For example, if I call my boss a snake, I am not saying that he is literally a reptile. Instead, I am using figurative language to communicate my opinions about him. Since we think of snakes as sneaky, slimy, and sinister, I am using the concrete image of a snake to communicate these abstract opinions and impressions.

The two most common figures of speech are similes and metaphors. Both are comparisons between two apparently dissimilar things. Similes are explicit comparisons using the words *like* or *as*; metaphors are implicit comparisons. To return to the previous example, if I say, "My boss, Bob, was waiting for me when I showed up to work five minutes late today—the snake!" I have constructed a metaphor. Writing about his experiences fighting in World War I, Wilfred Owen begins his poem "Dulce et decorum est," with a string of similes: "Bent double, like old beggars under sacks, / Knock-kneed, coughing like hags, we cursed through sludge." Owen's goal was to undercut clichéd notions that war and dying in battle were glorious. Certainly, comparing soldiers to coughing hags and to beggars underscores his point.

"Fog," a short poem by Carl Sandburg provides a clear example of a metaphor. Sandburg's poem reads:

> The fog comes
> on little cat feet.

It sits looking
over harbor and city
on silent haunches
and then moves on.

Notice how effectively Sandburg conveys surprising impressions of the fog by comparing two seemingly disparate things—the fog and a cat.

Symbols, by contrast, are things that stand for, or represent, other things. Often they represent something intangible, such as concepts or ideas. In everyday life we use and understand symbols easily. Babies at christenings and brides at weddings wear white to represent purity. Think, too, of a dollar bill. The paper itself has no value in and of itself. Instead, that paper bill is a symbol of something else, the precious metal in a nation's coffers. Symbols in literature work similarly. Authors use symbols to evoke more than a simple, straightforward, literal meaning. Characters, objects, and places can all function as symbols. Famous literary examples of symbols include Moby-Dick, the white whale of Herman Melville's novel, and the scarlet *A* of Nathaniel Hawthorne's *The Scarlet Letter.* As both of these symbols suggest, a literary symbol cannot be adequately defined or explained by any one meaning. Hester Prynne's Puritan community clearly intends her scarlet *A* as a symbol of her adultery, but as the novel progresses, even her own community reads the letter as representing not just *adultery,* but *able, angel,* and a host of other meanings.

Writing about imagery and symbols requires close attention to the author's language. To prepare a paper on symbolism or imagery in a work, identify and trace the images and symbols and then try to draw some conclusions about how they function. Ask yourself how any symbols or images help contribute to the themes or meanings of the work. What connotations do they carry? How do they affect your reception of the work? Do they shed light on characters or settings? A strong paper on imagery or symbolism will thoroughly consider the use of figures in the text and will try to reach some conclusions about how or why the author uses them.

WRITING ABOUT HISTORY AND CONTEXT

As noted above, it is possible to write an analytical paper that also considers the work's context. After all, the text was not created in a vacuum. The author lived and wrote in a specific time period and in a specific cultural context and, like all of us, was shaped by that environment. Learning more about the historical and cultural circumstances that surround the author and the work can help illuminate a text and provide you with productive material for a paper. Remember, though, that when you write analytical papers, you should use the context to illuminate the text. Do not lose sight of your goal—to interpret the meaning of the literary work. Use historical or philosophical research as a tool to develop your textual evaluation.

Thoughtful readers often consider how history and culture affected the author's choice and treatment of his or her subject matter. Investigations into the history and context of a work could examine the work's relation to specific historical events, such as the Salem witch trials in 17th-century Massachusetts or the restoration of Charles to the British throne in 1660. Bear in mind that historical context is not limited to politics and world events. While knowing about the Vietnam War is certainly helpful in interpreting much of Tim O'Brien's fiction, and some knowledge of the French Revolution clearly illuminates the dynamics of Charles Dickens's *A Tale of Two Cities*, historical context also entails the fabric of daily life. Examining a text in light of gender roles, race relations, class boundaries, or working conditions can give rise to thoughtful and compelling papers. Exploring the conditions of the working class in 19th-century England, for example, can provide a particularly effective avenue for writing about Dickens's *Hard Times*.

You can begin thinking about these issues by asking broad questions at first. What do you know about the time period and about the author? What does the editorial apparatus in your text tell you? These might be starting places. Similarly, when specific historical events or dynamics are particularly important to understanding a work but might be somewhat obscure to modern readers, textbooks usually provide notes to explain historical background. These are a good place to start. With this information, ask yourself how these historical facts and circumstances might have affected the author, the presentation of theme, and the presentation of character. How does knowing more about the work's specific historical context illuminate the work? To take a well-known example, understanding the complex attitudes toward slavery during the time Mark Twain wrote *Adventures of Huckleberry Finn* should help you begin to examine issues of race in the text. Additionally, you might compare these attitudes to those of the time in which the novel was set. How might this comparison affect your interpretation of a work written after the abolition of slavery but set before the Civil War?

WRITING ABOUT PHILOSOPHY AND IDEAS

Philosophical concerns are closely related to both historical context and thematic issues. Like historical investigation, philosophical research can provide a useful tool as you analyze a text. For example, an investigation into the working class in Dickens's England might lead you to a topic on the philosophical doctrine of utilitarianism in *Hard Times*. Many other works explore philosophies and ideas quite explicitly. Mary Shelley's famous novel *Frankenstein,* for example, explores John Locke's tabula rasa theory of human knowledge as she portrays the intellectual and emotional development of Victor Frankenstein's creature. As this example indicates, philosophical issues are somewhat more abstract than investigations of theme or historical context. Some other examples of philosophical issues include human free will, the formation of human identity, the nature of sin, or questions of ethics.

Writing about philosophy and ideas might require some outside research, but usually the notes or other material in your text will provide you with basic information, and often footnotes and bibliographies suggest places you can go to read further about the subject. If you have identified a philosophical theme that runs through a text, you might ask yourself how the author develops this theme. Look at character development and the interactions of characters, for example. Similarly, you might examine whether the narrative voice in a work of fiction addresses the philosophical concerns of the text.

WRITING COMPARISON AND CONTRAST ESSAYS

Finally, you might find that comparing and contrasting the works or techniques of an author provides a useful tool for literary analysis. A comparison and contrast essay might compare two characters or themes in a single work, or it might compare the author's treatment of a theme in two works. It might also contrast methods of character development or analyze an author's differing treatment of a philosophical concern in two works. Writing comparison and contrast essays, though, requires some special consideration. While they generally provide you with plenty of material to use, they also come with a built-in trap: the laundry list. These papers often become mere lists of connections between the works. As this chapter will discuss, a strong thesis must make an assertion that you want to prove or validate. A strong comparison/contrast thesis, then, needs to comment on the significance of the similarities and differences you observe. It is not enough merely to assert that the works contain similarities and differences. You might, for example, assert why the similarities and differences are important and explain how they illuminate the works's treatment of theme. Remember, too, that a thesis should not be a statement of the obvious. A comparison/contrast paper that focuses only on very obvious similarities or differences does little to illuminate the connections between the works. Often, an effective method of shaping a strong thesis and argument is to begin your paper by noting the similarities between the works but then to develop a thesis that asserts how these apparently similar elements are different. If, for example, you observe that Emily Dickinson wrote a number of poems about spiders, you might analyze how she uses spider imagery differently in two poems. Similarly, many scholars have noted that Hawthorne created many "mad scientist" characters, men who are so devoted to their science or their art that they lose perspective on all else. A good thesis comparing two of these characters—Aylmer of "The Birth-mark" and Dr. Rappaccini of "Rappaccini's Daughter," for example—might initially identify both characters as examples of Hawthorne's mad scientist type but then argue that their motivations for scientific experimentation differ. If you strive to analyze the similarities or differences, discuss significances, and move beyond the obvious, your paper should move beyond the laundry list trap.

PREPARING TO WRITE

Armed with a clear sense of your task—illuminating the text—and with an understanding of theme, character, language, history, and philosophy, you are ready to approach the writing process. Remember that good writing is grounded in good reading and that close reading takes time, attention, and more than one reading of your text. Read for comprehension first. As you go back and review the work, mark the text to chart the details of the work as well as your reactions. Highlight important passages, repeated words, and image patterns. "Converse" with the text through marginal notes. Mark turns in the plot, ask questions, and make observations about characters, themes, and language. If you are reading from a book that does not belong to you, keep a record of your reactions in a journal or notebook. If you have read a work of literature carefully, paying attention to both the text and the context of the work, you have a leg up on the writing process. Admittedly, at this point, your ideas are probably very broad and undefined, but you have taken an important first step toward writing a strong paper.

Your next step is to focus, to take a broad, perhaps fuzzy, topic and define it more clearly. Even a topic provided by your instructor will need to be focused appropriately. Remember that good writers make the topic their own. There are a number of strategies—often called "invention"—that you can use to develop your own focus. In one such strategy, called *freewriting,* you spend 10 minutes or so just writing about your topic without referring back to the text or your notes. Write whatever comes to mind; the important thing is that you just keep writing. Often this process allows you to develop fresh ideas or approaches to your subject matter. You could also try *brainstorming:* Write down your topic and then list all the related points or ideas you can think of. Include questions, comments, words, important passages or events, and anything else that comes to mind. Let one idea lead to another. In the related technique of *clustering,* or *mapping,* write your topic on a sheet of paper and write related ideas around it. Then list related subpoints under each of these main ideas. Many people then draw arrows to show connections between points. This technique helps you narrow your topic and can also help you organize your ideas. Similarly, asking journalistic questions—Who? What? Where? When? Why? and How?—can develop ideas for topic development.

Thesis Statements

Once you have developed a focused topic, you can begin to think about your thesis statement, the main point or purpose of your paper. It is imperative that you craft a strong thesis, otherwise, your paper will likely be little more than random, disorganized observations about the text. Think of your thesis statement as a kind of road map for your paper. It tells your reader where you are going and how you are going to get there.

To craft a good thesis, you must keep a number of things in mind. First, as the title of this subsection indicates, your paper's thesis should be a statement, an assertion about the text that you want to prove or validate. Beginning writers often formulate a question that they attempt to use as a thesis. For example, a writer exploring the theme of hospitality in Homer's *Iliad* might ask, Why are Glaukos and Diomedes able to remain friends despite their being on opposite sides of the Trojan War? While a question like this is a good strategy to use in the invention process to help narrow your topic and find your thesis, it cannot serve as the thesis statement because it does not tell your reader what you want to assert about hospitality. You might shape this question into a thesis by instead proposing an answer to that question: In the Homeric epics, hospitality (or *xenia*, "guest-host relationship") governs the entire range of human social scales, from the fate of the self (Odysseus becomes a homeless beggar; the young Patroclus was a fugitive until Achilles' father, Peleus, took him in) to the civic community (the suitors are bad guests in Odysseus's royal household, and removing them restores the Ithacan monarchy), to the whole region (the entire Trojan War is revenge for what a bad guest Paris was when he left Menelaus's home with his wife, Helen), and even the cosmos (Zeus's interview with Thetis, his own introspection during Sarpedon's ordeal, and his dealings with Athena all pertain to the bad *xenia* of the suitors, Aigisthos, and Paris). The poem ultimately suggests that the guest-host relationship is a fundamentally important yet imperfect institution for the prevention of violence in an otherwise almost-lawless society. This might seem lengthy, but if you read it without the parenthetical examples it is quite short. With the inclusion of the examples, notice that this thesis provides an initial plan or structure for the rest of the paper.

Second, remember that a good thesis makes an assertion that you need to support. In other words, a good thesis does not state the obvious. If you try to formulate a thesis about hospitality by simply saying, Hospitality is important in the *Iliad* and *Odyssey*, you have done nothing but rephrase the obvious. Since Homer's poems are, respectively, centered on a war for the retrieval of a host's wife who ran off with a bad guest, and on the homecoming of Odysseus to a household full of bad guests, there would be little point in spending three to five pages supporting that assertion. You might try to develop a thesis from that point by asking yourself some further questions: Without a police force (an 18th-century invention) or a formalized legal system, how could people in the ancient world regulate violence? How does *xenia* coexist with other Homeric norms of behavior, such as piracy, war, slavery, blood feud, and supplication?

As the comparison with the road map also suggests, your thesis should appear near the beginning of the paper. In relatively short papers (three to six pages) the thesis almost always appears in the first paragraph. Some writers fall into the trap of saving their thesis for the end, trying to provide a surprise or a big moment of revelation, as if to say, "TA-DA! I've just proved that in the 'Catalog of Ships,' Homer uses anecdotes to keep the audience engaged." Placing a thesis at the end of an essay can seriously mar the essay's effectiveness. If you fail to define your essay's point and purpose clearly at the beginning, your reader will find it difficult to assess the clarity of your argument and understand the points you are making. When your argument comes as a surprise at the end, you force your reader to reread your essay in order to assess its logic and effectiveness.

Finally, you should avoid using the first person ("I") as you present your thesis. Though it is not strictly wrong to write in the first person, it is difficult to do so gracefully. While writing in the first person, beginning writers often fall into the trap of writing self-reflexive prose (writing *about* their paper *in* their paper). Often this leads to the most dreaded of opening lines: "In this paper I am going to discuss . . ." Not only does this self-reflexive voice make for very awkward prose, it frequently allows writers to boldly announce a topic while completely avoiding a thesis statement. An example might be a paper (about the action of *Iliad* IX, the bulk of which is a story traditionally called "The Embassy to Achilles") that begins as follows: "The Embassy to Achilles," (*Iliad* IX) one of the most famous episodes in Homer, takes place over an afternoon when the strongest of the Greek warriors, Achilles, whose withdrawal from battle has been disastrous for them, is visited by three men—Odysseus, Ajax, and Phoenix—who try to persuade him to return. In this paper, I am going to discuss how Achilles reacts to them. The author of this paper has done little more than announce a general topic for the paper (the reaction of Achilles to the three ambassadors). While the last sentence might be a thesis, the writer fails to present an opinion about the significance of the reaction. To improve this "thesis," the writer would need to back up a few steps. First, the announced topic of the paper is too broad; it largely summarizes the events in the story, without saying anything about the ideas in the story. The writer should highlight what she considers the meaning of the episode: What is it about? The writer might begin with emotional observations: the visit reveals the depth of Achilles' feelings of outrage that motivate his refusal, and it shows the feelings of frustration in the three failed speakers. These emotions of resentment and frustration suggest spatial imagery of pressure and blockage, friction and resistance. Along these lines, the essay writer might find in *Iliad* IX an interesting tableau of stasis and motion: The Greeks are being slaughtered by the Trojans because Achilles has withdrawn. His action is his inaction; he is killing by doing nothing (later, he will accomplish nothing by killing, in the sense that no amount of Trojan corpses will ever bring back the slain Patroclus). He will not come to them with his force, so they come to him with their words. The Greeks want him to come back and fight. He will not move, though he is "Achilles of the swift feet." From here, the author could select the means by which Homer communicates these ideas and then begin to craft a specific thesis. A writer who chooses to explore the way rage is controlled by Achilles' hospitality might, for example, craft a thesis that reads, "The Embassy to Achilles" is a Homeric episode that explores the limits of verbal persuasion, but it also addresses the limits of force, since Achilles' argument is a dismissal of the whole warrior enterprise.

Outlines

While developing a strong, thoughtful thesis early in your writing process should help focus your paper, outlining provides an essential tool for logically shaping that paper. A good outline helps you see—and develop—the relationships among the points in your argument and assures you that your paper flows logically and coherently. Outlining not only helps place your points in a logical order but also helps you subordinate supporting points, weed out any irrelevant points, and decide if there are any necessary points that are missing from your argument. You can use an outlining method to contain and organize the flow of observations and ideas you experience as you read, so that the text on the page becomes better known to you and your insights are not forgotten. The early stages of generating an essay involve reading and note taking, an additive, cumulative process. The later stages involve sorting and cutting out what your eventual thesis excludes.

Most of us are familiar with formal outlines that use numerical and letter designations for each point. However, there are different types of outlines; you may find that an informal outline is a more useful tool for you. What is important, though, is that you spend the time to develop some sort of outline—formal or informal.

Remember that an outline is a tool to help you shape and write a strong paper. If you do not spend sufficient time planning your supporting points and shaping the arrangement of those points, you will most likely construct a vague, unfocused outline that provides little, if any, help with the writing of the paper.

An outline is a snapshot of the structure of a larger work. The metaphor of the snapshot is useful because it shows the way an outline provides an instant overview of how the work is constructed. An outline is also a map, in that it locates each part of your essay in relation to the others. You have to decide not only what to include and what to cut, but how to arrange your material—what to subordinate as an element in a larger topic, and what to elevate to the status of its own topic. To use yet another metaphor, you must choose what will be a twig and what will be its own branch.

Outlining can be used for gaining a grip on your material during the process of organizing your thoughts. Here is an outline whose purpose is to compare two divine *theophanies*, or visitations. They belong together as part of a larger heading:

> I. Visitations of gods to humans
>   A. *Iliad* Book I: Athena, as a proxy for Hera, visits Achilles
>   1. Overt purposes: save Agamemnon's life; promise Achilles vindication.
>   2. Covert purposes: Induce Achilles's withdrawal (as a substitute for regicide).
>   B. *Iliad* Book II: Dream, as a proxy for Zeus, visits Agamemnon
>   1. Overt purposes: to prompt Agamemnon to make a new assault on Troy.
>   2. Covert purpose: to gratify Achilles by having that assault miscarry.

Notice the way these outline items are arranged in parallel. This clarifies the data for you and will ultimately clarify your essay for the reader.

If your research paper is to follow the most basic structure in common use, you will need three parallel examples, not two. Since the *Iliad* has provided at least one theophany per book so far, consider the next book, number three. There, sure enough, Helen experiences two theophanies: First, she is visited by Iris, the messenger goddess, who comes in disguise and calls her out to the ramparts of Troy to survey the field and observe her former husband, Menelaus, in the distance. Then to Helen's side comes Aphrodite herself, also in disguise, to fetch her back inside. In the form of an old Trojan crone, the goddess affectionately urges the world's most beautiful woman to go into Alexander's bedroom and make love with him. But after hearing Aphrodite, Helen launches a direct verbal attack on Alexander (also know as Paris). This is parallel to Achilles's behavior in *Iliad* I, when he hears Athena's advice and promptly rails against Agamemnon. How would you arrange those similarities and differences in an outline?

I. Visitations of gods to human individuals ("theophanies")
   A. Book I: Athena, as a proxy for Hera, visits Achilles:
      1. to save Agamemnon's life;
      2. to promise vindication to Achilles;
      3. to induce Achilles's withdrawal (as a substitute for regicide);
      4. to move Achilles out of the Assembly and into his own shelter.
   B. Book II: Dream, as a proxy for Zeus, visits Agamemnon:
      1. to prompt Agamemnon to make a new assault on Troy;
      2. to get more Greeks killed;
      3. to gratify Achilles, since the assault will miscarry;
      4. to move Agamemnon out of his bedroom and into the Assembly.
   C. Book III: Iris visits Helen:
      1. to move Helen outside to the ramparts, so as:

        2. to show Helen's remarkably warm relationship with the Trojans;
        3. to show how the Greek heroes look from the Trojan side.
    D. Book III: Aphrodite visits Paris:
        1. to save Paris's life, by
        2. moving Paris from Menelaus's presence on the battlefield and into his own bedroom—repeating Paris's flight (with Helen) from Menelaus's presence in Menelaus's house, into Paris's house, with Helen—the war's original cause
        3. to prolong the war, by defeating the effort to reduce it to a duel
    E. Book III: Aphrodite visits Helen:
        1. to repeat the sexual adultery that caused the war
        2. to reassert the pairing of Helen with Paris

From the text you can build an outline like this one; from such an outline, you might construe a thesis statement, like the following:

Thesis: In Homer's *Iliad*, divine visitations advance the plot by moving persons around, distributing gratification, making promises, and reapplying the poem's emphasis on important relationships or themes.

Now suppose you add this idea to your other material, about "The Embassy to Achilles." That might yield a new thesis:

In Homer's *Iliad*, divine visitations advance the plot by moving persons around, distributing gratification, making true and/or false promises, and reapplying emphasis. In *Iliad* IX, "The Embassy to Achilles," the visitation of the three ambassadors (Odysseus, Phoenix, and Ajax) is like a mortal, and therefore failed, theophany. It is

like a visitation by a god, in that it aims to move a
person (Achilles), but it can't; it aims to distribute
gratification (the twice-enumerated list of Agamemnon's
bribes, in exchange for Achilles' return), but can't;
makes true and false promises; and reapplies an existing
emphasis, on the limits of human power. To expand on
this last point, "The Embassy to Achilles" shows the
limitations of words, since the ambassadors' speeches
fail to persuade Achilles, and the limitations of deeds,
since, as Achilles explains, deeds bring no gratitude,
only material goods that can never resurrect those who
die in defense or pursuit of them.

Either the thesis provides the seeds for a structure, or the structure suggests the thesis, or both. Your process may be different with every paper you write, and it is sure to be different from your neighbor's. The student's craft (of which the professional scholar's job is really just an extension) involves familiarizing yourself with an essential literary toolbox of interpretive techniques and learning to deploy it in a spirit that is playful enough to be imaginative, intuitive, and interesting, but rational enough to perceive the hidden patterns of the text and accurately relate them to what we all face as human beings.

Insight can come suddenly, or it can emerge as the product of a long process of gathering and sorting. Eventually a pattern emerges, and the writer finds a sentence that expresses that pattern's significance. This expression amounts to a claim that the writer defends using quotations from the text, selected and organized so as to substantiate the thesis. There is something gamelike and ritualized about this activity, and the classic three- and five-paragraph essay structures it celebrates. These are merely the ideal center around which turns the larger, more diverse reality of what people actually write and how they actually write it. The heart of the matter remains: Read the primary text—Homer's poetry—over and over, and practice writing about it until your thoughts take shape.

Body Paragraphs

Once your outline is complete, you can begin drafting your paper. Paragraphs, units of related sentences, are the building blocks of a good paper, and as you draft you should keep in mind both the function and the qualities of good paragraphs. Paragraphs help you chart and control the shape and content of your essay, and they help the reader see your organization and your logic. You should begin a new paragraph whenever you move from one major point to another. In longer, more complex essays you might use a group of related paragraphs to support major points. Remember that in addition to being adequately developed, a good paragraph is both unified and coherent.

Unified Paragraphs:

Each paragraph must be centered on one idea or point, and a unified paragraph carefully focuses on and develops this central idea without including extraneous ideas or tangents. For beginning writers, the best way to ensure that you are constructing unified paragraphs is to include a topic sentence in each paragraph. This topic sentence should convey the main point of the paragraph, and every sentence in the paragraph should relate to that topic sentence. Any sentence that strays from the central topic does not belong in the paragraph and needs to be revised, moved, or deleted. Consider the following paragraph about how the *Iliad* is the poem "Of the Anger of Achilles," explaining that there are two of these angers: one early, lesser rage, at Agamemnon; the other later, at Hector, and much greater:

> The first line of Homer's *Iliad* is "Rage, sing, Goddess, of Achilles the son of Peleus . . ," but it turns out that there are really two rages of Achilles. The first is directed at his own commander, King Agamemnon, who humiliated Achilles by improperly confiscating his prize; the second is aimed at Hector and the Trojans, who killed Achilles' best friend, Patroclus. The opening lines of the poem describe his *mênis* or "rage" as something that caused the deaths of myriad Achaeans, not Trojans, so the poem's famous opening does not directly refer to the later and greater of the two rages. From a modern perspective, that seems odd, since we expect the more important thing (the greater rage) to go in the most structurally important place (the opening of the poem, which announces the subject of the story). After Patroclus's death at the end of *Iliad* XVI, Achilles' new anger against Troy dwarfs his old anger at Agamemnon.

Indeed, it achieves cosmic scale: Within its horrible
power, Achilles fights the very river Skamander in the
Trojan plain; he commits acts of pitiless, monstrous
savagery, like killing suppliants (Lykaon) and exposing
corpses to the elements (Hector); he even appears briefly
on the battlefield without any armor, protected instead
by a fury so elemental it inspires Athena to cause magic
flames to shoot from Achilles' naked head. That greater
rage is not what the three ambassadors from Agamemnon
must confront and assuage when they visit Achilles' tent
in book IX, hoping to talk him back into the war. They
face only Achilles' lesser wrath, yet their words prove
useless in its face.

Coherent Paragraphs:

In addition to shaping unified paragraphs, you must also craft coherent
paragraphs, paragraphs that develop their points logically with sentences
that flow smoothly into one another. Coherence depends on the order of
your sentences, but it is not strictly the order of the sentences that is important to paragraph coherence. You also need to craft your prose to help the
reader see the relationship among the sentences.

Consider the following paragraph about Achilles' anger in book IX of
the *Iliad.* Notice how the writer uses the same ideas as the paragraph above,
yet fails to help the reader see the relationships among the points.

The first line of Homer's *Iliad* is "Rage, sing, Goddess,
of Achilles the son of Peleus . . .," but it turns out
that there are really two rages of Achilles, one against
Agamemnon and one against the Trojans, which is the
more potent, since it seems to kill more people and it
comes with strange happenings involving fire shooting
from Achilles' head, Achilles fighting against the river,
and so on. No wonder Odysseus, Ajax, and Phoenix cannot
talk him back into the war when they try to do so in
book IX. Even though this anger is not as bad as what
is coming next, it is the worst thing Achilles has ever
felt. When Odysseus comes to Achilles as an ambassador
from Agamemnon in book IX and offers him vast wealth in

exchange for Achilles' return to battle, and Achilles refuses, he seems right to do so, since Agamemnon has not apologized and he does not need the riches the king offers him. Achilles is miserable: "He cheated me and did me hurt." As bad as things are for him here, they get much worse in *Iliad* XVIII once he finds out about Patroclus's death. Things get darker and darker until at the very end in book XXIV we get to poor Priam. All this anger at Agamemnon in book IX looks sort of ridiculous in retrospect. Achilles should have sailed home when he had the chance.

A number of techniques are available to aid paragraph coherence. Careful use of transitional words and phrases is essential. You can use transitional flags to introduce an example or an illustration *(for example, for instance)*, to amplify a point or add another phase of the same idea *(additionally, furthermore, next, similarly, finally, then)*, to indicate a conclusion or result *(therefore, as a result, thus, in other words)*, to signal a contrast or a qualification *(on the other hand, nevertheless, despite this, on the contrary, still, however, conversely)*, to signal a comparison *(likewise, in comparison, similarly)*, and to indicate a movement in time *(afterward, earlier, eventually, finally, later, subsequently, until)*.

In addition to transitional flags, careful use of pronouns aids coherence and flow. If you were writing about *The Wizard of Oz*, you would not want to keep repeating the phrase *the witch* or the name *Dorothy*. Careful substitution of the pronoun *she* in these instances can aid coherence. A word of warning, though: When you substitute pronouns for proper names, always be sure that your pronoun reference is clear. In a paragraph that discusses both Dorothy and the witch, substituting *she* could lead to confusion. Make sure that it is clear to whom the pronoun refers. Generally, the pronoun refers to the last proper noun you have used.

While repeating the same name over and over again can lead to awkward, boring prose, it is possible to use repetition to help your paragraph's coherence. Careful repetition of important words or phrases can lend coherence to your paragraph by reminding readers of your key points. Admittedly, it takes some practice to use this technique effectively. You may find that reading your prose aloud can help you develop an ear for effective use of repetition.

To see how helpful transitional aids are, consider the following paragraphs about the visitation of the three ambassadors to the angry Achilles in *Iliad* IX. Notice how the author shapes the ideas and quotations into a coherent group of paragraphs whose point is easy to follow, interesting, and grounded in the text.

In Homer's *Iliad*, divine visitations advance the plot by moving persons around, distributing gratification, making promises, and reapplying emphasis. But in the "Embassy to Achilles," the visitors are not divine but quite human, and none of their intended purposes is fulfilled; their trip retards the plot, instead of advancing it, giving the poet an opportunity to show us aspects of Achilles we have not yet seen. Consider the notion that the visitation of Odysseus, Phoenix, and Ajax to the angry Achilles is like a mortal, and therefore failed, theophany. Its purpose is to move a person (Achilles), but it cannot move him; it aims to distribute gratification (the twice-enumerated list of Agamemnon's bribes, in exchange for the desperate relief provided by Achilles' return), but nobody is gratified; it makes promises (true in that the bribe is a real offer to Achilles from Agamemnon; false in that it goes unaccepted and so unpaid); and it reapplies an existing emphasis, namely (and appropriately, for a tale about a failed mission), the limits of human power.

How does "The Embassy to Achilles" reemphasize a standing Iliadic theme of the limits of human power? The story of the embassy shows the limitations of words, since the ambassadors' speeches fail to persuade Achilles, and the limitations of deeds, since as Achilles explains, deeds bring "no gratitude," only material goods that can never resurrect those who die in defense or pursuit of them. Later, at XVII 145, a point in the poem just after Patroclus's death, Homer presents Glaukos, the Lykian ally of the Trojans, complaining about the same sort of ingratitude happening on the war's other side: "We [Lykians] got no gratitude for our everlasting hard struggle against your [Troy's] enemies." Part of the strength of book IX lies in the appeal of the position Achilles articulates, even amid the pain and inertia of his grudge. Though Agamemnon's offer includes the return of the confiscated prize along with vast additional wealth, there is never any apology to Achilles, who seems to want one (IX, 387, "Until he make good to me all this heart-rending insolence" [Lattimore, p. 208]). As for the life of city sacking and spoils division, it can offer only material wealth and immaterial honor; Achilles has lost the taste for the first and feels that the second can no longer be had by fighting Agamemnon's war for him. There is no real reason to stay—except the one that leads to the death of Patroclus and that motivated the journey of the three speakers to Achilles' tent in the first place: pity for the dying Achaeans.

Achilles, however, is not Patroclus; he is much less susceptible to social pity and was moved to allow Patroclus to go into battle not by any pity for the Achaeans, as a larger group to which he and his men ultimately belong (that was Patroclus's motive), but out of pity for Patroclus himself, who yearned to go into battle and defend his friends. When Achilles himself rejoins the war, it is not out of pity for the Greeks but out of rage over Patroclus's death. Even when this rage ends at the close of the poem, Achilles does not relent because he has finished defending his surviving friends; he relents because he is touched by pity for an enemy, the individual man in front of him: not beautiful young Patroclus now, but old Priam, the most violated, miserable man of pity in all of literature, worse off than Shakespeare's King Lear and on par with Job from the Bible. Achilles never becomes the fully socialized hero celebrated by Nestor, who fights for his community first and his own glory second. It is futile, and yet tragically beautiful, to do as Homer's "kingliest" man Agamemnon has done: send three men to persuade Achilles to be what he is not.

Similarly, the following paragraph from the same paper demonstrates both unity and coherence. In it, the author argues that Homer has shown us a deeply tragic truth about the human condition:

> The pathos of "The Embassy to Achilles" comes from the audience's advance knowledge of the whole story. We know the three visitors will fail to persuade him, and we know he will bitterly regret his choice because of its unforeseen consequences. For all its grand, implacable resentment of Agamemnon, Achilles' anger in book IX is nothing compared to the rage that will possess him in book XVIII when he learns that Patroclus has been killed. Call Achilles' rebuke of Odysseus's offer (in the embassy scene in *Iliad* IX) hubristic and blind, or instead say it has a certain bracing dignity and reasonableness to it. Correct or mistaken, the position to which Achilles here clings so tenaciously is soon utterly swallowed up in the misery of deep personal bereavement. Only when he meets with someone more deeply wounded than he, namely Priam, can Achilles then give up this second, greater anger by giving up to Priam that exposed corpse of his son Hector without whose funeral the poem cannot end. Though in *Iliad* IX 315-20 and 400-18 we see Achilles seriously consider a break from the heroic world of martial fame, that opportunity is missed, and the poem ends in a tragic vision of human dignity amid the worst horrors of violation and loss. When Priam risks his life to ransom the body of his son Hector, and when Achilles is moved to pity by the old man, we feel we are in the presence of a deep affirmation of human dignity. Yet, this affirmation requires a world of pain for its emergence.

Introductions

Introductions present particular challenges for writers. Generally, your introduction should do two things: capture your reader's attention and explain the main point of your essay. In other words, while your introduction should contain your thesis, it needs to do a bit more work than that. You are likely to find that starting that first paragraph is one of the most difficult parts of the paper. It is hard to face that blank page or screen, and as a result, many beginning writers, in desperation to start somewhere, start with overly broad, general statements. While it is often a good strategy to start with more general subject matter and narrow your focus, do not begin with broad sweeping statements such as, Everyone likes to be creative and feel understood. Such sentences are little more than empty filler. They begin to fill the blank page, but they do nothing to advance your argument. Instead, you should try to gain your reader's interest. Some writers like to begin with a pertinent quotation or with a relevant question. Or, you might begin with an introduction of the topic you will discuss. If you are writing about Steinbeck's presentation of the effects of frustration in "The Chrysanthemums," for instance, you might begin by talking about how frustration is understood to affect people psychologically. Another common trap to avoid is depending on your title to introduce the author and the text you are writing about. Always include the work's author and title in your opening paragraph.

Compare the effectiveness of the following introductions.

1. Throughout history, people have hated being insulted. Think how you feel when you're insulted: It makes you kind of crazy, doesn't it? In this story, Homer shows Achilles' sense of outrage and alienation by focusing on his thoughts and actions. He cannot go back into the war, but he also cannot go home, so he is stuck doing nothing.

2. In "The Embassy to Achilles," Homer demonstrates the human predicament in the figure of Achilles, who seems to live at the mercy of two powers: his emotions and the imperatives of his civilization. Psychologists have observed that the emotional self is sometimes more powerful than the individual of which it is a part; the heart can be a tyrant and will not put up with being disregarded. Its quiet power is such that an individual who tries to circumvent his true feelings will, eventually, have to face up to who he is and what he needs. Yet culture often drives us to act in opposition

to our own emotional requirements, causing
inner conflicts that can prove disastrous. The
"Embassy" episode not only shows the failure of
the ambassadors to bring the hero back into the
war; it also shows Achilles grasping—but failing
to execute—the idea that heroic warfare is
ultimately both bad and avoidable. Homeric society
constrains Achilles' actions despite the tyranny
of his feelings; though he is too angry to help
the Achaeans by rejoining the war, he is still too
heroic to get back in his ship and leave. That
terrible balance is the focus of the ninth book
of the *Iliad*.

The first introduction begins with a vague, overly broad sentence. It cites
unclear, undeveloped examples and then moves abruptly to the thesis.
Notice, too, how a reader deprived of the paper's title does not know the
title of the story that the paper will analyze. The second introduction works
with the same material and thesis but provides more detail and is consequently much more interesting. It offers ideas about why Achilles is stuck,
rather than stopping at the observation that he cannot seem to go forward.
The paragraph begins with the thesis, which includes both the author and
the title of the work to be discussed.

The paragraph below provides another example of an opening strategy.
It begins by introducing the author and the text it will analyze, and then it
moves on by briefly introducing relevant details of the story in order to set
up its thesis.

Homer's epic poem the *Iliad* sings of human destructiveness,
focusing on two episodes of rage experienced by the
greatest of warriors, Achilles. The opening of the poem
names the lesser of those two rages as the poem's starting
point (and for some readers, the governing topic of the
whole work). Near the midpoint of the *Iliad* there occurs a
famous story, sometimes called "The Embassy to Achilles,"
in which King Agamemnon (the current object of Achilles'
anger) sends three men to plead with the young hero in
a desperate effort to get him back into the Achaean war

against the Trojans. They fail, since Achilles remains furious with his fellow Achaeans and their king, refusing to rejoin the war that the Trojans have begun to win in his absence. All that fresh Achaean misery and defeat stirs the heart of Achilles' dear friend Patroclus, whose pity extends from the bleeding individual before his eyes to the thousands of others in the same plight (whereas Achilles seems capable of pitying only one person at a time). Patroclus asks his friend for permission to rescue the Achaean army in battle, and Achilles consents, so long as Patroclus only defends the ships, stopping short of attacking Troy, a city and a people Apollo loves. Patroclus must fight within limits-a hypocritical and ironic requirement—since we have just seen Achilles' own lack of limits in his prideful outrage at Agamemnon, whose ambassadors he has just rebuffed (IX). Because of the same human limitations that made Achilles and Agamemnon quarrel, after a glorious killing spree on the field of battle (XVI), Patroclus commits hubris: He attacks the city of Troy and fights against Apollo and so is killed. The moment Achilles learns of his friend's death, the news awakens the second and far greater of his two rages, which he executes partly by slaughtering numberless Trojans including his great opponent Hector and partly by exposing Hector's corpse to the elements. Since we the readers are aware that this will happen, what are we to make of "The Embassy to Achilles" in book IX? The scene raises several unspoken questions: Why does the poem open with a reference to this, the lesser of Achilles' two rages? Might there be a sense in which this really is the more "destructive" (*oulomenen*) anger? Why does Achilles not yield to the ambassadors? How does their mission-oriented visit resemble other such visits in the poem?

Conclusions

Conclusions present another series of challenges for writers. No doubt you have heard the old adage about writing papers: "Tell us what you are going to say, say it, and then tell us what you've said." While this formula does not necessarily result in bad papers, it does not often result in good ones, either. It will almost certainly result in boring papers (especially boring conclusions). If you have done a good job establishing your points in the body of the paper, the reader already knows and understands your argument. There is no need to merely reiterate it without adding anything. Do not just summarize your main points in your conclusion, since a mechanical and redundant conclusion does little to advance your argument or interest your reader. Consider the following conclusion to the paper about rage in "The Embassy to Achilles."

> In conclusion, Homer presents Achilles as helpless against his own rage. His stubbornness in the embassy scene indicates that, even when we try hard, we cannot always change our lives. I guess that is true for all of us.

Besides starting with a mechanical transitional device, this conclusion does little more than summarize the main points of the outline (and it does not even touch on all of them). It is incomplete and uninteresting, leading nowhere.

Instead, your conclusion should add something to your paper. A good tactic is to build upon the points you have been arguing. Asking "why?" often helps you draw further conclusions. For example, in the paper on "The Embassy to Achilles," you might go on to ask whether, and how, Homer's *Iliad* raises the possibility that the endless cycle of violence— all this pain—may somehow be avoidable. During the embassy scene, Achilles considers just packing up and going home to Phthia. Does the *Iliad* contain other hints of a different kind of life, one without war and piracy? Or is it exclusively the job of Homer's *Odyssey* to make such a vision imaginable?

Another method for successfully concluding a paper is to speculate on other directions in which to take your topic by tying it into larger issues. You might do this by envisioning your paper as just one section of a larger paper. Having established your points in this paper, how would you build upon this argument? Where would you go next? In the following conclusion to the paper on "The Embassy to Achilles," the author reiterates some of the main points of the paper but does so in order to amplify the discussion of the story's central message and to connect it to other Greek texts on the same figures, written in the period after Homer:

> It is the inner blindness of Achilles that makes the *Iliad* so comparable to Athenian tragedy where, captive to some passion or other, the protagonist suffers a failure of perception that costs him everything. Like the hero of Sophocles' *Oedipus* (or Creon in *Antigone*), Achilles in his delusion persists beyond a point of no return and is transformed by the ensuing loss. The other half of Achilles' first *mênis* or instance of rage is Agamemnon's anger at him, and for his part Agamemnon acknowledges this to have been sheer insanity ("Since I was mad . . ." IX, 119). But Achilles' madness is more complicated, not so easily undone and put aside as Agamemnon's. It comprises the passion of his grudge against Agamemnon who wounded him with humiliation; the reckless extension of that grudge to the Achaean soldiers *en masse*; and the confidence that his own course of action is appropriate now, as he rebukes the three ambassadors and then once more, as he allows Patroclus to go and fight in his stead. At that point (XVI, 97–100) we are shown the depth of Achilles' singular state of mind in a chilling prayer whose unbounded violence foreshadows his genocidal depravity in books XVIII to XXIII: "Father Zeus, Athene and Apollo, if only / one of all the Trojans could escape destruction, not one / of the Argives, but you and I could emerge from the slaughter / so that we two alone could strip away from the city of Troy her sacred head-dress." Perhaps only the Cyclops of the *Odyssey* could be further from the pro-social warrior ideal urged by Nestor, Phoenix, and Peleus, indeed by every paternal figure in Achilles' life.

Citations and Formatting

Using Primary Sources:

As the examples included in this chapter indicate, strong papers on literary texts incorporate quotations from the text in order to support their points. It is not enough for you to assert your interpretation without providing support or evidence from the text. Without well-chosen quotations to support your argument you are, in effect, saying to the reader, "Take my word for it." It is important to use quotations thoughtfully and selectively. Remember that the paper presents *your* argument, so choose quotations that support *your* assertions. Do not let the author's voice overwhelm your own. With that caution in mind, there are some guidelines you should follow to ensure that you use quotations clearly and effectively.

Integrate Quotations:

Quotations should always be integrated into your own prose. Do not just drop them into your paper without introduction or comment. Otherwise, it is unlikely that your reader will see their function. You can integrate textual support easily and clearly with identifying tags, short phrases that identify the speaker. For example:

The narrator describes Hera as *boôpis*, "ox-eyed."

While this introductory phrase, "the narrator describes," appears before the quotation, you can also use tags after or in the middle of the quoted text, as the following examples demonstrate:

"Why, Patroclus, do you come to me like a young girl to her mother?" asks Achilles.

You can also use a colon to formally introduce a quotation:

Achilles' change of worldview is dramatic: "An equal portion goes to him who hangs back, as to him who is constantly fighting."

In poetry, the placement of line breaks (or of slash marks, which stand for line breaks) is called lineation. When you quote poetry, whether in its original language or in a translation, reproduce the same lineation you see on the page. If you quote a prose translation, there will be no line breaks to indicate, only paragraphs; these, too, should be accurately reflected in your quotations. In quoting a verse translation, lineate your quotations just as the translator has done.

> *Iliad* VII ends as the Achaeans finish their fortifications:
> "They spilled the wine on the ground from their cups, and
> none was so hardy / as to drink, till he had poured to
> the all-powerful son of Kronos."

Longer quotations (more than four lines of prose or three lines of poetry) should be set off from the rest of your paper in a block quotation. Double-space before you begin the passage, indent it 10 spaces from your left-hand margin, and double-space the passage itself. Because the indentation signals the inclusion of a quotation, do not use quotation marks around the cited passage. Use a colon to introduce the passage:

> Achilles seems all too serious in his threat to quit the war entirely:
>
> > But since I choose not to war with noble Hector, tomorrow, having performed sacrifices to Zeus and all the gods, [and] having well laden my ships, when I shall have drawn them down to the sea, thou shalt behold, if thou wilt, and if such things be a care to thee, my ships early in the morn sailing upon the fishy Hellespont, and men within them, eager for rowing; and if glorious Neptune grant but a prosperous voyage, on the third day I shall surely reach fertile Phthia [prose translation by Theodore Alois Buckley].

> The whole of Emily Dickinson's poem speaks of the imagination:

```
To make a prairie it takes a clover and one bee,
One clover, and a bee,
And revery.
The revery alone will do,
If bees are few.
```

```
Clearly, she argues for the creative power of the mind.
```

It is also important to interpret quotations after you introduce them and explain how they help advance your point. You cannot assume that your reader will interpret the quotations the same way that you do.

Quote Accurately:

Always quote accurately. Anything within quotations marks must be the author's exact words. There are, however, some rules to follow if you need to modify the quotation to fit into your prose.

1. Use brackets to indicate any material that might have been added to the author's exact wording. For example, if you need to add any words to the quotation or alter it grammatically to allow it to fit into your prose, indicate your changes in brackets:

   ```
   The sun goes down "[a]s these two [are] talking
   thus together," and they finish their work as
   book VII ends.
   ```

2. Conversely, if you choose to omit any words from the quotation, use ellipses (three spaced periods) to indicate missing words or phrases:

   ```
   Book XIII ends with an omen: "[A]n ominous bird
   winged by at his right hand . . . and the host
   of the Achaeans, made brave / by the bird sign,
   shouted . . ."
   ```

3. If you delete a sentence or more, use the ellipses after a period:

In *The Odyssey Re-Formed*, Frederick Ahl and Hanna Roisman write: "Telemachus is not at all ready to believe the stranger when he denies he is a god, declares he is Telemachus's father, and embraces him. . . . Telemachus's reluctance to accept the stranger as his father does not indicate that the possibility that this man is Odysseus had not suggested itself to him" (Ahl, 195).

4. If you omit a line or more of poetry, or more than one paragraph of prose, use a single line of spaced periods to indicate the omission, as in this quotation from the poet Emily Dickinson:

To make a prairie it takes a clover and one bee,
. . . .
And revery.
The revery alone will do,
If bees are few.

Punctuate Properly:

Punctuation of quotations often causes more trouble than it should. Once again, you just need to keep these simple rules in mind.

1. Periods and commas should be placed inside quotation marks, even if they are not part of the original quotation:

"Why," Achilles asks, "do you come to me like a young girl to her mother?"

The only exception to this rule is when the quotation is followed by a parenthetical reference. In this case, the period or comma goes after the citation (more on these later in this chapter):

Meyer Reinhold expressed it this way: "The essential thing with Homer—and most especially is this true of the *Iliad*—is the magical, bewitching,

```
irresistible, intoxicating sweep of music in his
meter" (17).
```

2. Other marks of punctuation—colons, semicolons, question marks, and exclamation points—go outside the quotation marks unless they are part of the original quotation:

```
What effect might translator Richmond Lattimore
be trying to achieve in rendering the line "and
went silently away beside the murmuring sea-
beach"? (60)
```

Documenting Primary Sources:

Unless you are instructed otherwise, you should provide sufficient information for your reader to locate material you quote. Generally, literature papers follow the rules set forth by the Modern Language Association (MLA). These can be found in the *MLA Handbook for Writers of Research Papers* (sixth edition). You should be able to find this book in the reference section of your library. Additionally, its rules for citing both primary and secondary sources are widely available from reputable online sources. One of these is the Online Writing Lab (OWL) at Purdue University. OWL's guide to MLA style is available at http://owl.english.purdue.edu/owl/resource/557/01/. The Modern Language Association also offers answers to frequently asked questions about MLA style on this helpful Web page: http://www.mla.org/style_faq. Generally, when you are citing from literary works in papers, you should keep a few guidelines in mind.

Parenthetical Citations:

MLA asks for parenthetical references in your text after quotations. When you are working with a primary text in prose (short stories, novels, or essays, or a prose translation of a poetic original) include page numbers in the parentheses:

```
Henry's effort with Elisa is clear: "You've got a strong
new crop coming" (2).
```

When you are quoting poetry, include line numbers:

Dickinson's speaker tells of the arrival of a fly: "There
interposed a Fly— / With Blue—uncertain stumbling Buzz—
/ Between the light—and Me—" (12-14).

Works Cited Page:

These parenthetical citations are linked to a separate works cited page at
the end of the paper. The works cited page lists works alphabetically by the
authors' last names. An entry for the above quotation from Steinbeck's "The
Chrysanthemums" would read:

Steinbeck, John. "The Chrysanthemums." *The Long Valley.*
New York: Penguin, 1995. 1-13.

The *MLA Handbook* includes a full listing of sample entries, as do many of
the online explanations of MLA style.

Documenting Secondary Sources:

To ensure that your paper is built entirely upon your own ideas and
analysis, instructors often ask that you write interpretative papers
without any outside research. If, on the other hand, your paper requires
research, you must document any secondary sources you use. You need
to document direct quotations, summaries or paraphrases of others's
ideas, and factual information that is not common knowledge. Follow
the guidelines above for quoting primary sources when you use direct
quotations from secondary sources. Keep in mind that MLA style also
includes specific guidelines for citing electronic sources. OWL's Web
site provides a good summary: http://owl.english.purdue.edu/owl/
resource/557/09/.

Parenthetical Citations:

As with the documentation of primary sources, described above, MLA
guidelines require in-text parenthetical references to your secondary
sources. Unlike the research papers you might write for a history class, literary research papers following MLA style do not use footnotes as a means
of documenting sources. Instead, after a quotation, you should cite the
author's last name and the page number:

"The tragic contradictions of warfare and heroism in the
Iliad are nowhere more apparent and more moving than in
the case of Achilles" (Schein, 90).

If you include the name of the author in your prose, then you would include
only the page number in your citation. For example:

In *The Odyssey: Structure, Narration, and Meaning*, Bruce
Louden has written about the *Odyssey*'s minor characters
Elpenor and Leodes, "Both characters exist in the poem
primarily to die and to lead or link other members of
their groups to death and the underworld" (46).

If you are including more than one work by the same author, the parenthetical citation should include a shortened yet identifiable version of the
title in order to indicate which of the author's works you cite. For example:

As G. S. Kirk points out, "It is near an imaginary coast
that the Cyclopes live their easy if unsociable lives"
(*Myth* 164).

Similarly, and just as important, if you summarize or paraphrase the particular ideas of your source, you must provide documentation:

The Cyclops Polyphemus suddenly changes his behavior
from that of a dairyman to that of a carnivorous animal
who eats human beings, guts and all (Kirk, *Myth* 166).

Works Cited Page:

Like the primary sources discussed above, the parenthetical references
to secondary sources are keyed to a separate works cited page at the end
of your paper. Here is an example of a works cited page that uses the
examples cited above. Note that when two or more works by the same
author are listed, you should use three hyphens followed by a period in
the subsequent entries. You can find a complete list of sample entries in
the *MLA Handbook* or from a reputable online summary of MLA style.

WORKS CITED

Kirk, G. S. *Myth: Its Meaning and Function in Ancient and Other Cultures* (Sather Classical Lectures, Volume 40). Berkeley, California: University of California Press, 1970.

———. *The Iliad: A Commentary* (Volume I: Books 1–4). Newcastle: Cambridge University Press, 1985.

Plagiarism

Failure to document carefully and thoroughly can leave you open to charges of stealing the ideas of others, which is known as plagiarism, and this is a very serious matter. Remember that it is important to include quotation marks when you use language from your source, even if you use just one or two words. For example, if you wrote, The tragic contradictions of warfare and heroism in the Iliad are nowhere more apparent and more moving than in the case of Achilles, you would be guilty of plagiarism, since you used Schein's distinct language without acknowledging him as the source. Instead, you should write: What a modern mind calls "the tragic contradictions of warfare and heroism" seem to inhere in the very air of the Iliad, pervading all the action and the entire psychic economy of all the characters, epitomized in Achilles (Schein, 90). In this case, you have properly credited Schein.

Similarly, neither summarizing the ideas of an author nor changing or omitting just a few words means that you can omit a citation. Alfred Heubeck and Stephanie West's *Commentary on Homer's Odyssey* contains the following passage about Homeric dreams:

> Dreams serve to motivate new developments in the action and provide a simple means for divine intervention in human affairs. Here Penelope has to be saved from total surrender to despair in a situation where no human friend could help her (242).

Below are two examples of plagiarized passages:

If a friend were available, Penelope might not need the
help of a dream; in her isolation, it is only this visitor
from the Gods that rescues her before she can give up.

Dreams motivate new movements in the action and enable
divine intervention in human affairs. Here Penelope must
be saved from complete capitulation to despair in a
situation where no human friend could help her (Heubeck
and West, 242).

While the first passage does not use Heubeck's and West's exact language,
it does list the same ideas they propose as the essential point about Penelope's dream without citing their work. Since this interpretation is their distinct idea, this constitutes plagiarism. The second passage has superficially
changed some wording, condensed the thought somewhat, and included a
citation, but some of the phrasing belongs to Heubeck and West. The first
passage could be fixed with a parenthetical citation. But because some of
the wording in the second remains the same, and because other phrases
are merely word-by-word synonyms for the words of Heubeck and West, it
would require the use of both quotation marks and a parenthetical citation.
The passage below represents an honestly and adequately documented use
of the original passage:

According to Alfred Heubeck and Stephanie West, Penelope's
dream is typical in the narratological work it performs:
advancing the plot and rescuing Penelope from despair.
"Dreams motivate new movements in the action and enable
divine intervention in human affairs" (242).

This passage acknowledges that the interpretation is derived from Heubeck
and West while appropriately using quotations to indicate their precise
language.

While it is not necessary to document well-known facts, often referred
to as "common knowledge," any ideas or language that you take from someone else must be properly documented. Common knowledge generally
includes the birth and death dates of authors or other well-documented
facts of their lives. An often-cited guideline is that if you can find the infor-

mation in three sources, it is common knowledge. Despite this guideline, it is, admittedly, often difficult to know if the facts you uncover are common knowledge or not. When in doubt, document your source.

Sample Essay

Phoebe Dyctinna
Mr. Polytropos
English II
February 20, 2011

ACHILLES'S *MÊNIS* ("RAGE") AND MORTAL LIMITATIONS
IN *ILIAD* IX, "THE EMBASSY TO ACHILLES"

The first line of Homer's *Iliad* is "Rage, sing, Goddess, of Achilles the son of Peleus . . ," but it turns out that there are really two rages of Achilles. The first is directed at his own commander, King Agamemnon, who humiliated Achilles by improperly confiscating his prize; the second is aimed at Hector and the Trojans, who killed Achilles' best friend, Patroclus. The opening lines of the poem describe his *mênis* or "rage" as something that caused the deaths of myriad *Achaeans*, not Trojans, so the poem's famous opening does not directly refer to the later and greater of the two rages. After Patroclus's death at the end of *Iliad* XVI, Achilles' new anger against Troy dwarfs his old anger at Agamemnon. It achieves cosmic scale: Within its horrible power, Achilles fights the very river Skamander in the Trojan plain; he commits acts of pitiless, monstrous savagery, like killing suppliants (Lykaon) and exposing corpses to the elements (Hector); he even appears briefly on the battlefield without any armor, protected instead by a fury so elemental it inspires Athena to make magic flames shoot from Achilles' naked head. For Achilles' first *mênis*, the Trojans do the killing; his fury is all emotion, without physical violence. Yet the words of Agamemnon's three ambassadors prove useless against it.

If there is something strangely familiar about the experience of reading "The Embassy to Achilles," it may be because it shares essential features with one of Homeric poetry's recurrent scenes or set pieces, the *theophany*, or "divine visitation." In both Homeric epics, theophanies advance the plot by moving persons around, distributing gratification, making promises, and reapplying emphasis. In "The Embassy to Achilles," however, the visitors are not divine but quite human, and none of their intended purposes is fulfilled. Their trip retards the plot, instead of advancing it, giving the poet an opportunity to show us aspects of Achilles we have not yet seen. The embassy's purpose is to move a person (Achilles), but it cannot move him; it aims to distribute gratification (the twice-enumerated list of Agamemnon's bribes, in exchange for the desperate relief provided by Achilles' return), but nobody is gratified; it makes promises ("All these things shall I do if he will put aside his anger," IX, 157); and it reapplies an existing emphasis, namely (and, appropriately, for a tale about a failed mission), the limits of human power. As a type of divine *Atê*, or ruin, Achilles' lesser *mênis* in *Iliad* IX epitomizes these human limits, just as his greater *mênis* in XVIII–XXIII epitomizes the breach of limits.

The story of the embassy shows the inadequacy of words, since the ambassadors' speeches fail to persuade Achilles, and the corresponding futility of deeds that, as Achilles explains, bring "no gratitude," only material goods that can never resurrect the soldiers who fight over them. Later, at XVII, 145, a point in the poem just after Patroclus's death, Homer presents Glaukos, the Lykian ally of the Trojans, complaining about the very same sort of ingratitude evident on the war's other side: "We [Lykians] got no gratitude for our everlasting hard struggle against your [Troy's] enemies." Part of the strength of book IX lies in the appeal of the position Achilles articulates, even amid the pain and inertia of his grudge. Though Agamemnon's offer includes the return of the confiscated prize along with vast additional wealth, there is never any apology to Achilles, who seems to want one (IX, 387, "Until he make good to me all this heart-rending insolence," Lattimore, p. 208). As for the life of city sacking and spoils division, Achilles has lost the taste for its material rewards; there remains only honor, which can no longer be had by fighting Agamemnon's war for him. There is no real reason to stay, except the one that brings about the death of Patroclus and that motivated the journey of the three speakers to Achilles' tent in the first place: pity for the dying Achaeans.

Achilles, however, is not Patroclus; he is much less susceptible to social pity and was moved to allow Patroclus to go into battle not by any pity for the Achaeans as a larger group to which he and his men ultimately belong (that was Patroclus's motive) but pity for Patroclus himself, who yearned to go into battle and defend his friends. When Achilles himself rejoins the war, it is not out of pity for the Greeks but out of rage over Patroclus's death. Even when this rage is dispelled at the close of the poem, Achilles does not relent because he has finished defending his surviving friends; he relents because he is touched by pity for an enemy, the individual man in front of him, not beautiful young Patroclus now but old Priam, the most violated, miserable man of pity in all of literature, worse off than King Lear and on a par with Job from the Bible. Achilles never becomes the fully socialized hero celebrated by Nestor, who fights for his community first and his own glory second. It is futile, and yet tragically beautiful, to do as Homer's "kingliest" man Agamemnon has done in sending three men to persuade Achilles to be what he is not.

It is the inner blindness of Achilles that makes the *Iliad* comparable to Athenian tragedy in which, captive to some passion or other, the protagonist suffers a failure of perception that costs him everything. Like the hero of Sophocles' *Oedipus* (or Creon in *Antigone*), Achilles in his delusion persists beyond a point of no return and is transformed by the ensuing loss. The other half of Achilles' first *mênis* is Agamemnon's anger at him, and for his part Agamemnon acknowledges this to have been sheer insanity ("Since I was mad . . ." IX, 119). But Achilles' madness is more complicated, not so easily undone and put aside as Agamemnon's. It comprises the passion of his grudge against Agamemnon who wounded him with humiliation; the reckless extension of that grudge to the Achaean soldiers *en masse*; and the confidence that his own course of action is appropriate now, as he rebukes the three ambassadors, and then once more, as he allows Patroclus to go and fight in his stead. At that point (XVI, 97–100) we are shown the depth of Achilles' singular state of mind in a chilling prayer whose unbounded violence foreshadows his genocidal depravity in books XVIII to XXIII: "Father Zeus, Athene and Apollo, if only / one of all the Trojans could escape destruction, not one / of the Argives, but you and I could emerge from the slaughter / so that we two alone could strip away from the city of Troy her sacred head-dress." Perhaps only the Cyclops of the *Odyssey* could be further from the pro-social warrior ideal urged by Nestor, Phoenix, and Peleus, every paternal figure in Achilles' life.

The pathos of "The Embassy to Achilles" comes from the audience's advance knowledge of the entire story. We know the three visitors will fail to persuade him, and we know he will bitterly regret his choice because of its unforeseen consequences. For all its grand, implacable resentment of Agamemnon, Achilles' anger in book IX is nothing compared to the rage that will possess him in book XVIII when he learns that Patroclus has been killed. Call Achilles' rebuke of Odysseus's offer (in the embassy scene in Iliad IX) hubristic and blind, or instead say it has a certain bracing dignity and reasonableness to it. Correct or mistaken, the position to which Achilles here clings so tenaciously is soon utterly swallowed up in the misery of deep personal bereavement. Only when he meets with someone more deeply wounded than he, namely Priam, can Achilles give up this second, greater anger by giving up to Priam the exposed corpse of his son Hector without whose funeral the poem cannot end. Though in Iliad IX 315–20 and 400–18, we see Achilles seriously consider a break from the heroic world of martial fame, that opportunity is missed, and the poem ends in a tragic vision of human dignity amid the worst horrors of violation and loss. When Priam risks his life to ransom the body of his son Hector, and when Achilles is moved to pity by the old man, we feel we are in the presence of a deep affirmation of human dignity. Yet this affirmation requires a world of pain for its emergence.

WORKS CITED

Ahl, Frederick, and Hanna Roisman. *The Odyssey Re-Formed.* Ithaca, NY: Cornell University Press, 1996.

Buckley, Theodore Alois, trans. *The Iliad of Homer.* New York: Harper and Brothers, 1896.

Heubeck, Alfred, and Stephanie West. *Commentary on Homer's Odyssey* (Volume I, Introduction and Books I–VIII). New York: Oxford University Press, 1988.

Kirk, G. S. *Myth: Its Meaning and Function in Ancient and Other Cultures* (Sather Classical Lectures, Volume 40). Berkeley: University of California Press, 1970.

———. *The Iliad: A Commentary (Volume I: Books 1–4).* Newcastle: Cambridge University Press, 1985.

Lattimore, Richmond, trans. *The Iliad of Homer.* Chicago: University of Chicago Press, 1951.

Louden, Bruce. *The Odyssey: Structure, Narration, and Meaning.* Baltimore: The Johns Hopkins University Press, 1999.

Reinhold, Meyer. *Barron's Simplified Approach to Homer: The Odyssey.* Woodbury, NY: Barron's, 1967.

Schein, Seth L. *The Mortal Hero: An Introduction to Homer's Iliad.* Berkeley: University of California Press, 1984.

HOW TO WRITE
ABOUT HOMER

HOMER IS the first great Western poet whose work has come down to us. Writing about him is not like writing about a modern author— Ernest Hemingway, for example—with a first and last name, a known birthplace, and an archive of carefully preserved personal letters. Compared to such a figure, Homer is practically a force of nature, the primal fountainhead of a 3,000-year poetic tradition. Because of this earliness, this position at what looks like the beginning, Homer can sometimes seem more than human.

Just as individuals trace their lineage to parents and ancestors, works of literature are derived from and influenced by other writings. That premise has been at the heart of Harold Bloom's argument in much of his critical writing over the past half century. A text, like one's personal identity, does not exist in a world of its own making, but rather reflects the conditions that surround its creation. Homer, however, had no known literary "parentage" against which he could wage his struggle for creative identity. He is (from the perspective of posterity, if not in historical fact) simply the first. Why does European literature start with Homer? Because the *Iliad* and the *Odyssey* were the orally composed works that were already on people's lips in the middle of the eighth century when Greek longshoremen, merchants, and sailors became aware that their Phoenician and Syrian trading partners were using something called an alphabet to record spoken language and thought. Shortly thereafter, it occurred to the Greeks that by slightly modifying this *aleph-bet* (the first two letters of the Hebrew alphabet) into an *alpha-beta* (Greek), they could adapt it into a system for writing down the Greek language. Apart from possible inscriptions on vases and graffiti, Homer's epic poetry was probably among the first texts to be written down in the new letters and almost certainly the first such texts of any length. The writing down of Homeric poetry circa 740 B.C. was an act of preservation, but it also served as a fixative or sort of freezing process, preventing in the work both growth and decay.

Eventually the two Homeric epics became the core of a Greek identity that transcended the considerations of locality and birthplace; without the *Iliad*, the peoples of so many tiny Aegean islands might never have united in mutual defense against a Persian invader (as they did in 590 B.C. and again a decade later in 580). As you read Homer in preparation for your own essay writing, be aware that the author you approach is both a historical phenomenon and a myth in his own right. Greek identity has been shaped by these poems almost as much as the identity of Arab culture has been shaped by the Koran or Jewish culture by the Torah.

The *Iliad* (or "Story of Ilium," a city also called Troy) and the *Odyssey* (or "Story of Odysseus"), along with some short hymns to various gods, are the oldest surviving remnants of the Greek part of a much wider ancient cultural formation. Archaeologists believe that some time during the third millennium B.C. in the region between the Black and Caspian seas—perhaps in what is now Armenia, where both horses and hardwood trees were abundant—arose a method of mounting soldiers on a lightweight, horse-drawn cart. Using some combination of this new chariot warfare, migration, and diplomacy, the people of that area seem to have expanded over what became a staggeringly vast terrain, eastward to the Ganges in India (hence the prefix "Indo-") and northwest to Ireland and Iceland (hence the other half of the prefix, "-European"). They brought with them their genes, language, and religion; all three quickly spread in proliferating branches, some to disappear, others to supplant their neighbors, and others to blend and merge. This is known as the Indo-European expansion, and its literary remains form a patchwork of ancient poems, separated by divergent languages and geography but all related. These poems include the Irish *Tain*, the Germanic *Edda*, the Iranian *Avesta*, and the Indic *Vedas* (and later *Mahabarata*). Like the *Iliad* and the *Odyssey*, these texts show us a dangerous young world afflicted with piracy, warfare, and political murder, where fragile human institutions like hospitality and marriage serve as attempts to fend off or limit chaos.

In general, the poems were composed decades and even centuries after the heroic violence they depict, and since that violence was part of a great wave that tended to decrease the level of civilization in a territory by destroying persons, social networks, and institutions, the poems represent a stratum of culture that is newer and yet more primitive than that of the legendary warriors they celebrate. Nobody in Homer's original eighth-century B.C. audience would have ever seen a functioning palace as grand as the royal homes we hear about in the *Odyssey* at Menelaus's Sparta or Agamemnon's Mycenae. Some of this is speculative (the Indo-European expansion may have begun without chariot warfare, which may have been invented farther to the east and deeper in the past, to be exploited later by the already-relocating Indo-Europeans), but there is agreement that the expansion happened in the third and second millennia B.C., with the proto-Greek branch probably arriving in the Aegean around 1600 B.C. Around 1200 B.C., a catastrophe occurred that included the destruction of around 40 major urban centers in the Aegean region, including both Troy (apparently destroyed by the Greeks under the Mycenaean leadership of Agamemnon) and Mycenae. Various hypotheses have been suggested to help explain some or all of these local disasters and the general depopulation that followed, including earthquakes, drought, social revolution, and invasions by various candidates. As you explore historical questions about the ancient world, get accustomed to the veil of uncertainty that stands between us and the distant past. "Learn to love the questions themselves," as the poet Rainer Maria Rilke once advised, rather than definite answers that may never arrive.

Perhaps the most important literary meaning of the historical background behind Homer's *Iliad* and *Odyssey* is that the poet and his hearers felt inferior to their own heroic ancestors and to the legendary Trojans they had destroyed. The people of Homer's time and beyond heard his trance-inducing poetry and dreamed of giant men who could lift huge boulders with ease and throw them with deadly accuracy in defense of their own people and in pursuit of pillage. To vulnerable men and women living in underpopulated, uprooted, or contracted settlements often chronically short of laborers and soldiers, such figures must have seemed valuable beyond price. The poet and his hearers understood that Troy would be looted and burned but that the victorious Greek kings would each suffer terribly in turn. Both the attackers and the defenders represented a long-lost world of legendary human stature, prowess, wealth, and beauty, as well as an amazing intimacy with the gods that no longer happens every day, if at all.

Though the poetry of Mesopotamia is much older, Homer's verse is the first that survives from the Aegean and Mediterranean region. The older of the two poems, the *Iliad* tells the story of the war that destroyed the city called Troy, or Ilium, on the western coast of present-day Turkey, sometime toward the end of the second millennium B.C. Many historians hold that this roughly 10-year siege took place between 1250 B.C. and the waning decades of the following century, with a traditional date that works out to around 1183 B.C., but scholarly estimates vary widely and there are considerable archaeological writings about the question. Like other settlements of great age and importance such as Jericho, ancient Troy was a layered city, repeatedly damaged or destroyed and reoccupied; the *Iliad* describes the fate of what most scholars now believe was "layer six" of the site. (For further reading, see Neil Asher Silberman, *Between Past and Present: Archaeology, Ideology, and Nationalism in the Modern Middle East,* New York: Doubleday, 1990; also David A Traill, *Schliemann of Troy: Treasure and Deceit,* New York: St. Martin's Press, 1995.) Its fall to the Greek invader was somehow part of the Indo-European expansion described above, and yet it came toward the end of that expansion, when the aggressors themselves would have their own doom to confront all too soon. The Trojan War can be seen as marking the end of the Bronze Age, a period of roughly 2,000 years when that metal represented the best available technology for weapons and armor.

Just as the sacred texts of the great religions are repositories of wisdom in addition to being jumbled storehouses of archaeological information, the Homeric poems, too, are great heroic stories that also serve as containers for a vast wealth of facts about the distant past and its peoples. When you write about Homer, your teacher or professor may expect you to acknowledge, if not explore, this archaeological dimension of the text. At the close of this chapter is an extensive bibliography including several archaeological books that will aid you in that pursuit.

The invocation of the goddess that begins each of the two epics makes much more sense, and is much more important, if you remember that the poem was composed orally. The Muse helps the bard to invent and then helps in the recitation of what the bard has invented. The request for the Muse's help inaugurates an economy of divine abundance to compensate for human scarcity; this model of human effort mixed with divine inspiration will be repeated in various ways throughout the poem.

A Note on Notation

It is customary to refer to the 24 books of the *Iliad* using capitalized Roman numerals (for example, "For most of *Iliad* XVI, Patroclus is in a trancelike state"), and to those of the *Odyssey* using either lowercase Roman, or, as here, Arabic numerals (for example, "By the time *Odyssey* 4 is over, Telemachus seems like a new person"). Some of the proper names in Homer are given here in transliterated Greek (Philoitios, for example) but most have been anglicized (Achilles).

TOPICS AND STRATEGIES

There are any number of directions and approaches to adopt in writing an essay about Homer. Of course, you will need to select a certain work or works to focus on, as you will not be able to discuss Homer's entire oeuvre in one essay. The sample topics will give you suggestions about the different parts of the text you might use in conjunction with a particular topic, but the decisions are yours to make. Remember to consider the anticipated length of your essay, the length of the works you are considering, and the number of quoted passages you want to examine as you plan your paper. Be sure that you have ample space to consider the work(s) you have selected in a meaningful way and provide a rationale for grouping the texts as you do in your essay. While your basis for selection may be obvious on some occasions (when you have chosen stories that relate to a particular theme or include the same character), at other times it is beneficial to explain your selection to your reader. You might indicate, for example, that you have chosen to study a set of battlefield moments from the *Iliad* and from the last section of the *Odyssey* in order to explore Homeric thought about death and the soul, or perhaps you have selected passages about women such as Antikleia, Penelope, and Helen in order to sketch Homer's understanding of gender roles. If you are sure in your own mind of your reasons for choosing certain texts, and your essay makes those reasons clear to readers, then you can be assured that your selection will not wind up appearing random, thereby weakening your argument.

Themes

Certain themes are accessible from almost any point in Homer's text. You might study, for example, artistic labor, the nature of eros (love between partners in a couple), the effects of war on the family, or the relationship between human beings and the rest of nature in almost any region of Homer's vast poetic landscape. The following sample topics offer you suggestions as to which works you might focus on for a given topic, but the lists they provide are by no means exclusive. Feel free to include another passage or substitute a passage you find particularly interesting in place of one suggested in the topic. Once you have selected the works you want to study, you will want to reread each of them carefully, paying special attention to any passages that pertain to your topic, analyzing these passages and keeping careful notes. Then comes the really exciting part of crafting an essay such as this; you will want to compare the notes you have taken about each of the texts you have selected and synthesize your findings in the hope of drawing fresh and insightful conclusions.

Sample Topics:

1. Artistic labor: How does Homer depict the artist and the artistic process?

Begin by selecting passages in which Homer presents people engaging in the arts, such as the figure of the poet Demodocus in the *Odyssey* or the elaborate description of the god Hephaestus crafting the shield of Achilles in *Iliad* XVIII. There may also be passages that do not explicitly bear on artistic creation but seem to you to have something to say about it. The poem begins with an invocation to the divine Muse without whose poetic inspiration the poet would be amnesiac and mute. Might this relationship between a creative Goddess and a dependent but resourceful mortal singer have parallels in the poem, such as the relationship between Athena and Odysseus? What might Homer's treatment of the practice of other arts—for example, Odysseus's construction of the boat with which he escapes Calypso's island—suggest about poetry?

2. Erotic love: What does Homer's work ultimately have to say about love?

For this essay, choose two or more couples in Homer: Zeus and Hera, Helen and Menelaus, Helen and Paris, Hector and Andromache, Achilles and Briseis, Achilles and Patroclus, or Odysseus and Penelope. Describe their relationships, with attention to the limitations of their communication. What are the incidents or factors that limit or enable communication for each couple? In the world of the *Iliad,* love seems to have no chance at all, while in the *Odyssey,* the question is whether Penelope will couple with someone new or somehow regain her long-lost husband.

3. **Nature:** Describe the tension between nature and culture in Homer.

The natural world seems to be of interest in the Homeric poems only insofar as it protrudes into human affairs. The battlefield before Troy is a rocky plain, but we are never told this; it is evident only because periodically a hero will heft an enormous stone and hurl it at his opponent. Until it gets used by someone, the stone is invisible to the poem. Explore how the natural world and the human interact in Odysseus's hunting of the stag in *Odyssey* 10, his emergence nearly naked from the woods to appear before young Nausicaa in *Odyssey* 5, and the *Iliad*'s repeated formulaic simile of "the lion in the pride of his strength."

Characters

In the novel or the drama, it always makes sense to ask questions about character development. This, however, marks another area in which Homer's ancient origins affect the criteria by which we understand him. There is a case to be made that Homeric heroes, at least some of them, do not in fact develop much at all. Do you see evidence of personal growth in any character in the *Iliad* or *Odyssey?* You might choose a particular character, consider his or her state earlier versus later in the poem, and ask questions about the implications. Does Helen change her mind about her own past conduct? Does Achilles change, learn, and grow between the poem's beginning and its end, or does he simply suffer and destroy? Is Odysseus wiser at the end of the *Odyssey* than at the beginning of the *Iliad?*

Another approach to character-driven essays is to choose a social role and ask questions about the particular characters that play that role in the text at hand.

Sample Topics:

1. **Homer's soldiers:** How does the "Homeric warrior ethic" shape the characters of different soldiers?

The entire *Iliad* and the latter part of the *Odyssey* present warfare. A striking feature of the experience of reading this poetry is the thrill of its combat scenes, horrifically paired with the vision of irreparable loss, pain, bereavement, and ruin. Homer makes us loathe war for the agony it brings, but he also compels us to admire it. How is this achieved? Talk of *kleos*—"fame"— seems utterly discredited by the sight of baby Astyanax in *Iliad* VI or of old Queen Hecuba's bare breast of pity in book XXII. Yet when Glaukos and Diomedes converse in book V, warfare almost seems both noble and inevitable again. Consider for example, Diomedes, Odysseus, Thersites, Paris, and Ajax. See Gregory Nagy, *The Best of the Achaeans: Concepts of the Hero in Archaic Greek Poetry* (Baltimore: The Johns Hopkins University Press, 1980).

2. **Homer's women:** How does gender shape our experience of Homer's characters?

Gender is a rich area for the discovery of interesting arguments and observations about any literary text, and the vast amount of time separating our world from Homer's gives these questions extra gravity. Most women were very limited in their opportunities in the Homeric world, and at the start of the *Iliad* we see girls being traded like chattel after their families have been killed by the girls' new owners. This is chilling, and we might expect to find the female side of the epics to be a wasteland of oppression and silence, but we do not. Penelope has a regal dignity and endearing cleverness that inspires reverence, and she even trips up Odysseus in her famous test of him at 23,176–80.

Helen is her own woman, though thousands die in the wake of her infidelity. Though Hera hates Thetis, the latter is a loving mother to Achilles and admirable for her tears on his behalf. (See *The Distaff Side: Representing the Female in Homer's Odyssey*, ed. Beth Cohen, New York: Oxford University Press, 1995.) While women in the *Iliad* are at risk of slavery, rape, and forced concubinage, they are exempt from the wholesale slaughter and humiliation of defeat in battle that seems to imprison the men from their infancy (for example, Astyanax) until death.

History and Context

Scholars argue about whether Homer was a single poet; a pair of poets who wrote one epic each; or a brilliant poet-editor who shaped a large amount of inherited material and composed a smaller amount of original material, uniting it all into the coherent literary whole we have today; or perhaps "Homer" is a collective name for tens or even hundreds of poets composing orally over decades and centuries until the Homeric poems were written down in the 740s B.C. in a process that we can never fully reconstruct. One way or another, the *Iliad* and *Odyssey* were produced by the social mind of a people as well as the shaping hand of one or more poets. When you read them in English, you are being exposed to elements of many cultural formations, indistinctly blended. These would include: the lost legendary world of the historical Trojan War (circa 1183 B.C.) and the 500-year "dark age" of relative hardship that followed, during which the oral poetry that became the *Iliad* and *Odyssey* emerged and those works moved toward their final form. Then there is the intermittent but enduring prestige of Homeric poetry during the successive phases of literary history in the West that we tend to call the archaic, classical, Hellenistic, late antique, medieval, and modern periods, during which the two epics have been revered, rebelled against, and imitated (and in some places, temporarily forgotten). In the 19th and 20th centuries, Homer's poetry was used widely in British and other European schoolrooms to teach young people (especially young men) to admire soldiering and warfare, until that ideal was shattered by the mechanized carnage of World War I; but to some degree, a selective use of the *Iliad* is still available even for this kind of exploitation. Now that mass education in the classical languages has long since become a quaint memory, the culture and psyche of the particular translator whose English Homer you happen to be reading (probably because it was the translation your teacher or professor chose—ask why!) is another factor that colors your perceptions. So is your own personal culture, through which your reading is always being filtered—sometimes in ways you cannot fully recognize without careful thought. The more those historical layers are known to you, the more sophisticated and deliberate you can be in the interpretive choices you make during your writing process.

Sample Topics:

1. **The historical context of epic poetry is its orality:** What effect does the meter of the Homeric poem have on the listener or reader?

There are no written historical records from the earliest period of the poems' composition, because there was no writing. The poems survived because they were brilliantly composed in *meter*, or "measure," according to an elaborate system of rules governing the placement of various kinds of syllables in different positions in the poetic line. These rules of Homeric versification are mysterious in origin and can be compared with the elaborate rules for articulating mantras in the distantly related Vedic culture of India. (See Frits Stahl, *Ritual and Mantra: Rules Without Meaning*, Delhi: Motilal Banarsidass Publications, 1996.)

Begin with some background reading on the idea of a society without writing: See Walter J. Ong, *Orality and Literacy: The Technologizing of the Word* (Routledge, 1982) and Eric A. Havelock, *The Muse Learns to Write: Reflections on Orality and Literacy from Antiquity to the Present* (Yale UP, 1988). You will find that some societies without writing are able to produce individuals with amazing powers of memorization, whose poetic performances may be partly improvised but are able to preserve large amounts of information, narrative, and other material that is central to the communal identity. These particular cognitive powers tend to contract or even vanish rather quickly once writing is developed or introduced to such a society.

2. **Translation:** Who translated the Homeric poems you are reading in English? When was the translation work being done, and what was going on in the world at that time? What was the response to that translation when it was first published?

Choose a passage that touches you or somehow strikes you as important, and compare the rendering of that passage in this translation to some other one. What do you consider the brilliancies and the infelicities, those spots where the translation does something especially well or especially poorly? This may seem impossible without a knowledge of the original, but it is not. Consider issues of pacing, tone, flow, the deployment of verbal tricks and double meanings, etc.

You might wish to begin with some background reading on translation, beginning with the classic essay "On Translating Homer," by Matthew Arnold. Alternatively, consult the anthology of translations, *Homer in English,* ed., Aminadav Dykman (NY: Penguin, 1996).

Philosophy and Ideas

If you are setting out to write an essay about the philosophy and/or ideas that Homer's work engages and expresses, it might feel odd to notice that both "philosophy" and "idea" are notions that came after Homer and were unknown to him. Socrates seems to have coined the term *philosophy* late in the fifth century B.C., and Plato invented "ideas" a few decades later. Still, those terms have become so central to our thought processes that they are more than likely to be part of the examination, the discussion, or the essay assignment you are given. For all their breadth, and despite this arcane bit of anachronism, they can still be useful terms. As a discussion of a modern author's philosophy might turn on her attitudes about conduct, so an essay on Homer's world-view might focus on soldiering, with its notion of fame which, in retrospect, we might call an idea or a concept. *Kleos* is the Homeric term for fame, that particular kind of battlefield glory whose renown endures, apparently forever (see, for example, *Iliad* VII, 91, "so that my *kleos* will never perish"). The poet gives us several different presentations of *kleos:* the conversation of Glaukos and Diomedes in *Iliad* V; the speech of Hector over Astyanax in *Iliad* VI, and of Nestor in various moments of didactic reminiscence. These values pertain to the production of one specialized kind of life: the immortality of fame, in which the body dies but the glory of a heroic reputation lives on, imperishable because of its immateriality. Such "unperishing *kleos*" is never to be forgotten, so long as the Muse continues to enable human poetry.

Kleos is a "Uranian" value, that is, it is driven by the Indo-European male sky god (Zeus); the converse value is "Cthonian," sponsored by the Indo-European female earth goddess and sponsoring procreation, nurturance, the indoors, and the night. While these two terms form a dichotomy with considerable explanatory power, the Uranian/Chthonian dichotomy is a device that can sometimes blind people to ambiguities in the poems if it is simply taken on trust and overused.

Sample Topics:

1. *Kleos:* What exactly is Homer's concept of *kleos*, and how is it incorporated into his larger worldview?

2. **Ethics of piracy, loitering, and extortion:** Considering the entire arc of Odysseus's character from the earliest events of the *Iliad* to the end of the *Odyssey*, is Odysseus "good"? What are the ethical parameters he seems to respect or represent? Why is it acceptable for Odysseus to sack the Cicones but not for the Suitors to consume Odysseus's livestock?

3. **Masculinity:** Identify and evaluate the multiple models of masculinity that are presented and represented in Homer's work. We hear a warrior ideal of masculinity articulated variously by Glaukos to Diomedes, Hector to Astyanax, Patroclus to Achilles. Are they all essentially the same, or are there salient differences? Or consider some of the following male figures in Homer as alternative models: Thersites, Chryses, or Paris.

Form and Genre

When you are asked to consider "form" and "genre," ask yourself how a literary work is put together and what kind of story it is. In the case of Homer, one significant element of form is narration. You want to examine how the story is told, who tells it, and why. While initially these factors might seem to be outside the story proper, they are in fact an integral part of the story itself. In a novel or a lyric poem, the author is an individual, a private citizen with an address, but the narrator is someone else. In ancient epic, by contrast, the author is an unknown entity, a cipher for whose mystery our minds compensate by simply construing the narrator as the author. If you are an artist of one kind or another, or if you simply remember the very beginning of the poem, you will well recognize that the Muse is the one speaking through the poet. Consider the example of the much later, medieval epic poet Dante Alighieri. Inspired by his muse, Beatrice, Dante the poet writes a long poem whose speaker is another Dante, narrating the experiences of a third Dante, internal to the poem, whom we call Dante the pilgrim. As for Homer, there probably was a living genius whose brain once composed the majority of the lines of the *Iliad* and *Odyssey* and set them into their current shape, but that person died so long ago that almost nothing is known except a vague association with certain places, especially Smyrna and Khios. The composer perished thousands of years ago, but we can still hear—and because of Homer's poetic powers, even imaginatively see or conjure—him (or her) invoking the goddess and singing to the lyre. (Some writers, for example, Samuel Butler, Robert Graves, and Andrew Dalby, have argued for a female Homer.) Clearly, there is more than one person involved in any practice of the art of poetry. Plato wrote a dialogue about just this issue called the *Ion,* after its main character, who was a "rhapsode," or professional reciter of Homer, to whom Socrates explains how inspiration works in matters of poetry:

> **SOCRATES:** Do you know that the spectator is the last of the rings which, as I am saying, receive the power of the original magnet from one another? The rhapsode like yourself and the actor are intermediate links, and the poet himself is the first of them. Through all these the God sways the souls of men in any direction which he pleases, and makes one man hang down from another. Thus there is a vast chain of dancers and masters and under-masters of choruses, who are suspended, as if from the stone, at the side of the rings which hang down from the Muse. And every poet has some Muse from whom he is suspended, and by whom he is said to be possessed, which is nearly the same thing; for he is taken hold of. [Jowett translation]

Narration is of especial interest in the eighth book of the *Odyssey* where the bard Demodocus vies with Odysseus for the microphone, as it were. The poet shows us a professional poetic performer and juxtaposes him with the odd, interloping, category-crossing figure of Odysseus—a person who was (like the Muses, but unlike Demodocus, a typical bard whom they inspire) present during the Iliadic events of which Demodocus sings. Homer shows us Odysseus himself acting as a singer, when we are given the most unlikely of the *Odyssey*'s materials (the stories of the Cyclops, Circe, the Lystragonians, and other monstrous creatures for whom the real world of the audience seems to have no place). The outlandish nature (not yet split off as the "supernatural") of Odysseus's exotic adventure stories raises the question of his reliability as a narrator; so does the fact that he is in disguise for much of the poem and quite often tells what we know to be outright lies. Look closely at the relationship between poetry and pain in Homer, including Odysseus's tears of recollection and longing amid the song of Demodocus, and Helen's use of a pain-killing drug ("analgesic") during the nostalgic storytelling that takes place in her home on Sparta in *Odyssey* 4. (Consider the feminist critique of the *Odyssey*'s treatment of audiences—internal, implied, and actual—in *Siren Songs: Gender, Audiences, and Narrators in the* Odyssey, by Lillian Eileen Doherty, Ann Arbor: U of Michigan P, 1996.)

Sample Topics:

1. **Narration:** What issues arise from the fact that Odysseus the hero is also a singer of epic poetry?

   To a degree, the *Odyssey* takes the *Iliad*'s language of pain and moves it from the domain of real life into the new domain of art. The back and forth movement of the privilege of narration between Odysseus and Demodocus is rich in hidden implications.

2. **Small-scale structures:** What are some effects of the meter of Homeric verse?

   Because Homeric poetry was oral in both composition and performance, each line of it must fit into the frame of the meter—in the case of Homer and most other epic poets (for example Hesiod in Greek and Virgil in Latin but not Dante in Italian), that meter is dactylic hexameter. Its line is made up of six sections (or "feet"), each foot taking the form of a "dactyl," which means a three-syllable unit with only one stressed syllable, namely the first one: *X-o-o*. Another way to remember this is that in the name of the meter, dactylic hexameter, the adjective *dactylic* is itself a dactyl: *DAC-tyl-ic*. Within the rules of versification, the poet can also substitute other feet at certain positions; the most common of these alternative metrical feet is the spondee: *X-X*. Like the dactyl, the spondee starts with a stressed beat, but it follows it with another single stressed beat, instead of the pair of unstressed half-beats that a dactyl uses to fill the same block of time in the poetic line. In dactylic hexameter, the fifth foot is often a spondee; the sixth is always a spondee.

Now, even if you never pursue the details of Homeric versification, you may find it worth noting that the highly metrical language of Homer's poetry is trance inducing. Though no translation compares to the incantatory power of the ancient Greek original, the best English translations (such as the *Iliad* of Richmond Lattimore and the *Odyssey* of Albert Cook) on the lips of an able reader can be captivating for hours at a time, even without musical accompaniment. Is there a comparison to be made between Homeric poetry and hip-hop? For further reading, see, for example, Mark W. Edwards, *Sound, Sense, and Rhythm: Listening to Greek and Latin Poetry* (Princeton UP, 2004).

3. Medium-scale structures: Describe the Homeric simile.

A simile asserts commonality, that one thing is like something else. When something is to be described that lies beyond our usual experience, we resort to comparisons with more familiar things, chosen for their special similarities to the strange thing in the poem. For example, in *Iliad* II, 458, Homer compares the swarming Achaean soldiers to flies around a milking pail. The audience of the poet's day knew every sensory-motor nuance of the experience of milking a sheep, including the ongoing effort to cope with swarming flies; using this knowledge, they could perceive through the simile the strange phenomenon on the other side: a mass of Bronze Age warriors from centuries before, alive and moving in the plains before Troy, with the Trojan War still undecided.

Homeric poetry contains some 240 similes, each as brief as a pair of lines or as dilatory and expansive as a sonnet's worth of lines. Homer will often deploy a simile at a moment of high dramatic tension or crisis in order to delay the resolution that a climax demands. The simile has this effect of a pause in the flow of time; as the poem shifts from diachronic narration to synchronic slideshow, time seems to stop and we are shown a static tableau, within which there are two superimposed images: the humble, rustic barn circa 800 B.C. and the Trojan beach circa 1180 B.C. Since you are in neither moment, you triangulate among them when you hear the words and visualize: the flies above the pail, the animal, the cream; the soldiers busily ranging about their camp or issuing en masse from the holds of the ships. Because the world of Odysseus in the *Odyssey* is generally closer to the world of Homer's audience than was the world of the *Iliad*, similes are about three times more common in the earlier than in the later poem.

For more on the Homeric simile, see: Ian Johnston, "Homer's Similes: Nature as Conflict," at: http://records.viu.ca/~Johnstoi/homer/Iliadessaystofc.htm; William C. Scott, *The Artistry of the Homeric Simile* (Dartmouth College Press, University Press of New England: 2009); Irene J. F. de Jong, ed. *Homer: Critical Assessments* (Routledge, 1999); and "On Homer's Similes" by Eleanor F. Rambo, *The Classical Journal*, vol. 28, no. 1 (October 1932): 22–31.

4. **Large-scale structure, the epic:** What claims can you make about the large-scale structure of the epic? Does Homer plan on that scale?

Note that there is an important approach to Homeric poetry that involves concentrating on large-scale structures. Scholars with work of this kind include Oliver Taplin, whose *Homeric Soundings: The Shaping of the* Iliad (London: Oxford University Press, 1995) is especially helpful. See also Bruce Louden, *The* Odyssey: *Structure, Narration and Meaning* (Baltimore: The Johns Hopkins University Press, 1999) and Frederick Ahl, *The* Odyssey *Reformed* (Ithaca: Cornell Studies in Classical Philology, 1996). These books argue that there is good reason to think of Homer as a highly conscious, individual artist who was well able to shape large-scale structures across the entire *Iliad* or *Odyssey.* This he achieved by situating repetitions, often with ironic contrasts, at points in the narrative that are far removed from one another. Homer also used the method of ring composition, where the repetitions are patterned like the rings on a tree stump, resulting in a symmetry that is sometimes grand in its scale, uniting elements that are hundreds and even thousands of lines apart. Your task for such an essay would include the search for such elements, along with an effort to interpret them.

Compare and Contrast Essays

The most important thing to remember when you are writing a comparison and contrast essay is that your essay should do a great deal more than merely point out similarities and differences among several literary works. It is your job to explain to your readers the significance of these similarities and differences, to turn your observations into an interesting interpretation or argument. This will be easier if you have a good reason for comparing the pieces you are discussing in the first place. For example, if you are comparing the work of Athena and Hermes at the opening of the *Odyssey* with the conduct of the same two gods at the same poem's end, you are likely to discover something about the Homeric perception of the way the world works—gods sometimes work along parallel tracks to bring about shared goals—as well as something about the characters of these two particular gods—both of them are young, clever, and somehow attached to Odysseus.

Sample Topics:

1. **Elements common to both of Homer's epics:** Compare and contrast an aspect of Homer's work, such as a social institution (*xenia* or "hospitality," marriage, supplication, or dining are possible topics), looking at its consistencies and variations in the *Iliad* and *Odyssey.*

   Start by choosing two or more passages that seem to you to have some significant connection. For example, both epics can be said to hinge on acts of violated hospitality. You might compare and contrast the conduct of the suitors with that of Paris when he was Menelaus's guest in Sparta before the war. Once you have studied each of the texts separately, set them side by side to draw conclusions.

2. **Homer's work with that of another author:** Compare and contrast Homer's work with that of Hesiod, another author working in roughly the same time period.

Begin by choosing two works with something in common. You might decide to compare and contrast Hesiod's *Theogony* with Homer's *Iliad* book I, since each is an early work about the gods. Who is Zeus in each of these two texts? What might explain the differences?

Bibliography

Crotty, Kevin. *The Poetics of Supplication: Homer's* Iliad *and* Odyssey. Ithaca, NY: Cornell University Press, 1994.

Drews, Robert. *The End of the Bronze Age: Changes in Warfare and the Catastrophe ca. 1200 B.C.* Princeton, NJ: Princeton University Press, 1993.

Ford, Andrew. Homer: *The Poetry of the Past.* Ithaca, NY: Cornell University Press, 1994.

Mallory, Thomas. *In Search of the Indo-Europeans: Language, Archaeology and Myth.* London: Thames & Hudson Ltd., 1989.

ILIAD I–II:

The Quarrel, the Dream, and the Catalog of Ships

READING TO WRITE

THE *ILIAD* is the first of the two Homeric epics, earlier both in its composition and in the events of its narrative chronology. Whereas the *Iliad*'s action covers a two-week period during the ninth year of the decade-long Trojan War, the *Odyssey* is one of several poems about the homecoming (in Greek, the *nostos*) of one of the victorious Greek heroes, Odysseus. So *Iliad* I is the first of the first; in it, certain issues are presented more directly than anywhere else in the poem. In the opening line, we are shown the principle on which epic poetry operates: an immortal female principle—called *Thea* ("goddess") in the first line of the *Iliad* but *Mousa* ("muse") in the first line of the *Odyssey*—tells the poet what to say. Though we might expect the omniscience of the goddess to be based on a strictly magical sort of power, according to *Iliad* II the Muses know all by virtue of their having been present when the narrated events occurred. This is why they can recite, through the poet, the amazingly detailed "Catalog of Ships" (the phrase does not occur in the poem and is, like most of the names for Homeric episodes mentioned in this book, a scholarly convention) with neither error nor loss of audience interest. As Aristotle pointed out, the *Iliad* begins *in medias res*, "in the middle of things," rather than at the beginning of the Trojan War. This means that the poem's first movement must be rich in exposition, otherwise the audience will not know what is going on. So we get the encapsulated story of Achilles' quarrel with Agamemnon, involving

Chryses, the priest of Apollo, his daughter Chryseis, Achilles' "bride" Briseis, the prophet Calchas, and the god Apollo.

Be sure you understand the mechanics of Homer's plot, but be equally careful to avoid merely summarizing that plot in your paper. Some plot summary is usually necessary, but you must resist the temptation to fill your available space with an uncritical recounting of the poem's action. The best that could yield would be a competent and accurate list of events, not an analysis based on insight. Having done some reading and acquired some information, you are now pursuing essay-writing skills that are themselves means to an end, namely insight.

Be aware that if the writing assignment is fairly open, most students will choose to write essays about the beginning of the book, in the mistaken belief that it is possible to do so effectively without reading the entire work. So if you choose to focus your essay on this region of the text, be sure to make it clear that you are familiar with the book as a whole, as well. Your instructor may be grading a stack of papers, half of which are about diverse passages from *Iliad* II through XXIV, while the other half are on the first book of the *Iliad.* Make your paper stand out from these by presenting book I in the context of the whole book. Since the subject of book I, as of book IX, is Achilles' first and lesser wrath, you might accomplish this by making a comparison to the greater wrath that forms the subject of the poem's final six books. Many more suggestions follow.

We can begin with a close reading of an important passage, book II, 484–93:

> Tell me now, you Muses who have your homes on Olympos.
> For you, who are goddesses, are there,
>   and you know all things,
> and we have heard only the rumor of it and know nothing.
> Who then of those were the chief men and the lords of
>   the Danaans?
> I could not tell over the multitude of them nor name them,
> not if I had ten tongues and ten mouths, not if I had
> a voice never to be broken and a heart of bronze within me,
> not unless the Muses of Olympia, daughters
> of Zeus of the aegis, remembered all those who came
>   beneath Ilion.

The first thing to notice is that this passage from the middle of book II gives substance and detail to the invocation at the opening of book I. Here we are being told that the Muses have eyewitness knowledge, whereas human beings (like the poet, and his recital-performing successors, the rhapsodes, and their audience) only have aural information secondhand. Poetic knowledge is mere hearsay, but it is the best hearsay there is. As for real knowledge, the Greek language is unmistakably clear about its deep-seated connection between seeing and knowing. In his tragedy of *Oedipus*, Sophocles made much of this verbal fact, and it is in the study of that text that most of us learn this: in Greek, an important verb for "I see" becomes synonymous with "I know" when it is put into the perfect tense, the tense where the action of the verb has been finished and thus brought to perfection: "I have seen" and "I know" are expressed by the same form, *oida*. Note also the language of scarcity and abundance in the quoted passage: "not if I had ten tongues and ten mouths . . ." Scarcity and abundance will be a governing motif through the entire poem, especially since the Trojan War is one giant piracy expedition sustained by an ongoing series of lesser raids on nearby towns: "I have stormed from my ships twelve cities / of men, and by land eleven more through the generous Troad [the vast plain surrounding Troy]" says Achilles in book IX. There we even see this same logical operator from the passage quoted above: "Not if he [Agamemnon] gave me ten times as much, and twenty times over . . ." (IX, 379); in other words, even if the scarce thing was abundant, it would make little difference.

The passage is also about the difference between mortals and the gods. They have abundant eyewitness knowledge; we have scarce hearsay. They also have abundant immortal life, whereas the *Iliad* shows human beings dying like the insects or withering leaves to which the poet compares us. That links this passage to others in which the difference between gods and humans comes into focus, such as *Iliad* V, 127: "I have taken away the mist from your eyes, that before now / was there, so that you may well recognize the god and the mortal." Athena says this to Diomedes in order to prevent him from suffering the fate that overtakes Patroclus in book XVI, namely the hubris of fighting directly against a god on the battlefield. Notice that she has taken away a "mist" that was preventing Diomedes from seeing through the disguises of the gods, and that this mist is not peculiar to this man or these circumstances. The implication of the passage is that the gods have at all times misted the eyes of mortal people as part of our chronic condition. Presumably, we cannot see the gods now (circa 740 B.C. with Homer's original audience, nor in the 21st century) because they have left this mist in place. Observe that the motif of the Divine as the disabler of the human is deeply traditional. It appears in the Judaic tradition in Genesis, where the forbidden fruit of the Tree of Knowledge inflicts mortality and scarcity on Adam and Eve; it also appears closer to Homer, in Plato's *Symposium*, where the gods punish the double-bodied ancestors of humanity by splitting them in half (giving us our current form), making us weaker and slower and full of yearning for that split-off partner whom we can only regain through sexual love.

TOPICS AND STRATEGIES

This section of the chapter presents various topics for essays and general approaches to those topics. Be aware that the material below is only a place to start from, not some kind of master key to the perfect essay. Use this material to prompt your own thinking. Every topic discussed here could encompass a wide variety of papers.

Themes

While Homeric poetry deals with the great issues of human life from love to death and all things in between, the main subjects of the *Iliad* are war, ambition, hubris, grief and mourning, and something resembling forgiveness. Homer's world is full of men, ships, gods, women, and animals. While you may arrive at a topic and accompanying essay title that are more complex than a single word might imply (for example, "Achilles and Helen as Category-Crossing Figures," rather than just "Gender"), such simple topics are a good starting point for your critical imagination, especially in the earlier stages of the sorting process by which you arrive at a thesis statement. Note also that some of the best essays ever written, those of Ralph Waldo Emerson, tend to have one-word titles such as "Compensation," "History," and so on. In approaching your essay, sort your interests and then isolate passages from Homer that speak to the themes you find engaging. The questions presented here are not a list of assignments to be executed one after the other but a set of prompts intended to trigger or enhance your own thought process in pursuit of an original, accurate, and interesting essay of your own.

Sample Topics:

1. Nature versus culture: Discuss the "scepter / studded with golden nails" (II, 245–46). What does it symbolize and how?

The first thing to do given this topic is to quote the passage in question:

> But I will tell you this and swear a great oath
>   upon it:
> in the name of this scepter, which never again
>   will bear leaf nor
> branch, now that it has left behind the cut
>   stump in the mountains,
> nor shall it ever blossom again, since the
>   bronze blade stripped
> bark and leafage, and now at last the sons of
>   the Achaeans
> carry it in their hands in state when they
>   administer
> the justice of Zeus. And this shall be a great
>   oath before you:
> some day longing for Achilles will come to the
>   sons of the Achaeans,
> all of them. Then stricken at heart though you
>   be, you will be able
> to do nothing, when in their numbers before
>   man-slaughtering Hector
> they drop and die. And then you will eat out
>   the heart within you
> in sorrow, that you did no honor to the best of
>   the Achaeans. (I, 233–39)

Next, read the passage several times and then see what stands out in your mind. After the formulaic line that introduces this passage are five lines about the scepter on which Achilles swears, followed by five lines of the oath itself. There are certain objects by which it is conventional for oaths to be sworn; these include swords, tombs, crowns, and scepters. Though the choice of oath object is conventional, note Achilles' striking account of the history of this scepter, its total transformation from a living plant to a dead instrument. The scepter is a symbol, therefore it corresponds to something other than itself, in such a way as to evoke deep issues about that thing. To what might this object correspond?

For an answer, consider the content of the oath Achilles is swearing on this scepter: "Some day longing for Achilles will come to the sons of the Achaeans, / all of them . . . when in their numbers before man-slaughtering Hector / they drop and die." Like the green sapling in the wild, the young soldiers Achilles is talking about—and addressing with this oath—have natural life in their veins. Though their war-fame may be limited as yet, their bonds with one another and with their loved ones back home are still intact, just as the scepter was once growing wild "in the mountains," not an object of use nor even an object of knowledge, still rooted, still bearing branches, still protected by bark. The wild young tree is still undifferentiated from the others by any woodworking or inscription or golden nails, as any boy soldier is still undifferentiated from the others by any disfiguring wounds, heroic exploits, and consequent fame *(kleos)*, nor any glorious monument (such as the one Hector fantasizes about at VII, 89–90). The comparison becomes explicit quite often: remember the common Iliadic simile where the dying young soldier is to the bronze weapon as a young tree is to an axe. As William Clyde Scott wrote, "Simoesius, Crethus Orsilochus, Imbrius, Asius, and Sarpedon drop like chopped trees [at] IV, 482; V, 560; XIII, 178; XIII, 389; and XVI, 482" (Scott, 70). Nature is transformed into culture through a death process that trades the warm, embodied life of experience and growth in exchange for a cold, disembodied immortality of fame that others can hear about but not touch or access. Indeed, the disabling of interpersonal touch as a consequence of war death appears in Achilles' futile attempt to embrace the ghost of Patroclus, as it does in the poem "Greater Love" by World War I poet Wilfred Owen: "Weep, you may weep, for you may touch them not."

2. **Rage** *(mênis):* Compare the two rages of Achilles.

Wrath, the traditional English term for major, consequence-bearing anger, has become a bit archaic, so we will use *rage* instead. As previously noted, the Greek term used is *mênis*, the first word of the *Iliad* (where we find it used as an object, in what is grammatically identified as the accusative case, with the form *mênin*). This is a compare and contrast assignment, but it is also a theme-based assignment asking about Achilles' rage. To perform it, you would look hard at our present text (*Iliad* I and II) for the first part of the comparison; for the second part, you would revisit Achilles's behavior after book XVIII, 20, the point where he learns of Patroclus's death.

3. Supplication: What is the role of supplication in *Iliad* I, II?

Scholar Kevin Crotty wrote *The Poetics of Supplication*, one of many books in the field of Homeric studies focused on exactly this theme. Still other books about Homer will have a single chapter on the topic, which might be a more manageable amount of material in some academic circumstances. Supplication is a formal yet intimate, ritualized, and adaptable form of begging for something specific. The suppliant makes an eloquent, explicit plea for relief, spoken in formal tones, generally in a self-humbling posture such as kneeling and holding the beard (or the knees) of the authority he or she has approached. Generally, supplication involves some plea for reciprocity, with the suppliant reminding the supplicated one of any services already performed, and/or promising services in the future. Depending on the strength of the reciprocity claimed, the obligation to grant the suppliant's wish can be very strong. Here in the *Iliad*'s first two books, we see Apollo's priest Chryses supplicate Agamemnon, asking for the return of his daughter Chryseis in exchange for ransom. But King Agamemnon refuses, which triggers the rest of the plot, beginning with the next supplication: Chryses supplicates Apollo in prayer, bringing plague on the Achaeans. Agamemnon did not accept Chryses' supplication; Apollo does. Nine plague days later, there is a kind of supplication in the request of the prophet Calchas that Achilles guarantee his safety in exchange for his frank public disclosure of his vision. Achilles, in turn, supplicates his divine mother Thetis with the wish for her to please, in turn, supplicate Zeus on Achilles' behalf, which she does. The examples go on and on; now that you know what supplication is, you can find important instances of it and interpret them, perhaps comparatively. A similar process applies with other Homeric institutions like hospitality *(xenia).*

4. **Politics:** What kind of political processes occur in *Iliad* I and II? What are the limitations of those political processes?

This essay is of course asking about the great Assembly of the Achaeans in book I, on the ninth day of the plague. But it is broad enough to include one-on-one political exchanges such as the supplications we discussed, or the amazing private interaction between Achilles and Athena (invisible to everyone but him) that occurs amid that public assembly. Like most questions about social institutions, this one raises the possibility that they are not adequate to prevent disaster.

Character

To teach the *Iliad* even once is to be amazed at the depth of feeling this poem can conjure in students of all ages, despite the 3,000 years separating contemporary readers from its subject. Homer achieves such emotional resonance and immediacy with a gift for characterization unrivaled in its graceful economy. Remember that the question is always asking you what you can demonstrate using quotations from the primary text, in this case Homer's poetry.

Sample Topics:
1. **The nature of Homeric characters:** Do they develop?

This was once an important question in Homeric scholarship, largely resolved in the past few decades with an affirmative answer. From the work of Milman Parry in the 1930s through that of his successors Adam Parry and Albert Lord in midcentury, academic opinion was mightily impressed by the collective nature of oral poetic composition. Milman Parry discovered that the *Iliad* and *Odyssey* were composed orally in a formulaic style that made use of a stock of phrases to fit various positions in the dactylic hexameter line. His successors went on to suggest that much of the creativity involved in the production of what became the two epics may have belonged to several generations of professional poetic performers, improvising around a common stock of stories, using a common stock of phrases. Instead of the blind old man from Smyrna, "Homer" became many bards at many times and places, who performed many different versions of many different chunks of poetic subject matter, arranging them in different patterns and sequences. In more recent decades that trend has largely been reversed, due to a 1982 study of *The Epithets in Homer* by Paolo Vivante, popularized by Seth Schein in his 1984 book, *The Mortal Hero.*

As some of Parry's readers subtracted individuality from their idea of the poems' author, many of them also subtracted it from their reading of the characters. If there was no unitary authorial intention to craft a character's developmental arc, just a field (a bit like the Internet, but with no "by" lines) full of free-floating blocks of story to be arranged into a sequence, then this sequence might give the illusion of character development, and that explains why we feel as if Achilles is growing up in the *Iliad,* or Odysseus is becoming wiser in the *Odyssey.* That is the "nondevelopmental" view. What do you think? Choose a character in Homer and focus on that character's story. Does the person change, or is he or she simply responding to changing circumstances without being inwardly shaped by them?

2. **Achilles in *Iliad* I–II:** How does Homer show us who Achilles is in this text? Why exactly does Achilles obey Athena's instructions, and are those reasons revealing of his nature?

Examine the specific words and behaviors of Achilles in the Assembly, and compare his interaction with Athena to his interactions with Agamemnon here. You might also compare the former to Athena's interactions with other heroes, such as Odysseus and Diomedes. What are Achilles' apparent ideas about authority?

3. Agamemnon as character in *Iliad* I–II: How does Homer show us who Agamemnon is? Why does Agamemnon risk angering Achilles, when he could have simply returned Chryseis, accepted the ransom, and gone on to other business?

Note Agamemnon's hubristic language at I, 182–87: "*Even as Phoibos Apollo is taking* away my Chryseis . . . / *I shall take* the fair-cheeked Briseis . . . *and another man may shrink back from likening himself to me* and contending against me." In a single sentence, the king first commits hubris by likening himself to Apollo; next, by insisting like a god that any man must "shrink back from likening himself to me"—the same divine privilege that he himself has just infringed. Look for other moments when Agamemnon's language is especially suited to his character or expressive of his predicament.

4. Women: Comment on the doubling effect of the rhyming women's names, Briseis and Chrysies, which suggests their subordinate condition as chattel to be traded between men.

Homer's brevity in the presentation of Briseis here in the *Iliad*'s opening books will yield to a rush of emotion in book XIX where we hear "Briseis's Lament for Patroclus." That sudden opening of the character's humanity has a stronger effect, because the Briseis we know until that point has been something of a stick figure; we know Achilles loves her but not why. (See Casey Dué, *Homeric Variations on a Lament by Briseis*, Rowman & Littlefield, 2002.) What do you make of Agamemnon's remark about Chryseis at I, 113–15: "I like her better than Klytaimnestra / my own wife, for in truth she is no way inferior, / neither in build nor stature nor wit, not in accomplishment"? Before you write about women in the ancient world, you should acquaint yourself with one of the many excellent works of general background on the subject, among them Sarah Pomeroy's *Goddesses, Whores, Wives, and Slaves: Women in Classical Antiquity* (Schocken Books, 1995), Susan Blundell's *Women in Ancient Greece* (Harvard UP, 1995), and

The Distaff Side: Representing the Female in Homer's Odyssey, edited by Beth Cohen (Oxford UP, 1995).

5. **Gods:** Choose among one of the following divine actions and analyze Homer's presentation of it: Apollo and the plague; Athena's intervention; Thetis's supplication of Zeus.

This writing assignment prompts you to think about the gods and their role in human affairs. Apollo is like a force of nature as he shoots his arrows of plague up and down the ranks of the Achaean army. Athena is like a part of Achilles' own mind (the part Freud called the superego, which is responsible for impulse control) as she grabs him by the hair and turns him around. The goddess Thetis is like a mortal woman in her plea to Zeus on her mortal son's behalf. Yet for the Homeric world the gods are far more than personifications of natural forces, offshoots of the human psyche, or mortal persons like us. They represent a European polytheist tradition that was eventually defeated by monotheism and driven underground, where it was maintained in a fragmented, erratic, residual form by fringe figures who lacked a place in the new order. See, for example, Keith Thomas, *Religion and the Decline of Magic* (Scribner's, 1970) and *God Against the Gods: The History of the War Between Monotheism and Polytheism* by Jonathan Kirsch (Penguin, 2005). In Homer, however, the Olympian gods are in their glory days, still triumphant over their predecessors the Titans and earth goddesses, and not yet faced with the bizarre idea that there might only be one god, after all. The great expression of Zeus's supremacy is, in the prose translation of Samuel Butler: "Make ye fast from heaven a chain of gold, and lay ye hold thereof, all ye gods and all goddesses; yet could ye not drag to earth from out of heaven Zeus the Counselor most high, not though ye labored sore. But whenso I were minded to draw of a ready heart, then with earth itself should I draw you and with sea withal; and the rope should I thereafter bind about a peak of Olympus and all those things should hang in space" (VIII, 19–26).

Olympian religion was never so codified and official as the modern religions with which most of us are familiar; there were shrines to various gods all over Greece, and priests in their employ, but nothing like the vast bureaucracies of the contemporary Vatican or the 19th-century Tibetan Buddhist hierarchy. Like Sufism or even Hinduism, the term *Olympian religion* is really a catch-all, intended to subsume hundreds of local cults and minor deities, some of them long forgotten. "Homer's Olympian religion is Panhellenic," writes Seth Schein, citing the great 19th-century philologist Erwin Rohde (who was, incidentally, a friend and colleague of Friedrich Nietzsche). "That is, the actual differences among the innumerable local cults of the Olympian Gods are ignored in the *Iliad* (and *Odyssey*), as Homer transcends the limits of regional and local worship to create in poetry a religious uniformity that did not exist historically" (Schein, 49). This Homeric trend toward a religious identity that would embrace the entire Greek-speaking region is paralleled in other similar movements from the same period: The establishment of the Olympic games in 776 B.C. both expressed and enhanced an emergent Panhellenic consciousness, as did the colonial expansionism of the period, which brought Greek-speaking settlers farther to the periphery of Hellenic civilization without eroding their identity as ancient Greeks. They had, or would very soon have, the Homeric poems for their mirror.

The topics offered are Apollo and the plague, Athena's intervention, and Thetis's supplication of Zeus. All three are examples of a god doing something to fulfill an obligation to someone else: Apollo reciprocates Chryses' prayer by shooting plague arrows at the Greek army; Athena enacts Hera's instructions by accosting Achilles; and Thetis carries out her promise to her son Achilles by supplicating Zeus on his behalf. Observe how many and varied are the links connecting gods and mortals in this little list of three divine actions. The cosmos comprises mortals and immortals together, and is itself a kind of society.

Philosophy and Ideas

Over the course of the past century, Homeric poetry has been the scene of some remarkable assertions about consciousness. Perhaps most important of these are *The Origin of Consciousness in the Breakdown of the Bicameral Mind* by Julian Jaynes (Mariner, 2000); *The Greeks and the Irrational* (Sather Classical Lectures) by E. R. Dodds (U of California P, 2004); and *The Discovery of the Mind: The Greek Origins of European Thought* by Bruno Snell (Harper, 1960). More recently, these issues were given new direction by Richard Gaskin in an essay, "Do Homeric Heroes Make Real Decisions?" in *Oxford Readings in Homer's Iliad,* ed. Douglas Cairns (Oxford UP, 2002). These books examine the way the Homeric poems present human mental functioning (especially decision making, but also willed physical movement) looking for clues about the kind of minds Homer's audience may have had and what their assumptions might have been in regard to the way the mind works. Putting those books aside for the moment, what do the pages of the *Iliad* suggest to you about the issues we call philosophical?

Sample Topics:

1. **Free will and constraint:** Consider the plight of the high king, Agamemnon. He says the same thing on two occasions: II, 110–19 and IX, 17–28. What are the crucial differences between the two iterations of these words? What ironies arise from the comparison of the two passages?

Quote the passages and you will find they are identical:

> Zeus son of Kronos has caught me fast in bitter
> futility.
> He is hard; who before this time promised me
> and consented
> that I might sack strong-walled Ilion and sail
> homeward.
> Now he has devised a vile deception, and bids
> me go back
> to Argos in dishonor having lost many of my
> people. (II, 110–19 / IX, 17–28)

What is dramatically different are the circumstances surrounding Agamemnon's two iterations of these lines. In the first (II, 110–19), he thinks he is cleverly testing his troops by pretending to despair, hoping they will prove so spirited for the war as to refuse his suggestion of flight and instead insist on staying until their eventual victory. Unfortunately, they are actually as eager to quit and leave as he had feared they might be. He is wrong about it all: the mood of the troops, the truth value of the dream, the fate of the impending assault it urged, and the entire quarrel with Achilles, who introduced the idea of dreams as a reliable source of information for decision making. Revisit that last fact for a moment.

At I, 63, Achilles tells the assembled Greeks that their present troubles require them to consult "a soothsayer, or an interpreter of Dreams," adding the peculiar phrase, "for a Dream, too, comes from Zeus." This seems to equate divine origin with truthfulness. Yet Zeus immediately sends one such dream to the sleeping general Agamemnon with a totally false and disastrous promise of success in his next campaign—a message that begins with the exquisitely true announcement: "I am a messenger from Zeus," followed by the false phrase "who pities you from far away . . ." This dream is mixing lies with truth, divine sponsorship (like what Odysseus gets from Athena in the *Odyssey*) with divine opposition (like what Odysseus gets from Poseidon in the *Odyssey*).

By the time Agamemnon expresses his despair in book IX, speaking the same words he spoke in book II, he is no longer merely feigning it to test his men; the despair is earnest, and he expects to lose. Zeus has in fact "caught [him] in bitter futility," and Agamemnon's dishonesty with his men in book II has compounded his own experience of being deceived, since just when he thought he was cleverly lying, he was speaking the truth without knowing it. Now in book IX the despair is real, but Diomedes is able to rouse the troops (doing Agamemnon's own job, as Patroclus does Achilles' job) so that they insist on victory as Agamemnon had hoped they would back in book II. The relevance of all this lies in the phrase "Zeus has caught me fast" (as in "held fast," meaning tightly, not quickly; think of the verb *fasten*). What do these repetitions—charged with the ironies we have just surveyed—suggest about man's position in the cosmos? It seems the shaping presence of the gods, who keep showing up in human lives to trigger new stages in Zeus's plan (I, 5), is like the shaping presence of an author in a story whose plot he implements. That idea is deeply traditional and will resurface hundreds of times as literary history unfolds. Should you choose to discuss this issue, you may want to quote Greek tragedy or Shakespeare; if possible, find a relevant quotation from a play being taught in the same course for which you are now writing your Homer essay.

2. **Transience:** One recurrent theme in the *Iliad* is transience, the passing nature of human beings, the way mortals come and go while the world and the gods continue.

Consider *Iliad* II, 695–710.:

> They who held Phylake and Pyrasos of the
>   flowers,
> the precinct of Demeter, and Iton, mother of
>   sheepflocks,
> Antron by the sea-shore, and Pteleos deep in
>   the meadows,
> of these in turn fighting Protesilaos was
>   leader
> while he lived; but now the black earth had
>   closed him under,
> whose wife, cheeks torn for grief, was left
>   behind in Phylake
> and a marriage half completed; a Dardanian man
>   had killed him
> as he leapt from his ship, far the first of all
>   the Achaeans.
> Yet these, longing as they did for their
>   leader, did not go leaderless,
> but Podarkes, scion of Ares, set them in order,
>   child of Iphikles, who in turn was son to
>   Phylakos

rich in flocks, full brother of high-hearted
  Protesilaos,
younger born; but the elder man was braver
  also,
Protesilaos, a man of battle; yet still the
  people
lacked not a leader, though they longed for him
  and his valour.
Following along with Podarkes were forty black
  ships.

This is one of several passages of biographical narrative that the poet has scattered among the data of the Catalogue of Ships in book II, creating a rich tension between the impersonal statistics of the infantry and the humanity of the aristocrats who lead them. No such passage has greater pathos than this one about the two sons of Iphiklos. We hear of Protesilaos for the first time in line 698 (ending in "while he yet lived"), but in the next line he is dead. This recapitulates his actual career at Troy, where he was the first of the Greeks to disembark but was immediately killed "as he leapt forth from his ship." Like so many other battlefield fatalities in the poem, the death of Protesilaos is made painful to the poem's audience by the inclusion of details about his family and his homeland. Yet something else makes this passage special. It is not only the dead man's intimates who yearn and mourn for him, it is the whole people *(laoi)*, which his subjects comprise. The image of Protesilaos is here conjured three times by the poem; three times, he is replaced by his lesser brother, Podarkos, until the poem seems to give up and accept that Protesilaos is truly gone. Only then do we get the formulaic, impersonal, and therefore heartbreaking formula: "And with him there followed forty black ships." There is no ambiguity in the pronoun *him*. It is not Protesilaos but Podarkos.

From the larger perspective of the poem itself, outside of the affections of those who knew the man, Protesilaos's only claim to a permanent image is that he was the first to set foot on the

Trojan shore—but the triviality of this is brutally clear from the immediate disclosure that he could not kill a single opponent before his fall. His name seems to mean "first of the people," but this ultimately did not matter. It is as if time itself is driving his image out of the mind, and the poem must counteract time. For G. S. Kirk, the meter of line 703 "provides an epigrammatic summary of [the people's] pathetic yearning as well as neatly leading on to present realities" (*Commentary*, 231). Consider comparing that comment, and the passage it describes, with the modern poems "Musée de Beaux Arts" by W. H. Auden and "Out, Out" by Robert Frost.

3. **Knowledge:** The Muses and Calchas both possess a kind of omniscience. Is it the same kind? See I, 69–72:

> Kalchas, Thestor's son, far the best of the
> bird interpreters,
> who knew all things that were, the things to
> come and the things past,
> who guided into the land of Ilion the ships of
> the Achaeans
> through that seercraft of his own that Phoibos
> Apollo gave him.

Kalchas is mortal, so he cannot have all his knowledge from direct experience. Like Teiresias in Sophocles, he is a *mantis*, a prophet, whose clairvoyance is the god Apollo's gift. This may remind you of the discussion above about the omniscient muse inspiring the poet and singing through him. Suppose you psychologize the poet's invocation to her for a moment, and think of the muse as the unconscious. Better yet, suppose that the muse and the unconscious are in effect two names for the same phenomenon, namely the hidden source of poetry. Invoking the muse is also placating the psychic defenses ranged in a ring around that fertile source (as in Genesis 3:24). The mantis is doing what the poet does, borrowing a god's knowledge for a moment.

4. Ethics: Describe the role of oaths in *Iliad* I–II.

Achilles swears on the scepter at I, 233–44, as quoted above. Because his emotional commitment to his position is so unwavering, it is easy to forget that Achilles is also bound to his position by a great oath. Note also Odysseus's oath to Thersites. Consider commenting on the formulaic language of Homeric oaths. See also II, 339.

Form and Genre

Dactylic hexameter was previously discussed in a section on meter. Turn then from that small-scale structure to the large-scale structure of the *Iliad*. Oliver Taplin has argued, in the remarkable *Homeric Soundings: The Shaping of the Iliad* (Clarendon, 1992), that the poem has three movements, each about as long as an audience could enjoy, or a performer could perform, in a single long performance. The movements correspond to narrative time before the *Iliad*'s central ninth day (I–IX), the day itself (XI–XVIII), and time thereafter (XVIII–XXIV). Book X, the Doloneia, ("story of Dolon") is apparently an interpolation, a discrete section that interrupts the action.

Sample Topics:

1. ***Iliad* I–II as oral poetry:** What are some characteristics of this text that show it to be an oral composition?

The English language has been blessed with a broad range of Homeric translations, many of which are excellent, faithful, and thrilling. Richmond Lattimore's *Iliad* and Albert Cook's *Odyssey* predominate, but there are many others to admire and enjoy (for example, the recent *Iliad* by Rodney Merrill). Most translators make an effort to carry across the formulaic nature of the original, that is, they imitate Homer's tendency to deploy units of poetry (as small as two words or as large as sixty lines together), tactically rolling them out to suit his shaping purposes. If a translator fears repetition and introduces variation where it does not occur in the original, that is usually lamentable. Repetition is essential to Homeric poetry.

2. **The catalog form:** The ships are not the only thing cataloged in Homeric poetry; there are also lists (or "catalogs"; a *kata-logos* is literally a "down-telling") of women, shades, and nymphs. Some writers have held the catalog of ships in aesthetic contempt, as little more than a mere list of data. Instead, what can we find to appreciate in it?

In the catalog of ships, the poetry temporarily shifts its function from narrative to inventory—from relating the cherished story of the past, to conserving the quantitative details thereof lest they, too, be forgotten. The poet interjects passages of emotionally compelling narrative into the catalog in order to prevent boredom and daydreaming. Common in the ancient poetry of many cultures, such number-driven catalogs can have various purposes, and it is not always a simple matter to decide which one of these is uppermost: to preserve what were (or, what the bards thought were) real statistics; to create an illusion of verisimilitude by seeming to do so; or simply to signify utterly general quantities, using integers chosen for their poetic qualities, the nuances of which may have been lost over the intervening centuries. Genesis 5:3–29, for example, is strikingly specific about the various longevities of Adam's proximate descendants—but readers tend to dismiss those numbers with the inference that each connotes nothing more specific than "a long time," and that taken together, they signify a gradual decline of human longevity as it diminished toward the status quo (with the salient exception of Methuselah) of three score and ten.

For the poetic purposes of the *Iliad*, the rationale for enumerating the various contingents of ships is better integrated into the story than are the biblical life spans of Noah's ancestors. After all, apart from the vocational tags in Genesis 4 (for example, 4:21: ". . . Jubal: he was the father of all such as handle the harp and organ"), we never hear any stories about people born between Abel and Noah, so their ages at death are of no narrative importance. The size of each Achaean leader's military contingent, by contrast, not only indicates his relative importance to the expedition, it also contributes to an impression of just how many men were fighting—a matter of some significance in a war poem.

Language, Symbols, and Imagery

Homer's dialect is Panhellenic and ahistorical. That is to say, it is a composite of Greek dialects spoken at various locations around the Aegean, at various times. In that regard, it resembles the Italian in which Dante Alighieri (A.D. 1265–1325) composed the *Divine Comedy*. Having been exiled from his home city of Florence, Dante wandered all over Italy, absorbing one by one the speech habits and writing conventions of the people among whom he lived and travelled. Homer may have been a wandering performer (and for all we know, a political exile like Dante, but that is speculation) and had a similar experience of accumulating exposure to dialects that he then integrated into his poetic language. Some writers have credited Dante with the veritable "invention" of modern Italian as a language, going on to ascribe the same sort of codifying-as-founding achievement to Martin Luther's 1534 German Bible. Homer seems to deserve the same distinction.

Sample Topics:

1. **Similes in *Iliad* I–II:** Comment on the bee simile at II, 87–94:

> Like the swarms of clustering bees that issue
>   forever
> in fresh bursts from the hollow in the stone,
>   and hang like
> bunched grapes as they hover beneath the
>   flowers in springtime
> fluttering in swarms together this way and that
>   way,
> so the many nations of men from the ships and
>   the shelters
> along the front of the deep sea beach marched
>   in order
> by companies to the assembly . . .

Notice that here is one simile within another; the troops are like bees that are like grapes. From the point of view of Homer's eighth-century audience, the strange thing is the daunting swarm of busy soldiers, while the familiar things are apiculture (beekeeping) and vitnery (grape growing).

2. Symbols: Comment on the omen at Aulis:

> "Zeus of the counsels has shown us this great
>   portent: a thing late,
> late to be accomplished, whose glory shall
>   perish never.
> As this snake has eaten the sparrow herself
>   with her children,
> eight of them, and the mother was the ninth,
>   who bore them,
> so for years as many as this shall we fight in
>   this place
> and in the tenth year we shall take the city
>   of the wide ways."
> So he spoke to us then; now all this is being
>   accomplished.

Odysseus says this to the Achaeans, successfully winning them over to the idea of staying in the war rather than going home. The reminder of the omen at Aulis is strikingly effective, serving as a sort of hypnotic suggestion to the army that there will be huge rewards for persistence. It also reinforces their respect for Calchas, on whose credibility rests the link between the plague and young Chryseis' captivity to Agamemnon, with all its consequences for Achilles and others. What do you make of the contrast between the mother bird and her eight baby birds, all full of procreative life, and the death-bringing snake? If the birds are the years of the Trojan War, and their loss is the bereavement of all the Trojan families, where does that leave the Greeks in this omen? Why is nobody concerned about the fate of the snake,

whom Zeus turns to stone? If it represents the victorious Achaeans, doesn't it behoove them to notice its petrifaction and what
that might imply for their own fate?

Bibliography for "*Iliad* I–II: The Quarrel, the Dream, and the Catalog of Ships"

Blundell, Susan. *Women in Ancient Greece*. Cambridge, Mass.: Harvard UP, 1995.

Cohen, Beth, ed. *The Distaff Side: Representing the Female in Homer's* Odyssey. Oxford: Oxford UP, 1995.

Dodds, E. R. *The Greeks and the Irrational* (Sather Classical Lectures). Berkeley: University of California Press, 1951.

Dué, Casey. *Homeric Variations on a Lament by Briseis*. Berkeley, Calif.: Rowman & Littlefield, 2002.

Jaynes, Julian. *The Origin of Consciousness in the Breakdown of the Bicameral Mind*. New York: Houghton Mifflin Company, 1976.

Kirk, G. S. *The* Iliad: *A Commentary* (Volume I: Books 1–4). Newcastle: Cambridge University Press, 1985.

Lattimore, Richmond, trans. *The Iliad of Homer*. Chicago: University of Chicago Press, 1951.

Pomeroy, Sarah. *Goddesses, Whores, Wives, and Slaves: Women in Classical Antiquity*. New York: Schocken Books, 1995.

Rohde, Erwin. *Psyche: Seelencult und Unsterblichkeitsglaube der Griechen*, 1898. Trans. W. B. Hillis as *Psyche: The Cult of Souls and Belief in Immortality among the Ancient Greeks*. London, 1920.

Schein, Seth L. *The Mortal Hero: An Introduction to Homer's* Iliad. Berkeley: University of California Press, 1984.

Scott, William C. *The Oral Nature of the Homeric Simile*. Batava: Mnemosyne, Bibliotheca Classica Supplementum, 1974.

Snell, Bruno. *The Discovery of the Mind: The Greek Origins of European Thought*. New York: Harper and Brothers, 1960. Trans, T. G. Rosenmeyer.

Taplin, Oliver. *Homeric Soundings: The Shaping of the* Iliad. Oxford: Clarendon, 1992.

ILIAD III–IX, X:

Before the
Central Ninth Day

READING TO WRITE

THIS IS the first of the *Iliad*'s three movements, comprising books I through IX, along with the strange tenth book of the *Iliad* or Doloneia, the "Story of Dolon." There is good reason to believe that the Doloneia is a post-Homeric interpolation (see Taplin, *Soundings*, 152). In this broad sweep from "Anger, sing, Muse," to the point just before book XI begins, much action transpires and yet little changes. The plot is made to slow down in its advance—twice, because two attempts are made to preempt the progress of the war by substituting a duel of two men for the war of thousands. Both attempts fail because of sabotage, a tragic waste that makes the regulation of violence impossible. When *Iliad* VI fills us with a vision of pity and hope, yearning for a future for Hector's infant son, Astyanax, we remember these wasted opportunities (the two duels, Antenor's ill-fated proposal to return Helen, and the failed embassy to Achilles, for example) in all their tragic implications for the human predicament.

Hector scolds his brother Paris at III, 38–57, and Paris responds with the disarming tactic of simply agreeing with his accuser (III, 58–66):

> Then in answer Alexandros the godlike spoke to him:
> "Hector, seeing you have scolded me rightly, not beyond
> measure—

still, your heart forever is weariless, like an axe-blade
driven by a man's strength through the timber, one who,
    well skilled,
hews a piece for a ship, driven on by the force of a man's
    strength:
such is the heart in your breast, unshakable: yet do not
bring up against me the sweet favors of golden Aphrodite.
Never to be cast away are the gifts of the gods, magnificent,
which they give of their own will, no man could have them
    for wanting them . . ."

Here an essay writer might pick up on the remarkable rhetorical facility of Paris, his ability to use language to deflect the anger of his brother Hector, who has the better case. From a social point of view, taking account of the consequences of Paris's behavior for his people, the man is a disaster. Yet here he nearly wins us over, seeming to go to the heart of the matter: "Never to be cast away are the gifts of the gods." Paris is avoiding the responsibility for his adultery with Helen by calling attention to the divine origin of the transgressive, rule-breaking charisma he shares with her. In exploring this potent if somewhat dubious proposition, consider the cases of men in the Trojan War whose excellent skills are wasted there because they are inadequately relevant to warfare, for example, augury (II, 158–62), hunting (V, 48–50), workmanship (V, 59–61), good looks (II, 673–75), etc. Those, too, were gifts of the Gods, impossible to cast away, definitive of their possessors, valuable in their right niches, destructive only in their narrowness of scope ("Nastes came like a girl to the fighting in golden raiment, / poor fool, nor did this avail to keep dismal death back" II, 872–73), whereas the sexual charisma of the composite Paris-Helen is woefully destructive in causing the war in the first place. Their behavior toward Menelaus is an outrage against sacred conventions of hospitality called in ancient Greek *xenia*, the guest-host obligations.

Paris and Helen indulged their own Aphroditic nature rather than respect the *xenia* they owed Menelaus, and the Trojan War was the genocidal result. This kernel of offense is not the war; it is a dispute over a husband's immaterial honor, a host's righteous indignity; it is the quarrel of Menelaus and Paris, and the duel is the perfect solution. It fits the scale of Paris's crime, as the Trojan War does not, and compared with the War, the duel sorts for the aggrieved parties with beautiful economy. Instead, the truce (a fragile bubble in the continuum of battlefield mass violence, within which alone the duel is possible) fails, because Pandaros had to use the archery taught him by Apollo to fire an arrow at Menelaus with the bow given to him by Apollo (since, as Paris reminds us, "Never to be cast away are the gifts of the gods, magnificent"). A massive looting action at Troy is the climax of ten years of piracy leveled by the Greeks against the surrounding villages of the Trojan plain and the nearby islands. Plenty of misery, since it is not old King Priam alone but thousands of bereaved people left alive on the dunghills of grief and slavery, mourning their children and spouses and friends. Andromache is painfully clear about this at VI, 407–39. Yet Paris reminds us that, "Never to be cast away are the gifts of the gods, magnificent." In eloping with his host's wife, he was just being his own Aphrodite-besotted self. In a world where all adults behaved responsibly, with vigilant, altruistic, prosocial attention to the priorities of justice, nobody could behave with the sensuality, lightheartedness, and freedom of a Paris. A look at today's celebrity culture might easily yield parallels to famous people who play a role in the popular imagination similar to what Paris does for the *Iliad.*

TOPICS AND STRATEGIES

This section of the chapter will discuss various possible topics for essays and general approaches to those topics. Be aware that the material below is only a place to start from, not some kind of master key to the perfect essay. Use this material to prompt your own thinking. Every topic discussed here could encompass a wide variety of papers.

The topics below are intended to help you arrive at a question of interest that can serve as the basis of an original paper on this region of the *Iliad,* namely books III through IX, and book X, the "Doloneia." These including the heartbreaking sixth book, where we see Troy from the inside and are brought face-to-face with what the Trojan War will cost, in the person of Hector's infant son Astyanax and his wretched wife Andromache. It also includes the crucial book IX, which has already been the subject of our first chapter and will therefore be only lightly touched upon here. In general this first, copious one-third of the *Iliad* can be thought of as a display of Homeric culture's admirable but limited resources for controlling the circulation of violence. Certain semiformalized institutions of behavior, binding as norms but essentially unenforceable except by the gods themselves, are hard put to contain the flow of violence and of its emotional precursors, especially the *mênis* of Achilles and the *atê* of Agamemnon. These semiformalized institutions include *xenia* (hospitality, or guest-host relationship); supplication (as discussed in the chapter on writing about *Iliad* I–II); and oaths, such as the one surrounding the truce between the armies, which permits the duel between the principal parties to the grievance of the war, namely Paris and Menelaus.

Themes

As you watch the unfolding implications of Paris's remark, "Never to be cast away are the gifts of the gods," think of all the moments when Homer presents us with someone who has been given a gift by a god. Notice how those gifts seem always beset with a strange duality; whatever comes from beyond the human ken seems to be both curse and blessing. Consider the poem's prized, unique works of handicraft like Pandaros's bow or Hector's helmet. The latter is a defensive object, a component of armor, and yet it appears to the baby Astyanax utterly terrifying, a sign of the death system that we know will ultimately consume him. The bow of Pandaros is a weapon in the defense of Troy, yet it destroys the city because it is the instrument by which the duel-truce is broken. These vexing objects are divine gifts, like the skills that they symbolize; though Pandaros's bow is said to be given him by Apollo directly at II, 827, Pandaros crafts it from the wild goat at IV, 105–11 (Schein, 56–57). The helmet, conversely, is never directly called the gift of a god, but the descriptor would seem to fit, given the helmet's role in this scene.

Sample Topics:
   1. **Nature versus culture:** Why does Homer include the business about Hector's helmet at VI, 466–76?

   The name of Hector means "the holder," and as he holds Troy together by fending off the Achaeans, the helmet that holds the Holder is perhaps more emblematic of his personality and role than any other object in the poem. He must take it off in order to confer his blessing on his infant son, Astyanax (since the boy is too terrified of his father's helmet to permit the blessing to proceed otherwise), but that blessing itself reinstates exactly the values Hector had seemed to put aside in taking off the helmet. As Paris/Alexander cannot cast off the gift of Aphrodite that caused the war, Hector cannot cast off the heroic role in which he has his being, the doomed defender of a doomed city, by doffing his helmet. Only two characters seem capable of seriously calling into question the entire heroic enterprise of warfare: Achilles the aggressor, who reconsiders the Iliadic life in general from his withdrawn position in book IX, and Thersites the dissident, whom Odysseus beats for his insolence in book II. Hector is held by the same Trojan city he holds together; he is held by his helmet, and held by the warrior ideology that constrains everyone in the poem.

2. **Supplication and prayer:** Comment on Dolon's failed supplication in *Iliad* X. What is its significance?

There are several failed supplications in the *Iliad,* among them that of Adrestos to the Atreidae at VI, 45; Lykaon to the enraged Achilles, at XXI; and between them, the failed supplication of Dolon to Odysseus and Diomedes at X, 378–81. All are perhaps exemplary of the fraying of the culture's limits on violence as the Trojan War begins to corrode them. Among other strategies, you might compare the failed supplications with successful ones, seeking similarities and differences.

   Diomedes kills dozens of people in the war, yet compared with Achilles, he is a figure of restraint and continuity. Both are gifted by Athena with the magic of pyrotechnics; both are extraordinarily strong. But when Agamemnon treats Diomedes with the haughty contempt that proved so disastrous with Achilles, Diomedes is unfazed; in his view, this is simply the way kings behave. When Diomedes is at risk of fighting too directly against Apollo on the field, he heeds the same warning from the god that Patroclus will fatally ignore. It is odd, therefore, that Homer has Diomedes kill a suppliant in book X; the hubris of such a killing is appropriate to Agamemnon (not Menelaus) in book VI, since he has been hubristic in several other ways by that point, and to Achilles in book XXI, who is dishonoring corpses and fighting with rivers in an all-out orgy of destruction. It is perhaps not appropriate for Diomedes in book X, but then the interpolation reading solves this problem, relieving Homer of the inconsistency with the claim that book X is not really Homeric anyway.

3. **Politics and war:** This portion of the *Iliad* contains at least three meetings in which there seems to be some hope for the prevention of all-out slaughter. Yet each of them comes to nothing: the truce of the duel is broken in book III; the court scene on Olympus in book IV is supposed to prevent further intervention, but does not do so; and in the Trojan politics of book VII, Paris quashes Antenor's proposal to end the war by returning Helen. Is politics futile?

As one reads through the *Iliad,* coming into closer and closer contact with its crushing emotional powers of pity and terror, one is tempted to attribute its horrific violence to fate, or to the will of Zeus, or to something more subtle, like "the tragic consciousness." The alternative is to emphasize mortals' individual and collective responsibility for war, and accept history's judgment: people are fools. In fighting wars, we trade gold for bronze. We give up the warm, animal life of pleasure and generativity in exchange for an abstraction called *kleos,* or fame, or glory, whose price tends to include somebody's death and bereavement, eventually one's own.

A reader of Homer with sufficient enthusiasm for political passages like assemblies and embassies might be able to claim with the great 19th-century military theorist Carl von Clausewitz that "war is a continuation of politics by other means." If he or she takes a more utilitarian view, whose goal for politics is simply the minimization of human suffering, then war represents the failure of those political institutions that should prevent it. Today's foremost exemplar of such a politics is probably Jurgen Habermas, the German social thinker whose 1981 tome, *The Theory of Communicative Action,* posited an ideal communicative rationality and then explained all violence as the results of all-too-common failures of such rationality, in what he called "distorted communication." The *Iliad* is rich in distorted communication and, as one might expect, rich in violence. The 19th-century German poet Johann Wolfgang von Goethe said that the world of the *Iliad* is "Hell." The poem's landscape is home to a mammoth question whose silence cannot hide its large size: is the human condition's Iliadic Hell avoidable? Can the carnage ever stop? That question won't be answered here, but its urgency has never failed, since the *Iliad* is happening right now, at the instant you are reading this, in several places at once all over the earth, using not swords and spears but Kalashnikovs and knives, rockets and rocks. Somewhere, a Pandaros is breaking a truce; an Agamemnon is provoking a Diomedes, who looks the other way; and myriad corpses are made prey for dogs and birds. Since the ancients apparently underwent the same sufferings, and reading their poetry causes kinship with them to arise in us, we do well to avail ourselves of their free sympathy, which in turn confers upon them the unforgotten status they craved in making their poems (and fighting their wars) for us to hear.

Distorted communication accounts well for Pandaros's breaking of the truce. As Dream deceived Agamemnon in book II, Athena deceives Pandaros in book III:

> Speaking in winged words she stood beside him
> and spoke to him:
> 'Wise son of Lykaon, would you now let me
> persuade you?
> So you might dare send a flying arrow against
> Menelaus
> and win you glory and gratitude in the sight of
> all Trojans,
> particularly beyond all else with prince
> Alexandros.

Beyond all beside you would carry away glorious
   gifts from him,
were he to see warlike Menelaus, the son of
   Atreus,
struck down by your arrow, and laid on the
   sorrowful corpse-fire.
Come then, let go an arrow against haughty
   Menelaus,
but make your prayer to Apollo the light-born,
   the glorious archer,
that you will accomplish a grand sacrifice of
   lambs first born
when you come home again to the city of sacred
   Zeleia.'

By Habermas's lights, the distortion in this communication is the omission of two highly relevant facts: first, that the gods destroy those who break oaths and, second, that a shot at Menelaus will violate the oaths of Priam and of Troy itself, bringing death on everyone. The breakage of the truce was not only a human accident, it was also the will of Zeus:

She spoke, nor did the father of gods and men
   disobey her,
but immediately he spoke in winged words to
   Athene:
"Go now swiftly to the host of the Achaeans
   and Trojans
and try to make it so that the Trojans are
   first offenders
to do injury against the oaths to the far-famed
   Achaeans."

As an explanation for violence, "distorted communication" is at its weakest when it has to account for the kind of conflict that arises in competition over scarce resources. This is because, whatever the quality of communication among the claimants to scarce resources, the resources are still scarce. Either they will be divided evenly or there will be other claims exerted; those claims will be contested, and so on. As Achilles says at book I, line 124, abundance is the exception, scarcity the rule: "There is no great store of things lying about I know of."

Character

Homer is aware that we are interested in his characters in themselves, and not only for the ways they help to propel the narrative. When Homer shows us Helen and Priam's survey of the heroes at *Iliad* III, 146, we may feel as if we are back in the cheap seats, far from the battlefield; on the other hand, we are also like fans who have made it backstage, to see the king of Troy and the most beautiful woman in the world discuss three heroes in succession as they watch them work: Agamemnon, then Odysseus, then Ajax, but not Kastor and Pollux, who, unknown to Helen, are already dead.

Sample Topics:

1. **Diomedes:** In regard to his self-possession and poise in IV, *aristeia* in book V, and *xenia* in book VI, what does the depiction of Diomedes suggest? Is he the best of the heroic ideal, or does he, too, bear some features so damning as to discredit that ideal? In what ways is he inferior to Achilles?

Diomedes is like Achilles but without the complexity. When Agamemnon speaks outrageously to Diomedes, trying to get a rise out of him, Diomedes manages to do what Achilles could not; he lets it go. In Diomedes' great *aristeia,* he is honored by Athena with the clearing away of a mist that normally prevents humans from distinguishing between mortals and gods. Flames shoot from his head, a magical effect sponsored by Athena for him and Achilles alone. Go through the books of the *Iliad* in which Diomedes acts decisively and ask yourself about the values implicit in his behavior. How do you see his achievements? Does he tend to respect boundaries or transgress them? You should be able to find relevant examples in Diomedes' dealings with Athena, Apollo, Glaukos, and Agamemnon. Anyone else?

2. **Compare Hector's "Warrior's Creed" in book VI, 440–65 with Thersites's speech in book II:** To what degree is Hector, or Achilles, or anyone else in the *Iliad* truly the captive of the ideas presented in these speeches?

Quote the text of Hector's speech. Quote Achilles' rejection of war in the "Embassy to Achilles" scene. Why is it so hard to leave all this behind?

3. **Women:** Compare the characters Helen and Andromache. They are two very different women, whose lives are touched by some of the same men. What have they in common? How are the two most different?

Ask yourself what social roles women played in the ancient world, and which of those roles each of these two women has played. Is Helen a mother? Is Andromache anyone's daughter or sister anymore? What happened to her family? What was Helen's past experience in war, and what was Andromache's?

4. **Gods:** Why does Homer show Aphrodite wounded in the hand by Diomedes? Wounding a god is a frighteningly hubristic thing to contemplate, yet Diomedes goes ahead and does this without much thought. Athena's approval ("Her, you may stab") must have concentrated his mind. But why does the poet present this strange image? Does it belong with anything else in the poem? What about Apollo and Poseidon at the end of *Iliad* VII, and their decision to obliterate the wall the Achaeans have built on the beach? What is the significance of that scene?

Look up the word *etiology*. Using a search engine, perhaps in a reference Web site or an encyclopedia, compare some examples of a later culture being baffled by the ruins of an earlier one whose monumental building methods had been forgotten in the meantime. You can find an Anglo-Saxon example by reading the two great medieval poems "The Wanderer" and "The Seafarer," and a Koranic example in the story of "the people of Ad and Thamud." Generally, if you live in a relatively dark age, and you come upon the broken remains of buildings so massive that nobody you know would be capable of constructing them, then you must attribute them to a people of the past. The problem is, since they were capable of doing what you cannot, they must have been superior. Yet they, too, were ruined and wiped out, or at least their buildings have been abandoned to disrepair and their great methods forgotten.

Philosophy and Ideas

Homer is a poet; for him, art and science have not yet been separated, and there is no split between emotion and idea. Reality flows through the Homeric hero as the dactylic hexameter flows through the mind, or as the *polyphloisbois* "much-murmuring" ocean waves wash along the beach. Of course the poem is informed by a deep intelligence, and in its action, its choice of words, and its structural arrangements it suggests various ideas about suffering, glory, loss, and mortality. Yet it is by no means a work "of ideas," concerned to argue a position or exhort an audience to take a course of action. The *Iliad* is an epic poem, a built package of experience, made more vivid by the dynamic changes in its tempo, mood, and scope of concern.

Sample Topics:

1. **Free will and constraint:** Consider the issue of free will once more, this time with regard to Pandaros and the breaking of the truce.

As you reread the passages of *Iliad* III that concern Pandaros, especially the sections on the origins of his bow and of his archery, consider this more famous passage from *Odyssey* 1: "It's disgraceful how these humans blame the gods. / They say their tribulations come from us, / when they themselves, through their own foolishness, / bring hardships which are not decreed by Fate" (Johnston). In that case, the man Zeus has in mind is Aigisthos, whom the Gods warned not to commit a particular crime; Aigisthos ignored their warning and was consequently destroyed. How well does Zeus's claim apply here in *Iliad* III, to Pandaros? Athena herself, at Zeus's own bidding, came to Pandaros and instructed him that it would be an excellent thing to shoot an arrow at Menelaus. As you read the poetry of this ancient civilization, the requirements of the story interact with the contours of your own orientation toward the supernatural when you hear about the gods. On the one hand, they are simply supernatural, immortal beings who exist outside of our minds, and they control and influence human life using their own free agency. On the other hand, since that presumably cannot be true, they are a fiction. Yet they are well able to assert their effects on the environment without being supernatural entities whom mere skepticism can subtract from the world. The gods are the way history works, the tendency of *hubris* to bring *nemesis;* the moral calculus of consequences and repercussions that karma constitutes; they are the contours of human psychology, the endocrine charts of puberty and menopause, and the neurology of epilepsy, and of the poet's trance, and of the soldier's fight-or-flight response.

2. **Transience:** The greatest expression of transience in the *Iliad* is VI, 146–211, where Glaukos, before boasting of his ancestry to Diomedes, begins by dismissing all human generations as trivial and fleeting in a famous and deeply traditional image:

> "High-hearted son of Tydeus, why ask of my generation?
> *As is the generation of leaves, so is that of humanity.*
> *The wind scatters the leaves on the ground, but the live timber*
> *burgeons with leaves again in the season of spring returning.*
> *So one generation of men will grow while another*
> *dies.* Yet if you wish to learn all this and be certain
> of my genealogy: there are plenty of men who know it. . . ."

To what other passages of world literature would you compare this? Here are some biblical passages to consider: Job

14:1–2; Psalms 37:1– 2; Psalms 90:5–6; Psalms 92:7–8; Psalms 102:11; Psalms 103:15–16; Psalms 129:5–7; Isaiah 37:26–27; Isaiah 40:6–8; Isaiah 51:12–13; James 1:9–11; I Peter 1:24–25.

Notice how male this image is. Though the focus is on birth and death, the generation of life and time, the metaphor of the tree makes women and wombs vanish from the picture. If this metaphor shows us human individuals as leaves, then perhaps the branches of the tree stand for those bonds of origin and attachment that a "family tree" configures. But we are not directed toward the branches: there are the leaves with which we are to identify, fleeting, anonymous, futile and perhaps beautiful, and there is "the live timber," the unfailing continuity of human presence in the world (as in the thirteenth line of Shakespeare's Sonnet 18: "so long as men can breathe or eyes can see . . ."), perhaps especially the tree's phallic trunk. This is still securely rooted: until the advent of nuclear weapons, the thought of the total erasure of the human species does not seem to have arisen except in the Flood story, located well in the past and, in Genesis if not in all books, sealed into the past with the covenant of God's rainbow. Mankind is apparently here to stay. Yet the destruction of the branches of the tree— the wrecking of human relationships—simply does not appear in Glaukos's great austere figure. All the misery of bereavement that turns Achilles into a lion, Niobe into a weeping rock or poplar tree, and Priam into "the most wretched man in the world" remains invisible in a world of isolated falling leaves. There is no violence in the figure, only the passage of time by which the leaves naturally die away; there is therefore no personal agency and no question of changing in pursuit of a different form of life with less violence and more mutuality. What results arise when you compare this "generation of leaves" passage with that of Achilles and the golden-studded scepter? What about the scepter, whose origins in handicraft are explained in some detail, compared with Pandaros's bow, which receives a similar narrative treatment?

3. Knowledge: Consider Thetis's prophecy for Achilles in book IX:

> My mother Thetis tells me that there are two ways in which I
> may meet my end *[telos]*. If I stay here and fight, I shall lose my
> safe homecoming *[nostos]* but I will have a glory *[kleos]* that is
> unwilting: whereas if I go home my glory *[kleos]* will die, but
> it will be a long time before the outcome *[telos]* of death shall
> take me.

This is the basis for Achilles' decision to go home and quit
the war: "And this would be my counsel to others also, to
sail back / home again, since no longer shall you find any
term set / on the sheer city of Ilion, since Zeus of the wide
brows has strongly / held his own hand over it. Let Phoenix
/ remain here with us and sleep here, so that tomorrow / he
may come with us in our ships to the beloved land of our
fathers . . ." (Lattimore). Yet Achilles stays and dies. Since he
is unable to exploit his awareness of the prophecy, it is almost
as if he did not really know of it. Consider other prophecies in
the *Iliad*, especially in the part of it under discussion, books
III–IX and X. Are they put to any more successful use than
this one?

4. **Ethics and responsibility:** Consider the oath of Achilles in
   book II and the oath at book III, 298–302, 303. The Trojans
   violate their oaths and this explains their eventual defeat.
   Yet Achilles fulfills his oath and he, too, is killed in the same
   war. Perhaps his despair in book IX is correct when he says
   the results are the same, whether one tries to be great or not.
   Discuss.

The premise of this question is that all oaths are of comparable
value. Achilles swore that the Achaeans would yearn for him
when they became overwhelmed by the Trojan forces in his
absence, and they do. The Trojans have sworn not to break the
truce; their oath is negative, so it cannot be accomplished once
and for all like a positive oath. Worse, the truce is binding for
the entire populace. All it takes is one Pandros (and Athena,
apparently), and the day is lost.

Form and Genre

The *Iliad* is a marvel of construction, with a structural elegance that has been compared to that of the great ceramic art of the period. Reviewer Minna Skafte Jensen, of the University of Southern Denmark, recently wrote in the pages of the *Byrn Mawr Classical Review* about the book by Bruce Heiden, *Homer's Cosmic Fabrication: Choice and Design in the Iliad* (A.P.A., *American Classical Studies* 52, New York/Oxford: Oxford University Press, 2008):

> In critical dialogue with Oliver Taplin and Keith Stanley, Heiden first returns to his argument from 1996 for an *Iliad* in three "movements" (here called "cycles")—books 1–8, 9–15, and 16–24. Since the beginning and end of the poem, books 1 and 24, are characterized by Achilles and Zeus respectively making important decisions, he looks for similar beginnings and ends in the course of the poem and finds them in book 8 (Zeus making a decision), 9 (Achilles), 15 (Zeus), and 16 (Achilles) . . . The three cycles are of unequal length, counted in books. However, the last book in each cycle refers to the corresponding first book (book 8 to 1, 15 to 9, and 24 to 16), and with the exception of the middle cycle the next to last book refers to the second (book 7 to 2 and book 23 to 17) and the third to last to the third (book 6 to 3 and book 22 to 18).

The complexity goes on from there. It is not as if the entire *Iliad* was a hologram, but there is a greater level of large-scale balance and symmetry, and smaller scale intricacy, than is obvious at first. Look at the artifacts of Greek physical culture from the Mycaenean period and the ensuing dark ages and Archaic period. Do any designs or design features strike you as similar to the construction of the *Iliad?*

Sample Topics:

1. **The Doloneia as interpolation:** One of the best books about this aspect of the *Iliad* is Oliver Taplin's *Homeric Soundings.* There we find a sharp critique of the tenth book as a non-Homeric poem: "The Doloneia has undoubtedly been fashioned to fit its setting within the *Iliad.* . . . But I can see no sign that the rest of the *Iliad* has been fashioned to include the Doloneia" (153).

From within the limits of a translation, does the *Iliad* seem
to show a change of style or a shift of voice in book X? How
would you describe it, and where do you see it in the text? Do
you believe the Doloneia has the same origin as the rest of the
poem? It has been suggested that the two Greek heroes in it
are more brutal than their typically Iliadic behavior would
lead us to expect. Do Odysseus and Diomedes act like themselves in this book—in dispatching the sleeping Thracians
with mass-murder efficiency, and in killing the suppliant
Dolon—or do they seem darker, colder, more like . . . Meriones? Do you feel as if Odysseus is not the same person in
this text as he is in the surrounding *Iliad?* That might form
part of a larger case against the Doloneia's having been composed as part of a separate non-Iliadic work either by Homer
or another person.

2. **Stock scenes or recurring types of scenes:** Certain kinds of
scenes are recurrent in the *Iliad,* such as kills in battle, visits,
and debates. Taplin is among the critics who have compared, for
example, the three parallel visit scenes at I, 327–38; IX, 182–91;
and XXIV, 471–79. These types of scenes are of compositional
value in that they help to build out the poem in its structural
progression; perhaps more importantly, they help the poet
emphasize salient points by setting them into place as departures from the pattern. That would not be possible without a
pattern from which to deviate. Looking at these three scenes,
what elements form the pattern? What elements form the significant deviations from it?

If this sort of work feels unfamiliar, consider whether the same
principle operates in cinema. In how many different films have
you seen a "type scene" in which a warrior arms himself? Long
before whatever blockbuster is currently playing on your ear-
lobe-implanted microchip video-bead, there were thousands
of such scenes in James Bond movies, superhero action flicks,
and so on: the briefcase goes on the bed, the hero opens it,
and inside are a whole bunch of silencers, clips, scopes, and

other paraphernalia which he assembles to theme music in an almost religious mood of ceremonial earnest. The arming scenes in Martin Scorcese's *Taxi Driver* (1976) are a darkly ironic play on such scenes in more traditional, less morally ambitious movies such as the James Bond films of the decades that preceded it. As a device for gaining the attention of the audience, the arming scene is as old as Homer. How many movies have you watched that contained an elaborate scene of a woman getting ready for a seduction? See Hera's visit to Aphrodite and the use she makes of what she gains from the younger goddess. Of course the parallel between these two kinds of recurrent scenes—arming for battle and primping for sexual activity—is just as ancient.

3. **Language, symbols, and imagery:** Note the language of the laying of the lambs in the chariot at *Iliad* III, 310. Compare it with Achilles's action of loading Priam's wagon with Hector's body at XXIV, 589–90.

This is essentially a compare and contrast essay, asking you to set two passages side by side and note similarities and differences. Once you have done that (or as you do it), try to assert something conclusive about your observations. Do they amount to an important aspect of a "Homeric world-view"? Is there an ethical dimension, a theory of mind, an analogy to geometric visual arts? Do the two passages imply that Hector and the lambs are ultimately alike? What use might some academic writers and scholars have made of such a resemblance in the past? Homer drives this wagon back and forth across the *Iliad*.

Bibliography and Online Resources for "*Iliad* III–IX, X: Before the Central Ninth Day"

Damen, Mark. *A Guide to Writing in History and Classics.* http://www.usu.edu/markdamen/1320AncLit/chapters/04homer.htm

Jensen, Minna Skafte. Review of Bruce Heiden, *Homer's Cosmic Fabrication: Choice and Design in the* Iliad (A.P.A., American Classical Studies 52.

New York/Oxford: Oxford University Press, 2008), in *Bryn Mawr Classical Review.*

Taplin, Oliver. *Homeric Soundings: The Shaping of the* Iliad. Oxford: Clarendon, 1992.

Taxi Driver (1976). Warner Home Video, DVD/VHS, 2000.

ILIAD XI–XVIII:

The Central Ninth Day

READING TO WRITE

THIS CHAPTER concerns the great central day—the day of Hector's temporary triumph—which spans the central movement of Homer's *Iliad*. It will leave book XVI, the Patrokleia (or "story of Patroclus"), for a separate chapter since the importance of that episode is so great. As you approach this middle section of the epic, bear in mind that it serves many purposes—raising and lowering the dramatic tension as well as the fortunes of the Greek army; getting the major Achaean heroes out of the way so that they will need to be rescued by Patroclus; and building the individuality of the characters. Ask yourself, as you read, about how the poet is accomplishing these things. As usual, one of the interesting elements in this region of the Homeric textual landscape is the deployment of gods and their agents to bring about the accomplishment of the will of Zeus *(Dios d'eteleieto boule)*; in other words (and in another sense), to effect the poet's purposes. When book XI begins, we witness a theophany not from Athena or Apollo but from a goddess whose name shows that she is essentially an allegorical figure, the personification of an abstraction and not a pleasant one: "Now Dawn rose from her bed, / where she lay by haughty Tithonus, / to carry her light to men and to immortals. Zeus sent down / in speed to the fast ships of the Achaeans the wearisome goddess / of Hate, holding in her hands the portent of battle." The Greek name here translated as "Hate" is *Eris*, more commonly translated "Strife." The poet has placed the two goddesses Dawn and Hate in close proximity on opposite sides of the mention of Zeus, to begin a long day of battle. The war cry of this early-rising Eris emboldens the Achaeans, whose first expression of renewed vigor is the *aristeia*, or "episode of greatness" of Agamemnon. Just as it begins, Eris appears again: "The pressure held their heads on a line, and they whirled and fought like / wolves, and Hate, the Lady of Sorrow, was gladdened to watch them" (book XI, 72–73). What effect does the emphatic presence of this goddess have on the proceedings? Note the Zeus-sent "dews of blood" at XI, 54.

The most direct approach to literary interpretation is close reading, where you open the primary text to a passage that seems important and then read it until it gradually yields its secrets to you. The opening pages of *Iliad* XI present a set of interesting elements that your essay might combine and coordinate: Dawn, Zeus, and Eris appear. Eris emits a rallying cry in line 10, which is transmitted to Agamemnon, who cries out in a similar manner five lines later. He then arms himself in a little type scene, underscored and completed by an array of Mycenaean physical culture—the decorated corselet, the gold-studded sword, the knobbed shield—and a thunderclap sent by both Hera and Athena, "doing honor to the lord of deep-golden Mykenai." Already we can notice several things: here is a much more sympathetic Agamemnon than the one we saw before the apology of book IX. The power behind him is not that of Zeus, who has toyed with Agamemnon in book II with the false dream and is much more interested in Thetis's son than in him. King Agamemnon is not really the aggrieved party to the war; Homer has split off that function, embodied in his brother Menelaus. Perhaps it is because Menelaus has something to fight about—a real, concrete issue called Helen, his wife—that he represents not *mênis* but the containment of violence, since he is willing to trade the whole war for a duel that might have saved thousands of lives if the gods had not sabotaged things. When the sons of Atreus have a choice about killing a suppliant, Menelaus is merciful but Agamemnon is not. His *aristeia* here in book XI provides some much-needed support for the heroic social ideology that Achilles has derided, since it shows Agamemnon earning the rewards for which he is so greedy. After that, his function has been served, and he is largely eclipsed from the forward movement of the poem, beyond the first half where Achilles hated him to the second half, where Achilles hates the Trojans.

Lattimore's phrase "deep-golden" is a slightly weird rendering of *poly-chrysoio*, "much-golden" or "abundant in gold." Classical audiences in the fifth century B.C. would have been acquainted with Mycenae, if at all, as a poor town far from the emergent powers of Athens and Sparta, not a palatial center of interethnic commerce and hoarded treasure extorted from distant cities by Mycenaean raiders like Agamemnon and his men. For this reason, and because of the old genitive ending in *-oio*, the phrase "gold-abundant Mykenai" is probably very ancient, perhaps as old as the 14th century B.C., prior to the Trojan War itself. This may also be true of the poetic language that describes Agamemnon's gorgeous armaments and armor, whose exotic materials (cobalt, gold, and tin) were available at the height of Mycenaean civilization but far more rare in the dark ages that followed. An excellent if somewhat dated orientation in these issues of archaeology is Thomas Webster's 1958 book, *From Mycenae to Homer: A Study in Early Greek Literature and Art.* See also Oliver Dickinson, *The Aegean Bronze Age* (Cambridge UP, 1994) and A. M. Snodgrass, *Archaeology and the Emergence of Greece* (Cornell UP, 2006).

When Agamemnon's *aristeia* begins, what are we shown? Book IX has just impressed us with the depth of Achilles's separateness from everyone, stuck as he is in a liminal space between Greek and Trojan, night and day, past and future, Uranian male and Chthonian female powers, Phthia and Troy, and between the two poles of his fate as foretold by his mother: a short life of eternal fame or a long one of peaceful obscurity. This is followed by the *Doloneia*, another tale of the liminal space between categories—even its compromised authenticity fits here, since it is possibly non-Homeric in being composed by someone else, yet Homeric in forming the de facto 10th book of the only *Iliad* we have. Its action happens in the darkness between one day and the next, in a narrative gap between the first and second of the *Iliad's* three movements, set in no man's land, where Odysseus, Diomedes, and Dolon the Trojan cross and recross the nameless territory between the armies. All of that ends with the opening of book XI, whether or not we include book X. In other words, whether the issue of isolation and liminality is on our minds because we have just finished the embassy to Achilles or the story of Dolon, we are primed for the resumption of the grueling normal action of wartime in the joining together of the armies in combat. Homer provides this even while he sustains the motif of separation: "And the men, like two lines of reapers who, facing each other, / drive their course all down the field of wheat or of barley / for a man blessed in substance, and the cut swathes drop showering, / so Trojans and Achaeans driving in against one another / cut men down, nor did either side think of disastrous panic."

This clash of the armies represents the resumption of general hostilities after several lapses including the two duels (of Menelaus and Paris in III, and of Ajax and Hector in VII), the burial of the dead (VII), the embassy (IX), and the night raid (X). When the armies converge we get a simile from familiar domestic life, in which sharecroppers or hired hands are toiling in the fields of a rich man who is elsewhere and does not appear.

You might compare this image to the point in Achilles' speech in IX where he reminds us that the Achaeans fight not for their own personal reasons but only in support of the sons of Atreus and their quarrel with Paris. The image of the reapers of grain is, of course, a deeply traditional image of death as harvester of human lives, consistent with the botanical rhetoric of Glaukos in the "generations of the leaves" simile in book VI. The gods have been prohibited from the battlefield, and at this second mention of Eris, her separateness is emphasized: "She alone of all the immortals attended this action." At this same moment, the other gods are isolated too:

> but the other immortals were not there, but sat quietly
> remote and apart in their palaces, where for each one of
> them
> a house had been built in splendor along the folds of
> Olympos.
> All were blaming the son of Kronos, Zeus of the dark mists,
> because his will was to give glory to the Trojans.

As soon as Zeus is introduced, he is set apart:

> To these gods
> the father gave no attention at all, but withdrawn from them
> and rejoicing in the pride of his strength sat apart from the
> others
> looking out over the city of Troy and the ships of the Achaeans,

watching the flash of the bronze, and men killing and men killed.

Follow through this theme of separateness and isolation to see where it leads.

TOPICS AND STRATEGIES

This section of the chapter will discuss various possible topics for essays and general approaches to those topics. Be aware that the material below is only a place to start from, not some kind of master key to the perfect essay. Use this material to prompt your own thinking. Every topic discussed here could encompass a wide variety of papers.

Themes

At book XI, 192, Zeus declares that Hector must refrain from fighting until Agamemnon leaves the battle, wounded: "then I guarantee power to Hector / to kill men, till he makes his way to the strong-benched vessels, / until the sun goes down and the blessed darkness comes over." That power lasts all day until sunset at XVIII, 240. The promise of it is repeated for maximum audience comprehension, when Iris tells Hector the same message she has just heard directly from Zeus. That structure-bearing promise is in some sense the theme of the text before us, since it shapes the entire plot under a sovereign edict of Zeus. A similar structure is already in place at book XI, 84–91: "So long as it was early morning and the sacred daylight increasing, / so long the thrown weapons of both took hold and men dropped under them. / But at that time when the woodcutter makes ready his supper . . . at that time the Danaans by their manhood broke the battalions." Book XI brings us back to Zeus's devastatingly false promise to Agamemnon in book II, both because we now see Agamemnon vindicated (refuting Achilles' denouncement of him in book II) and, because of the contrast with this (XI, 192), Zeus's true promise to Hector.

Sample Topics:

1. **Nature versus culture:** Consider the presence of animals in this part of the *Iliad,* and comment on their significance in XI, 145–62.

Quote the passage and begin the search for observations that can be developed into a thesis. The opening phrase is "Hippolochos sprang away," a name whose first element *hippos* means "horse"; the second, *lochos*, means "place of ambush." The similes in book XI insist that Trojan victims of Agamemnon's fury are as deer to Agamemnon's lion. Note the heartbreaking image of the riderless horse, or driverless chariot, at book XI, 159–62. Coordinate it with the fact that this passage ends on a very different zoological note, where animals are neither friendly slaves nor meat, but the eaters of men, the same carrion birds witnessed in book I, line 6, when their canine competitors (I, 5) were still around (only to die in droves at I, 50).

2. **Supplication and prayer:** At the beginning of Agamemnon's *aristeia*, he kills a suppliant. This is a savage behavior, characteristic of the Achilles portrayed after book XVIII when he kills the suppliant Lykaon. Yet there is a strong political reason why Agamemnon rejects these particular suppliants:

*"Take us alive, son of Atreus, and take appropriate ransom.
In the house of Antimachos the treasures lie piled in*
*   abundance,*
bronze is there, and gold, and difficultly wrought iron,
and our father would make you glad with abundant
*   repayment*
were he to hear we were alive by the ships of the Achaeans."
Thus these two cried out upon the king, lamenting
and in pitiful phrase, but they heard the voice that was
    without pity:
"If in truth you are the sons of wise Antimachos,
that man who once among the Trojans assembled advised
*   them*
that Menelaus, who came as envoy with godlike Odysseus,
should be murdered on the spot nor let go back to the
*   Achaeans,*
so now your mutilation shall punish the shame of your father."

One essay-building strategy would be to assemble examples of failed supplications and compare the degree of excuse available to the transgressor. Here, the antisocial act of killing a pair of suppliants is offset by the guilt of the two victims in this attempted murder of an envoy, the brother of Agamemnon himself. There is a strong contrast between the rationality of this passage (draconian as that rationality may be) and the irrational cosmic nihilism of Achilles' answer to Lykaon. The political facts at Agamemnon's disposal go a long way toward justifying his transgression against "Zeus as god of suppliants" *(Zeus Hikateos)* in this passage. Paris himself, having stolen Menelaus's wife, bribed the Trojan Antimachos into opposing Antenor's excellent proposal for Helen's return. He also sponsored an abortive assassination attempt against Menelaus. Still, perhaps nothing does more to diminish the significance of this flouting of supplication than its placement: These two suppliants are one of three pairs of brothers whom Agamemnon kills in his *aristeia.*

3. **Ideology:** This middle region of the *Iliad* contains several passages that are commonly examined for insights into what is loosely referred to as "Homeric psychology." Consider the isolation of Odysseus in *Iliad* XI, a key text for Richard Gaskin's essay "Do Homeric Heroes Make Real Decisions?" in *Oxford Readings in Homer,* edited by Douglas Cairns (2001).

Compare the ambivalence of Odysseus in this passage with similar passages of heroic ambivalence. Athena is Odysseus's divine patron yet she is absent in this moment, though she is vividly present to Achilles (not only is she visible to him alone, but he can feel her pull his hair) in the assembly scene, where she prevents him from murdering Agamemnon. Do you see heroic ideology as an extrinsic force that makes Odysseus's decision for him, or does he decide to stay and fight because that seems the best course? What are Odysseus's criteria here?

Character

By the end of this second movement in the triptych of Homer's *Iliad*, the central focus has shifted to just a pair of characters: Achilles (of whom several characters including Briseis, and the ghost of Patroclus have become extensions) and Hector, until the one kills the other and makes him into another of many surrogates for himself, or a proxy who represents or embodies certain aspects of himself. Thereafter, our interest is focused on Achilles and Hector's father, Priam. Before we reach that point, however, other major and minor characters must have their say, turn a developmental corner if they can, and serve the plot.

Sample Topics:

1. **Agamemnon:** Book XI shows us a new Agamemnon, changed or at least demarcated by the qualified "Apology" he sends toward Achilles in book IX. Consider his *aristeia*. How does it differ from that of Diomedes in book V or that of Idomeneus in book XIII? How do you interpret the relationship between Agamemnon's *aristeia* and Zeus's rain of blood? Does it honor the king, or is it irrelevant to him, or is it perhaps a countervailing element against his *aristeia*?

Address these questions by quoting the text. Note that another natural phenomenon of this moment, the thundering of Hera and Athena, is explicitly said to happen in honor of Agamemnon. The rain of blood, however, has a different rationale: Zeus sent it "since he was minded to throw into Hades many heads of the strong." The Greek for "throw into Hades," which ends the line as well as the sentence is *Aidi proiapsen*, positioned at the end of this line and of the third line of Homer's *Iliad*. This is the will of Zeus being accomplished, as at I, 5. The poem seems to be taking stock of itself, restating some of its earliest guiding themes as a preparation for the launch of the next part of the plot, namely the return of Patroclus to battle. Agamemnon in book XI is perhaps yet another surrogate for the absent Achilles, a prodigious but inadequate surrogate to whom Patroclus (a very different man from Agamemnon and a more gentle one by far) is martially superior.

2. **Meriones:** Research the figure of Meriones in Mycenaean archaeology. How is your impression of the Homeric character changed by learning that Meriones is among the most ancient heroes in the poem? Does his savagery seem primitive?

Consult the bibliography at the end of this chapter for some relevant books. Meantime, consider that Meriones is the henchman of Idomeneus, the Cretan king who is younger than Nestor (and consequently, he is currently stronger by far), but older than the others. What do you make of his famous horned helmet? Why does he give it to Odysseus, and what might these two Achaeans have in common?

3. **Ajax:** Note Ajax at book XI, line 497, "slaughtering men and horses alike." Research the plot of Sophocles' tragic drama, *Ajax*. What might this Homeric line prefigure?

Here you are asked to familiarize yourself with the plot of a later work that was profoundly influenced by Homeric poetry. You might begin by looking up a summary on the Web, or by reading the introduction and the text of a good edition of Sophocles' play, such as the Hackett Edition (2007) translated by Meineck and Woodruff, *Four Tragedies: Ajax, Women of Trachis, Electra, Philoctetes.* You will find that Ajax, having lost to Odysseus a competition for the armor of the late Achilles, feels so deeply cheated that he is driven mad (by Athena) and proceeds to slaughter a herd of cattle in the false belief that he is slaughtering Odysseus and the two Atreidae. Notice that Achilles in the *Iliad* does something like the inverse of this: he sacrifices twelve Trojan boys on the funeral pyre of Patroclus as if they were animals, knowing that they are human beings. Notice also that in *Iliad* XIII, Hector derides Ajax as an "inarticulate ox," while the Iliadic narrator describes Ajax at bay "like a wild beast" (XI, 545–65), particularized first as a lion, then as a donkey (in a passage bracketed by a pair of references to his great ox-hide shield). Does anyone use zoomorphic language to describe Ajax in Sophocles' play? Notice also that the *Iliad* depicts two different kinds of shield used by warriors in battle; one is a huge, oblong body shield of leather, Mycenaean in origin and probably obsolete at the end of the Bronze Age; the other smaller, round, and hand-held, still in use in one form or another during the eighth century B.C. when the Homeric poems were reaching their final form. With this earlier, obsolete shield the *Iliad* always associates Ajax, and sometimes, Hector. To what degree can you substantiate an argument that, already in Homer, Ajax is a primitive figure with animal-related associations, more closely linked to the "dry cow" of his ox-hide shield than to any metallurgical artifact like Achilles' armor (which he wanted but could not achieve)? Remember to take note of all the animals you see in the text, and note their spatial layout: The vaunt of Ajax mentions horses and hawks. The vaunt of Hector centers on vultures and dogs (the irony here centers on the eventual treatment of Hector's corpse by Achilles, prior to its eventual redemption when Achilles lays it in the wagon of the sad, old king).

4. **Nestor:** Examine the end of book XI, in which Patroclus is detained by old Nestor as he tells a long story of the heroism he performed in his youth. Why does Nestor tell this story at this time, when Patroclus is in a hurry? Why does Homer?

The question is asking for at least two things: an account of why Nestor chooses to detain Patroclus for so long with his nostalgic tale, and an account of the poet's artistic motivation for placing that same narrative at this spot in the larger poem. There are bad reasons that can be cited in response to both questions: namely, that Nestor is a garrulous old man using memories of his glorious past to compensate for his current inadequacy and, conversely, that the poet is simply a naïve arranger of inherited story blocks who has plunked this one (about the earliest exploits of a young Nestor defending his homeland of Pylos and its community) at a somehow illogical spot. The opposite answers, the ones that dignify both the poet and his aging Gerenian horseman, tend to be more elaborate, more interesting, and in some respects, more true.

The issue of old age in Homer is fascinating, and there seems to be no clear decision in the text as to which is better for a man, a "beautiful death" in battle "in the pride of his strength," or the long ordeal of gradually failing physical power, the serial bereavement from those whom one survives, and an eventual death in the quiet of peace that follows twenty thousand sunshine days, which those who were killed in their youth can never experience. The *Odyssey* is perhaps designed to enable us to prefer a long and peaceful life, provided there is enough creation and destruction in it to keep us moving, whether that motion is occurring inside us as passion or outside as wanderings and adventure. What the *Odyssey* does not want for its hero (and therefore, what it mutely discourages for the conduct of our own lives) is stagnation, the long spell of concealment, withdrawal, abeyance, and idleness in which Odysseus languishes on Calypso's island, an episode not entirely different from Achilles' period of idleness from *Iliad* II to XVIII. See Thomas M. Falkner's essay "Homeric Heroism, Old Age, and the End of the *Odyssey*," in the volume *Old Age in Greek and Latin Literature* (SUNY P, 1989), ed. Falkner. See also *Iliad* XIV, 86.

Philosophy and Ideas

When philosophy was eventually invented by Plato's friend and mentor, Socrates, one of its central issues was transience, the way that people, things, and states of affairs in this world seem to be always breaking down and dying, whereas the gods are by definition immortal. To the immortality of the gods, Plato eventually added that of certain unchanging abstractions: round things, such as the apple, a ball, and even the sun, may change and perish, but the roundness of all round things is, simply and eternally, the Round. The abstraction is eternal, though the examples perish. Eventually Plato became convinced that the true, the beautiful, the good, and other large or abstract notions were as eternal as Zeus and Athena. So it is striking that already in Homer, there is a deep appreciation of inevitable decay as the price for existence altogether.

Some objects of human effort, such as a poetic gift that carefully avoids competition with the Muses, can hope to last long, as the undying reputation of Homer has proven. But material objects do not fare so well, and ultimately Troy itself is like one more young man cut down long before time has done its job on him.

Sample Topics:

1. Transience: Consider *Iliad* XII, 1–9, the description of the doomed wall and ditch. The passage is unusual for the attention it gives to the destructive process, because its object—the wall and ditch—is being destroyed after the Trojan War. Most material objects remain more or less invisible to the poet until they figure into the action of the *Iliad*; here, we are brought forward to a time that was futurity to the heroes and remains deep in the past for the poet and his audience. We are shown Apollo and Poseidon actively wrecking what the Greeks built. Why should the gods be so eager to break down what is no longer being used by anybody for any purpose?

There may be ironies to discover in the fact that this wall-and-ditch construction (which sounds vaguely like a neolithic causewayed camp) is the only constructive part of a destructive expedition. This passage establishes the interconnection of time with space. History is given an endoskeleton by those decrees of Zeus that fit this formula: *So long as X is the case, for that long Y shall be in abeyance. But after X is over, then Y will go forward.* That was how Hector's great long day of triumph was articulated into being by Zeus, and that is how the wall and ditch of the Achaeans is razed by Apollo and Poseidon. Line 6 is one place to look for a peg on which to hang a possible argument: the Achaeans "had not given to the gods grand sacrifices" in the construction of their stone wall and their earthworks, and this doomed these constructions to the amazing assault of divine and natural forces we witness in the light of Homer's genius in *Iliad* XII, 1–35. To write an essay from a starting point such as this, take what you have before you and follow where it leads, within the text. The Achaean wall and ditch was doomed because the gods were not honored appropriately in its construction. What else had this wall to do with the issue of honor and dishonor? Why was it built, and in what year of the war?

In telling us the wall will be destroyed after the war, the poet is also telling us that it will survive the war itself. He then promptly shows us the war ravaging the wall but not destroying it—just yet. Does that sound reminiscent of the condition of any particular persons at the end of the poem?

2. **Free will and constraint:** Consider the case of Euchenor, son of Polyidos. How would you compare his choice to that of Achilles?

Each of these two heroes has a prediction about his destiny, and both predictions are of the same form: die young at Troy, or face an undetermined future. In the case of Achilles, the second part stands for a long life that merely happens to lack *kleos* (glory, war fame). But Euchenor's choice is easier because his alternatives are death at Troy or a lingering fatal illness. Combine this passage with Sarpedon's speech to Glaukos at XII, 310–28, and see what implications arise.

3. **Knowledge:** Consider Agamemnon's claim to understanding and his brother's admission of ignorance. Compare these and speculate about the economy of knowledge in the *Iliad*.

A first move might be to introduce a pair of useful terms, which in this case you will have heard in a previous chapter: knowledge is abundant among the gods (though in XIV Hera and Sleep successfully deceive Zeus for a little while) and scarce among mortals. Menelaus rails against the Trojans for their violations of *xenia*, guest-host relationship (*hospitality* is a more convenient term, but though it names the right domain, it bears too little weight; *xenia* is a cosmic affair, and not merely a social one), of which Zeus is the sponsor and guarantor: ". . . you haughty Trojans . . . you defiled me, wretched dogs, and your hearts knew no fear / at all of the hard anger of *Zeus loud-thundering, / the guest's god,* who some day will utterly sack your steep city." The name of Zeus and the phrase "guest's god" are in grammatical apposition, sharing the same case: this is the Zeus of xenia, yet he appears to be aiding the same people who violated the very standard of behavior of which he is the god. There follows a touchingly direct admission of Menelaus's bafflement at how all of this fits together:

> You who in vanity went away taking with you my wedded
> wife, and many possessions, when she had received you in
>   kindness.
> And now once more you rage among our seafaring vessels
> to throw deadly fire on them and kill the fighting Achaeans.
> But you will be held somewhere, though you be so headlong
>   for battle.
> Father Zeus, they say your wisdom passes all others',
> of men and gods, and yet from you all this is accomplished
> *the way you give these outrageous people your grace,*
>   these Trojans
> whose fighting strength is a thing of blind fury . . . (XIII,
> 623–33)

Achilles raging on the Trojan plain or sulking in his shelter while the pleas of Odysseus, Ajax, and Phoenix go unheeded are cases of a sovereign figure giving up his responsibilities and finding that the world makes far less sense than he had been led to expect. Menelaus is not Achilles, however, and his dejection does not impede what we nowadays might call his "functionality." He still fights, but under a god whose plans he has stopped understanding since they became deceptive and intricate. Menelaus simply does not know about Achilles' influence on Zeus through his mother, Thetis. He does not know about the reversals caused by Hera's subterfuge and by Zeus's eventual reawakening. He does not know that the favor Zeus shows the Trojans will last only until fire touches the ships, so that this peak of Trojan success will also mark the beginning of disaster for their city. His apparently new position—trusting in a Zeus whom he cannot understand—is thus the best available.

By contrast, his brother Agamemnon has a different perspective. He has taken away a woman to whom he was not entitled (like Paris but unlike Menelaus). He has received, and acted on, a dream from Zeus that proved false and destructive. At that time, he chose to test the Achaeans' resolve by faking an episode of despair; now in book XIV that despair is restated, this time sincerely, yet Agamemnon still sounds arrogant, claiming to know what he does not, though his hubris is tempered by the misery inherent to that alleged knowledge: "For *I knew it,* when with full heart he defended the Danaans, / and *I know it* now, when he glorifies these people as if they / were blessed gods, and has hobbled our warcraft and our hands's strength."

4. **Ethics and responsibility:** Consider Hector's threat to his own soldiers at XV, 345–51, that if any man holds back from fighting straight toward the ships, Hector will see that he is killed and his corpse abused by scavengers.

How does Hector's use of this kind of language change your feelings about Achilles' abuse of Hector's corpse?

Form and Genre

This middle span of the *Iliad* is rich with implications about imaginative literature and the making of art. One of the most striking figures it presents is that of the on-land naval scene in book XV, 387–89, where the Achaeans fight the Trojans from the decks of their ships using "long pikes that lay among the hulls for sea fighting" as the ships stand on solid ground, not water. Why is this image so suggestive? Where does it lead? At line 505, Ajax cries out to his fellows: "Do you expect, if our ships fall to helm-shining Hector, / you will walk each of you back dryshod to the land of your fathers?" Note the power of Homer's poetic technique in the closing section of *Iliad* XV: there is the mention at line 600 of the "single ship burned" as the long-anticipated trigger for the reversal of fortunes in the Trojan War. It is followed at 617–28 by a simile about Hector, one whose image is not from farming or hunting but from seafaring—and suddenly we are on a ship on the water, in a storm that Hector resembles because both are divinely sponsored natural forces onrushing without mercy against a ship. Only one of those ships is metaphorical, but it is the one with the water under it. This all adds up to a strange tableau of stillness and motion, permanence and change. If Heraclitus and Parmenides had a favorite book of the *Iliad,* this would likely be it.

Sample Topics:

1. ***Iliad* as tragedy:** Is it possible to regard the *Iliad* as a tragedy? What is the relationship between the two genres, epic and tragedy?

The relationship between epic and tragedy has been the subject of many critical works, including *The Birth of Tragedy from the Spirit of Music,* by the great philosopher and classicist of the nineteenth century, Friedrich Nietzsche. One book commonly taught in relevant courses is James Redfield's *Nature and Culture in the* Iliad: *The Tragedy of Hector.* In his 2007 book, *Achilles in Greek Tragedy,* Pantelis Michelakis considers the figure of that hero as he appears in the surviving Greek dramas; unfortunately, these cannot include Aeschylus's *Achilles,* since that text is lost to us. A stock of oral myth eventually became the major source of subject matter for the art of epic poetry. The earliest layers of myth are very old—probably Neolithic in origin, perhaps as old as the inventions of agriculture and animal-herding; for all we know, the first (and now long-lost) epic poetry may be almost as old as myth itself. Greek tragedy emerges from this same mythic background, a compound of Indo-European elements expressed in Greek form, and non–Indo-European elements borrowed from peoples in contact with those who wound up in Greece—but it also draws on epic, as Sophocles does in his *Ajax,* for example. Tragedy has origins in the structural genius of Homer, his arrangement of an intricate yet simple plot that creates and sustains remarkably high levels of audience/reader interest over a poem of 15,693 lines. The *Ajax* has

1,421 lines, a tenth as large, yet Sophoclean shaping technique has a Homeric tone, an austere grace, merciless to the hero yet somehow honoring him even in the depths of his destruction. "The audience or the reader knows, perhaps from the traditional story and certainly from *Iliad* VIII, 473–75 and XIV, 64–77, that the wishes of Achilles have already been superseded in the plan of Zeus. This knowledge sets Achilles' prayer in an ironic perspective that renders it tragic" (Schein, *The Mortal Hero*, 120).

Each Greek drama has one hero, whereas the *Iliad* is an assemblage of many stories; some of these are developed into central aspects of the epic's structure, like the Patroclus plot, while others, like the Aeneas material or the story of Memnon, are representative of some narrative tradition that may have been resonant at other times and in other forms but is only thinly present in the *Iliad*.

2. *Iliad* **as didactic—what does it teach:** There are vocational passages in the Homeric epics that teach particular skills. What lessons can you find in the *Iliad*? Discuss the degree to which the technique is explained by Homer rather than merely described by him.

Given the necessary materials of horn, sinew, reed, and so on, do you suppose you could manage to assemble a composite bow using the information in the episode of Pandaros and his inspired archery, including its dual origins in Apollo's generosity and Pandaros's own handicraft? Could you and some friends read *Odyssey* book 5 and deploy the expertise therein to successfully create a seaworthy boat? At what point in that process would such efforts be likely to come to grief, if at all?

Bibliography for "*Iliad* XI–XVIII: The Central Ninth Day"

Michelakis, Pantelis. *Achilles in Greek Tragedy*. London: Cambridge UP, 2007.
Nietzsche, Friedrich. *The Birth of Tragedy from the Spirit of Music*, trans. Francis Golffing. New York: Random House, 1956.

Redfield, James. *Nature and Culture in the* Iliad: *The Tragedy of Hector.* Durham, NC: Duke UP, 1994.

Webster, Thomas Bertram Lonsdale. *From Mycenae to Homer: A Study in Early Greek Literature and Art.* London: Methuen & Co., 1958.

ILIAD XVI:

The Patrokleia

READING TO WRITE

THE NAME of the poem is in effect "the Story of Troy," a city also called Ilium (in one or another grammatical form, sometimes latinized or anglicized as Ilium or Ilion) because its founding ancestors include one man named Tros as well as another named Ilos. It is not called the tragedy of Hector, the tragedy of Achilles, the comedy of Paris, nor the travels of Helen, though it includes all these things and many others. The city is the subject of the title, yet the rage of Achilles is the first word and, in that regard, a keystone of the poem's meaning. Yet of all the *Iliad*'s several sustained, interwoven plots, the greatest is the Patroclus story, or Patrokleia. It binds the lesser rage of Achilles to the greater, and it gives us a counterpart to Hector who shares Patroclus's most sympathetic trait, gentleness. As you read, ask yourself about the basis for this (quite common) claim that Hector and Patroclus are both noted for their compassion. To whom is each of these men kind? What is the artistic effect of having one of them kill the other? Would it have been different if Patroclus had been killed by any other hero, or if Hector lacked the sympathetic dimension Homer confers on him so deeply in *Iliad* VI? How? Agamemnon, Meriones, and the Lesser Ajax are cruel people who do ghastly things to their opponents; why has Homer given us a Trojan leader who is free of those traits?

Book XVI is the heart of the Patrokleia; it includes his arming, entry into battle, *aristeia*, and death. Here is its opening: "So they fought on both sides for the sake of the strong-benched vessel." One might wonder whether this line was ever placed as the last line of book XV instead of the first of book XVI. The division of the *Iliad* into 24 books is post-Homeric anyhow, and yet time has conferred on that editorial division an antiquity that drives it into the way we read the poems. Perhaps carrying over into the new section a final line from the previous one enhances the effect of the break. What immediately follows this orphan line about the battle by the ship is a deeply moving image:

> Meanwhile Patroclus came to the shepherd of the people,
>   Achilles,
> and stood by him and wept warm tears, like a spring
>   dark-running
> that down the face of a rock impassable drips its dim water;
> and swift-footed brilliant Achilles looked on him in pity,
> and spoke to him aloud and addressed him in winged
>   words: "Why then
> are you crying like some poor little girl, Patroclus,
> who runs after her mother and begs to be picked up and
>   carried,
> and clings to her dress, and holds her back when she tries to
>   hurry,
> and gazes tearfully into her face, until she is picked up?
> You are like such a one, Patroclus, dropping these soft
>   tears . . ."

There is a world of pain, and a ream of philosophy, in that phrase "Meanwhile, Patroclus . . ." It transliterates the hero's name and translates a common Greek grammatical particle *de*. That particle is usually paired with another particle *men*, so that the construction "*men* [this] . . . *de* [that]" is translated "on the one hand, this; *on the other hand,* that." The tiny term *de* can also occur by itself, to be translated as "but" or "and." Lattimore's rendering, "meanwhile Patroclus" is correctly repeated at several points in the poem, until it takes on an ominous quality as the hero's death draws ever closer. Here at book XVI, line 2, it serves as a pivot on which the entire plot of the *Iliad* turns, as it shifts, or prefigures the shift, from the earlier Achilles to the later one.

The rest of the line, too, seems loaded: "Meanwhile Patroclus came to the shepherd of the people, Achilles" is faintly jarring, because Achilles has put aside his social responsibilities and been shepherding neither his own people, the Myrmidons (who came to fight and are idle) nor the Achaeans in general (for whose death he has prayed, with success). Achilles is also failing to shepherd Patroclus, for which he later becomes furious with himself, so there is an artistic touch in this use of the shepherd epithet here (rather than some other Achillean epithet the poet could have chosen instead, whether a metrical equivalent one in an otherwise identical line, or with a different line altogether). For the bad shepherd who fails to protect his flock, depicted within a simile but darkly reminiscent of "Achilles, shepherd of the people," see book XVI, 354.

Why does Achilles invoke the image of the little girl, and why is it such a poignant image? Partly because the image of the crying child causes the audience to regress, having once been crying children as well. The same image also arouses, in those who are parents, a passion of protective instinct. Yet we know Achilles, the mother in the simile, is going to lose Patroclus. From a technical point of view, the poet is going to take us through several thousand lines of Achilles' mourning, so the weeping child image is part of Homer's process of priming us for that, endowing the relationship of the two young men with color, nuance, and love so that the eventual loss achieves the tragic, and the *mênis*, the rage, it arouses can be understood and inhabited by the imagination of the audience.

Having elaborated his simile of Patroclus to a crying toddler and himself to her reluctant but eventually nurturing mother, Achilles continues:

> "Could you have some news to tell, for me or the
>   Myrmidons?
> Have you, and nobody else, received some message from
>   Phthia?
> Yet they tell me Aktor's son Menoitios lives still
> and Aiakos's son Peleus lives still among the Myrmidons.
> If either of these died we should take it hard. Or is it
> the Argives you are mourning over, and how they are dying

against the hollow ships by reason of their own arrogance?
Tell me, do not hide it in your mind, and so we shall both know."

"Could you have some news to tell, for me or the Myrmidons?" Think of the wrongheaded lightness of these lines. The worst Achilles contemplates is the natural order of things, where aged fathers die and sons survive. Look again at that first line after the simile: "Could you have some news to tell, for me or the Myrmidons?" What does it foreshadow? See *Iliad* XVII, 640.

TOPICS AND STRATEGIES

This section of the chapter will discuss various possible topics for essays and general approaches to those topics. Be aware that the material below is only a place to start from, not some kind of master key to the perfect essay. Use this material to prompt your own thinking. Every topic discussed here could encompass a wide variety of papers.

Themes

One powerful theme in the *Iliad* is doubling, the technique by which the poet establishes some kind of symbolic equivalence between two characters. Neither confusing the audience about which is which nor diluting or weakening the individuality of character that the poet has achieved for his heroes, Homer's doubling raises thought-provoking implications, and your essay can trace these. Consider the ways that Homer implies some level of equivalence, or at least strong parallels, between and among the following pairs of persons: Achilles and Patroclus; Hector and Patroclus; Hector and Achilles; Achilles and Meleager; Achilles and Helen; Patroclus and Sarpedon.

Sample Topics:

1. **Nature versus culture:** Consider Patroclus's answer to Achilles at the start of XVI. After reciting a brief catalogue of the wounded, Patroclus compares Achilles to a raw force of nature. Why?

The question is asking about lines 33–35: "Pitiless: the rider Peleus was never your father / nor Thetis was your mother, but it was the grey sea that bore you / and the towering rocks, so sheer the heart in you is turned from us." Looking forward, where else in the poem is Achilles compared to an elemental, prehuman power? Remember his fight with the river in book XX. Make comparisons to those scenes. The term *foreshadowing* is applicable, but you will want to come up with some alternative phrases that might shed more light on why Homer implements these techniques and how they are achieved.

Looking back in the text, note that Patroclus's mention of Peleus picks up on Achilles's mention of him the moment before. These and all other mentions of Peleus in the poem (except perhaps some occurrences of the formula "Achilles son of Peleus") point toward the end of the poem, when old father Priam supplicates Achilles in the name of his own father Peleus.

2. **Supplication and prayer:** Consider Achilles' two-part prayer to Zeus for Patroclus: that he fight gloriously and return safely. Why does it fail?

Unlike the wall and ditch of the Achaeans, the prayer of Achilles was ritually correct. So were the prayers of Hecuba in book VI, but these, too, failed because there are limits to the willingness of the gods in general and Zeus in particular to adapt the world's ways to human desires. Affection, loyalty, prayer, and sacrifice go only so far with the gods; one cannot use piety to compel good fortune from the Divine in Olympian religion any more than one can do so in the Book of Job. Perhaps one deep theme of the *Iliad* might be framed as *the failure to protect*. Zeus weeps tears of blood over Sarpedon, but will not prevent his death because, as the poem suggests, it is a crucial part of a larger scheme whose derailment is somehow dangerous to the cosmos. When Glaukos makes a successful prayer to Apollo for pain relief, healing, and battle strength, he mourns for his friend: "the best of men has perished, / Sarpedon, son of Zeus; who will not stand by his children." Recall that Apollo, like Sarpedon, is a son of Zeus.

3. **Mass death:** At XVI, 97–100 Achilles expresses to Patroclus the wish that everyone, on both sides of the war, should die except for the two of them. Is he serious?

It seems he is not seriously wishing this: on the Achaean side, he did wish limited yet significant losses during his rage at Agamemnon, but that (lesser) *mênis* must be finished now, since the designated limit of its violence has been achieved. Besides, he is sending out Patroclus to defend the Achaeans, a thing he could not do while the first rage lasted. Nor, on the other hand, has he at this point that greater *mênis* for the Trojans that drives him to behave as though he is trying to wipe them out. Patroclus is alive and well, standing before him weeping with empathy for the Achaeans, and Achilles does not know that his warning to Patroclus—again, a set of limits to violence—will not be heeded. Now ask yourself the converse: what is there to suggest that on some level, Achilles would indeed welcome such an outcome as the genocidal disaster he wishes for at XVI, 97–100? Also, how does this shocking (even if merely sarcastic) remark shape our perception of what follows?

4. **Corpse abuse and desecration:** Hector's threats of corpse exposure, chilling as they are, raise important questions. Why does Homer introduce this concern through Hector?

To the horror of many, Achilles drags Hector's corpse around the city of Troy three times. How do Hector's threats to his own troops and to the dying Patroclus ("as for you, here the vultures will eat you") affect your experience of the poem's outcome? The *telos* or eventual resolution of the poem is about the fate of Hector's own corpse: abuse followed by restoration to honor. Does that remind you of anyone in the work?

Another topic in this section considered whether Achilles was serious in his bleak wish. Ask the same question with regard to Hector's threats of corpse exposure.

Character

Late in the poem we learn from a ghost that Patroclus only met Achilles because he was a fugitive who Peleus took in; fugitive, because the young Patroclus had accidentally killed another boy in anger at having lost to him in a dice game. A paper about the dice and the role of chance could benefit from the words *contingency, teleology,* and *epistemic* (if you do not know these words, look them up and then use them). This is just one way to explore how character intersects with the various other elements incorporated in Homer's epic.

Sample Topics:

1. **Diomedes and Patroclus:** Why does Diomedes successfully avoid conflict with Apollo, while Patroclus succumbs to it?

One obvious and therefore incomplete answer is, because of Athena's nurturance: "I have taken away the mist from your eyes . . ." she says hauntingly, to her favorite son of Tydeus. Note that this is the same kind of answer to the question why Odysseus survives whereas his companions (in the *Odyssey,* who are, of course, the same men he leads in the *Iliad,* only older) do not.

At book XVI, line 684, there is another occurrence of the pivot phrase *Patroclus de,* and we are told of his new onslaught. Then comes one of several strange moments in the *Iliad* when the Homeric narrator comments on a character's behavior: "Besotted: had he only kept the command of Peleiades / he might have got clear away from the evil spirit of black death." Homer's word for the keeping of the command is a figurative use of *phylasso,* the same verb that more commonly means "to guard, keep watch over," and in this sense Patroclus has failed to protect the command of Achilles, as Achilles has failed to protect Patroclus himself. Note that English shows the same usage as Greek here, since we too have the figurative idiom of "to keep a command" as well as this other, nurturing and social sense of the same verb, in the King James of Genesis 4:9, "Am I my brother's keeper?"

Homer's original word, which led to Lattimore's choice of "besotted," is *nepios,* and here is the range of its meaning as given in the standard *Homeric Dictionary* of Autenreith: "an epithet of little children or young animals, 'infant,' 'helpless'; often used figuratively, indicating the blind unconsciousness on the part of men that suggests an analogy between the relation of men to higher powers and that of infants to adults, 'helpless,' 'unwitting,' and sometimes disparagingly, 'simple,' 'childish'" (198).

Most Anglophone translators use "fool" for *nepios* here (as they use "children and fools" for Odysseus's men in the *Odyssey*). Lattimore likely chose "besotted" because it connotes a passing (not chronic) state of folly, like the *Atê* that seized Agamemnon; he wants to avoid giving the false impression that Homer is calling Patroclus stupid, which he certainly is not. "Besotted," however, does not capture the notes of tenderness and infantilism of Homer's word choice, which fits well with the image of the crying little girl that opened book XVI. The explanation given for Patroclus's death is this formula: "But always the mind of Zeus is a stronger thing than a man's mind." It includes Zeus's personal agency, beyond which there can be no appeal; the relative weakness of the human mind; and the actual, acute foolishness of Patroclus's captivity to his own exaggerated sense of battle frenzy. We are told that Zeus is responsible (told even more clearly in the rendering by A. T. Murray: "he [Zeus] it was that now put fury in the breast of Patroclus"), but that is also to say that Patroclus's failure was extraordinary. Consider the fresh yet suddenly broken bowstring of Teukros: Zeus is obviously responsible, since the string was fresh and should have lasted far longer. Patroclus was explicitly warned; he received early enough the knowledge necessary to avoid disaster; he even made some use of that knowledge, at 710–11 when he yields to Apollo. Yet he forgot it. A god is involved. Similarly, a god "stole away the wits of Glaukos" when he traded his gold armor for Diomedes' bronze, since it was plain to see what metal was being traded for what, yet Glaukos traded down anyway. Find more examples of self- or divine-induced folly.

Sample Topics:

1. Sarpedon, son of Zeus: What do you make of the particular achievement that Homer (or the tradition he inherited) has chosen to attribute to Sarpedon, namely the breaking of the Achaean wall?

The *Iliad*'s structurally central moment is arguably the story of the doomed wall and ditch, that emblem of the perishing nature of all things humanity can do or make. Sarpedon's breaching of the wall is counterbalanced by or symmetrical to the attempt of his killer, Patroclus, to penetrate the wall of Troy on the opposite end of the battlefield from the site of Sarpedon's moment of triumph.

Instead of saving his own life by killing Patroclus, as Sarpedon had intended his spear throw to do, it kills a horse, "blameless Pedasos," the one mortal of the three horses Patroclus drives into battle. Find a logical arrangement of this tableau of mortality contrasted with immortality. Note: They are Achilles' horses.

2. Gods: "Apollo loves these people." That was part of Achilles' warning to Patroclus in book XVI. In *Iliad* XV, Hector is wounded in the chest by a boulder thrown by Ajax, and Apollo comes to him and saves his life in an intimate theophany without disguise: "such an avenger am I . . ." One day later, Hector is dead, and Troy, doomed. What does it all amount to? Why does love not equal protection?

On every level between microcosm and macrocosm, authority figures in the *Iliad* are seen failing to protect their dependents. But the poem is not prescriptive; it does not seem to urge people to do better and make different choices that will cause less harm. Instead it seems to present human suffering as an inevitable feature of the cosmos, arising from the confluence of forces—time, the gods, chance, and human decision—that together constitute what the 19th century called "the world-process." In Homer, failure to protect is a central aspect of the way the world works. Before the Achaeans could sail to Troy from the becalmed Aegean, says a part of the story outside the *Iliad*, Agamemnon was told by Calchas the seer that he must sacrifice the life of his own daughter, Iphigenia. Far beyond the mere failure to protect, Agamemnon kills his own child and in return the gods provide a strong wind toward Troy. In the *Iliad* we do get to hear of one other early event in the history of the Trojan War. When Zeus wishes to impart to the Achaeans the information that the siege war upon which they have just embarked will last ten years and end in victory, how does he express himself? In an omen, at Aulis, where a mother bird watches helpless as a great snake devours her eight young, eating the mother bird ninth and last. So far, that's predation: the dark but unchangeable fact that all animals have to eat other organisms to stay alive (a key element in God's answer to Job in the book of Job). Just then, however, Zeus moves it beyond the merely natural by turning the gluttonous snake to stone, birds and all. Who else in the *Iliad* was also spoken of as having been turned to stone, and what had she in common with this poor bird?

Philosophy and Ideas

There is a tangled but interesting web of arguments about just how much "ego integrity" can be claimed for the Homeric heroes, with writers such as Jaynes, Dodds, Snell, and (more recently) Yoav Rinon minimizing the *I* of the Homeric hero, and others (most powerfully, Oliver Taplin) regarding the Homeric hero as a well-integrated psyche, not so different from later literary characters. In this thorny matter, be guided by the principle that the *Iliad* is indeed a work of genius: It achieves a tragic consciousness—that strange, bleak-as-the-lunar-landscape, painless place where the reader's mind goes when it has been wrung out like a saturated rag, so that its accumulated blood, sweat, and tears gush down and flow away, in the purgative process Aristotle called catharsis. If the Homeric heroes were like Hephaestus's robot helpers, the mere puppets of Zeus or of luck (to caricature Snell's nuanced position for a moment), this effect could probably not be achieved. At its best, the primitivist position (which maintains that someone like Hector is less of an autonomous moral agent than is a modern character such as Prince Hamlet or Jay Gatsby) affords insight into what might have been the general evolution of modern consciousness. At its worst, conversely, it is a shell game in which the various ancient Greek terms for elements of the human person—*thumos, orgê, psychê, noös, phrên,* and others—are shifted about so as to configure a theory of mind that suits the critic's purposes.

Sample Topics:

1. **Etiology of violence:** To ask how something originates is to ask about its etiology. In looking for the hidden roots of violence, sociologists generally look at the parenting practices of a society. Consider parenthood in the *Iliad,* especially fatherhood.

Glaukos tells an immortal son of Zeus (Apollo) that Zeus "will not protect his children," since a mortal son of Zeus (Sarpedon) has died. Yet we have some knowledge, even if this knowledge is incomplete and largely intuitive, of why Zeus has chosen to weep tears of blood rather than prevent Sarpedon's death as he had yearned to do. The Father Sky God can be excused and, in the Christian imagination, even passionately thanked, for his role in the bloody sacrifice of his own child, since he is God. Like Zeus permitting the death of his son Sarpedon as per Hera's warning, the Christian god, too, acts as the steward of the cosmos by permitting/arranging the crucifixion of his own son. Reading Hector's prayer for Astyanax, it is hard to see how a world of Homeric fathers could produce anything but a world of Homeric sons, some of them killed in infancy and others on the battlefield, a tiny handful surviving to the old age of Priam. And in such a world of utter bereavement, Priam's longevity is an evil to be endured, not a good to be enjoyed; he will escape into death only when he is killed by Neoptolemus, the son of Achilles. Is Homer suggesting that it is as impossible for mankind to have culture without warfare as it is for Zeus to save Sarpedon? In both cases there is a wisp of possibility that merely enhances and ennobles the futility.

2. **Divine intervention:** Consider the Homeric formula at XVI, 120: "Telamonian Aias / shook there in his hand a lopped spear,

while far away from him / the bronze spearhead fell echoing to the ground; and Aias / knew in his blameless heart, and shivered for knowing it, how this / was gods's work, how Zeus highthundering *cut across the intention* / in all his battle, how he planned that the Trojans should conquer." What does it mean?

First, ask yourself whether the phrase italicized above has been used by Homer elsewhere in the poem. The same formula occurs in the passage about Teukros's snapped bowstring. What have the two passages in common? Look closely at the two incidents and the spatial layout of the events they describe. What inferences can you draw?

3. **The dual form:** Consider the use of the dual form (a form of the pronoun "you" that meant "you two" without saying the number separately) in the embassy scene when Achilles addresses Ajax, Phoenix, and presumably the third man with them, Odysseus, and yet the grammar of the Greek excludes him.

Some commentators infer the interpolation of a fragment from a different poem in which only two ambassadors come to Achilles. Some suppose that this is instead (or is in addition) a brilliant slight to Odysseus (whose characteristic mode of operation is *mêtis*, "cleverness," which Achilles contemns here in book IX), deliberately put here by Homer. There is a resemblance to the moment when Achilles is accepting Patroclus's wish to go out and fight: he warns him not to attack Troy itself, "for fear some one of the everlasting gods on Olympos / might crush you. Apollo who works from afar loves these people . . ." That is of course exactly what occurs, and Apollo kills him. Yet just after this Achilles pronounces his sarcastic wish: only two survivors of the Trojan War, Achilles and Patroclus; not more. This wish is itself pronounced in the names of two gods who love Achilles (Zeus and Athena) and one more, who loves Hector instead: Apollo, who was just identified by name as Patroclus's antagonist to be avoided. Consider also the two immortal horses of Achil-

les, accompanied by a third, the mortal Pedasos whom Sarpedon accidentally kills.

Form and Genre

Epic poetry requires a structure to contain its various threads. From
within the world of the poem, that structure is known as *Dios boulê*, "the
will of Zeus"; from outside, it is simply the plot. Consider the figure of
Zeus in *Iliad* XVI actively weighing competing alternatives of how and
when Patroclus is to die. Is there an analogy to be made between Zeus
and the poet? What speaks for, and what speaks against, the possibility
that the poet was aware of this analogy?

Sample Topics:

1. **Chiasmus:** Compare the following two passages and observe
   what they have in common: XVI, 722; III, 415.

   Look up the term *chiasmus*. What role do parallel phrases and
   verbal structures play in the presentation and reception of the
   work? What is the potential effect of repetition and variation
   in the *Iliad*? How does each of the cited passages display mirroring and inversion on the level of content and in the words
   the poet chooses?

2. **The central day:** On the *Iliad*'s vast central day, the direction
   of the battle shifts from seaward (toward the Greek ships) to
   inland (Troy) when, despite an *aristeia* of Ajax, Hector sets
   one of the ships on fire. To whom does the ship belong? Why
   has the poet made it that man's ship, rather than someone
   else's?

   An essay on this topic will consider parallelism and symmetry
   in the structure and language of Homer's narrative. How and
   why is the transition from sea to land effected?

3. **The wall as emblematic of the work itself:** What lies at the
   exact center of the *Iliad*? The doomed wall and ditch of the

Achaeans. What is the significance of the episode's placement in the work overall?

For a comparison of this wall to the *Iliad* itself, see Andrew Ford, *Homer: The Poetry of the Past.* Time has conferred on the poem an antiquity that must have begun as the poet's mere hope. Yet all productions of the human mind, even Shakespeare, even Homer, even the languages of ancient Greece and of present-day America, will be forgotten one day.

Language, Symbols, and Imagery
Sample Topics:
1. **Death, grief, and mourning:** What are the ways Homer suggests that Achilles is dead before he is ever even wounded?

How does Achilles behave when he learns of Patroclus's death? How and where does the language of that grieving behavior correspond to the language of death in battle? What are things people typically do, but which Achilles stops doing when he learns of Patroclus's death? Does any of this apply to Hector? He, too, is mourned before he actually dies. Are the water nymphs beside Thetis actually mourning for Patroclus, or for Achilles in anticipation?

2. **The death of Patroclus:** Consider the exact manner in which Patroclus is killed. What are the implications for the themes and preoccupations the *Iliad* embodies?

One of the central facts to consider in pursuing this topic is that three persons kill Patroclus, "destiny and Apollo," Hector, and Euphorbos; that Apollo's direct intervention was required; and that the god began by causing the straps on Patroclus's armor to fail (a specialty of the Olympian gods, this failure of Bronze Age war equipment), stripping him.

3. **Comparing the deaths of Patroclus and Hector:** What are the similarities between the deaths of these two characters?

Begin by setting the passages beside each other and scanning them for matches. Describe what you find and speculate on its artistic advantages for the poem, given that the two heroes are on opposite sides of the war and are, in a sense, each other's individual killers. Though Patroclus only kills Hector through his proxy, Achilles, the same proxy relationship that cost Patroclus his life also avenges his death. Look at the helmet of Hector in book VI and then consider the helmet, which had belonged to Achilles, with which he replaces it.

Bibliography for "*Iliad* XVI: The Patrokleia"

Benardete, Seth. *Achilles and Hector: The Homeric Hero.* South Bend, Ind.: St. Augustine's Press, 2005.

Edwards, Mark W. *Homer: Poet of the* Iliad. Baltimore: The Johns Hopkins UP, 1990.

Ford, Andrew. *Homer: The Poetry of the Past.* Ithaca, NY: Cornell UP, 1994.

Fowler, Robert, ed. *The Cambridge Companion to Homer.* Cambridge Companions to Literature. Cambridge: Cambridge UP, 2004.

Nagy, Gregory. *Greek Mythology and Poetics* (Myth & Poetics S.). Ithaca: Cornell UP, 1992.

Willcock, Malcolm. *A Companion to the* Iliad. Chicago: U of Chicago P, 1976.

ILIAD XVIII–XXIV:

The Greater Wrath
and Priam's Mission

READING TO WRITE

A s YOU read the *Iliad* with the intent to write about it, notice the way the poem is resolved when Achilles is visited by old King Priam, who successfully petitions him for the return of his son Hector's body. This successful visit and instance of supplication in the poem restores Achilles to humanity, though he has a short time left to live. Part of the meaning of the poem, not to be missed in the experience of reading it, is a concern with time as an element through which human life plays out. The poet composed in the eighth century B.C., yet he was reconstructing the drama of a war that ended at least 400 years before his birth (perhaps as many as 700, depending on your interpretation of the evidence). His is an ancient voice, speaking to us of things that were already ancient for him. Unpacking the implications of that particular authorial relation may lead to an effective essay, and it may deliver you a satisfaction beyond the mere resolution of some assignment. The ending of the *Iliad* is one of the most memorable scenes in all literature. It plumbs the depths of human misery. We read it and emerge changed from our confrontation of the text, as Aristotle suggested in his *Poetics* when he said that tragedy "purges us of pity and terror."

TOPICS AND STRATEGIES

This section of the chapter will discuss various possible topics for essays and general approaches to those topics. Be aware that the suggested subjects and directions mark only a starting point, not some kind of master key to the perfect essay. Use this material to prompt your own thinking. Every topic discussed here could encompass a wide variety of papers.

Themes

In the last movement of the *Iliad*, its final one-third, themes arise that all seem to converge on the scene that unfolds inside Achilles' tent. Along the way, we are confronted with the appearance of Patroclus's ghost, who happens to mention a story that suggests that he met Achilles only because of a roll of some dice one day long ago. The reference is a reminder of the mysterious nature of the world, where human lives unfold according to multiple orders of causality comprising the gods, our own will, and chance. Chance itself is mired in determinate factors that shape randomness, right down to the gravitational constant in the downward force acting on the dice. Spears, like dice, are cast by human hands, and yet they hit or miss their targets according to the overdetermined interplay of human will, divine will, and chance; similar conditions pertain to anything launched by human hands, whether in warfare or gaming. A paper on the subject would do well to revisit the funeral games for Patroclus in *Iliad* XXIII.

Sample Topics:

1. **Patroclus's ghost and the afterlife:** What inferences can be made from the *Iliad* about the eighth-century B.C. idea of an afterlife? Consider Hector and Patroclus as two cases that seem like opposites. Are they?

Consider the passage in which Achilles witnesses Patroclus's ghost. Just after that, Homer seems to link two elements through their juxtaposition: the failure of Achilles' effort to cause Patroclus's funeral pyre to burst into flames and the failure of Achilles' effort to expose Hector's body to the dogs. When the winds are assembled by Iris, "They came with a sudden blast upon the sea, and the waves rose / under the whistling wind. They came to the generous Troad / and hit the pyre, and a huge inhuman blaze rose, roaring." What effect do these lines have on you? Do the awesome natural forces of wave and flame seem to stand for aspects of Achilles' inner life? How is that effect achieved?

Hector and Patroclus seem like opposites because the one kills the other; because Achilles hates the one and loves the other; because one is exposed to dogs and birds and the other is given a full sacrificial funeral complete with competitive games in his honor. Yet each of these points comes with its own limiting conditions and considerations. Hector kills Patroclus (with Apollo and Euphorbos), yet this triggers Hector's own death, in which their positions eventually converge. When the poem ends, Hector has a grand honorific funeral, joining Patroclus in that category too.

Achilles lashes Hector with the taunt, "So there is no one who can hold the dogs off / from your head" no matter the ransom Troy might offer for Hector's body. This is doubly wrong, a pair of mistakes about the world. First and more importantly, it is Zeus who holds off the dogs from Hector's head, though he is dragged from a chariot for miles. Second, even as Achilles stabs Hector in the throat and swears undying hate, it is "Achilles himself" who will lay the body in the wagon of Hector's father, Priam, one night in the near future.

2. **Skill and the horse race:** During the funeral games for Patroclus, old Nestor advises his young son Antilochos about the horse race. In an unwitting parallel to the biblical book of Ecclesiastes, we are told essentially that "the race is not always to the swift." Why is this observation included?

Nestor has given this advice in order to help his son win the race. Homer has most likely included the father's words for that reason but also to give the passage a didactic or instructional dimension. Decades ago, the scholar Eric Havelock wrote a book called *A Preface to Plato* in which he called attention to the "vocational" passages in Homer where the preliterate Greeks used oral poetry to pass down their traditions of craft and technical skill in such areas as horseracing, boat making, and archery. Whatever Homer is saying, he says it at a length that will best manage the attention of his live audience. That point can be combined with another consideration that sometimes underlies a Homeric choice of imagery or wording: He often seems to be quietly commenting on his own artifice. When he says, "The woodcutter is far better for skill than he is for brute strength," it makes sense to ask whether the woodcutter is also a stand-in for the poet. Surely "[b]y skill charioteer outpasses charioteer" can be read as a comment on poetic competition, since we have evidence elsewhere of bards trying to outperform one another in front of an audience that prefers newer material. Read the rest of this image as if it were a simile (which it is not) and ask yourself, where does the audience fit in? Are they the "slow horses"? Nestor continues: "He who has put all his confidence in his horses and chariot / and recklessly makes a turn that is loose one way or another / finds his horses drifting out of the course and does not control them." Remember the business about the poet's narratological management of the audience's attention? "But the man, though he drive the slower horses, who takes his advantage . . ."

The passage contains a kind of authorial shout: "I will give you a clear mark and you cannot fail to notice it." What is that clear mark? On the literal level, it is "a dry stump standing up from the ground about six feet, / oak, it may be, or pine, and not rotted away by rain-water, / and two white stones are leaned against it, one on either side. . . . / Either it is the grave-mark of someone who died long ago, / or was set as a racing goal by men who lived before our time." In case the tree and stone imagery reminds you of the male reproductive system, you could pursue this topic by consulting *The Reign of the Phallus: Sexual Politics in Ancient Athens* by Eva C. Keuls; *Ancient Symbol Worship: Influence of the Phallic Idea in the*

Religions of Antiquity by Charles Staniland Wake; and *Primitive Symbolism as Illustrated in Phallic Worship* by Hodder Michael Westropp. In any case, a fathom (Lattimore gives "six feet") tall is quite a "stump," about the height of a man, which fits with the idea that it might be a grave marker. If it was, then it has deteriorated since nobody seems sure whether it is a grave marker or not, let alone just whose grave it marks (this should remind you of Hector's fantasy of a grave marker for his victim). If it was not a grave marker, it was and remains a racing post; even then, the issue of anonymity is not dispelled because of the way Nestor phrases his description.

Note also the similarities between this dead racing post and the dead stick that Achilles uses as the staff that gives him the authority to speak during the Achaean assembly. Both are formerly living trees that have been turned into symbolic objects by a process of death; both have a utility that arises from an arbitrary act of meaning, since the Achaeans could just as easily use an appropriately sized stone or metal artifact for a grave or race marker, but they do not.

3. **Supplication/Zeus in command:** Consider how directly Zeus involves himself in making sure supplication is effective. How can you reconcile this with the failure of supplication elsewhere in the poem?

Perhaps this is why Lykaon is in the suppliant's situation for the second time: to diminish the threat to Zeus's honor that Achilles incurs by killing him this time. After all, he let him go the last time. Just as there are many gods and not one, there are many "aspects" of particular gods; Poseidon, for example, is lord of the sea, and of earthquakes, and of horses. Zeus Xenias is the keeper of hereditary guest-host friendship and protector of strangers; Zeus Horkos is the Zeus of oaths. The divine sponsor of hospitality and oaths also sponsors supplication, the institution of pity and mercy. This suggests successful protection, and yet the failure to protect is ever-present; Hector cannot protect Astyanax, and nobody protects Hector but the god Apollo, whose limits are well short of opposing destiny. Though "Apollo loves these people," and though he appears to Hector saying "such an avenger am I," the protection he receives will pertain to his corpse. The failed supplication by Hector to Achilles for the ransom of his own dying body is fulfilled by Priam's successful supplication for it. What fulfils, or answers for, the oath Pandaros broke?

Character

Sample Topics:

1. **Andromache's death-in-life and Achilles' death-in-life:** What are the implications of Homer's duplicating the behavior of the characters in these two scenes?

   The most important characters to die in the *Iliad* are Hector and Patroclus, and each has someone who loves him so much that he or she seems to die upon hearing the news that the beloved has been killed. What features do the two scenes have in common? Why is Homer employing (and why repeating or duplicating) these features?

2. ***Theophany*/divine visitation:** Consider the sublime moment of Hermes' divine self-disclosure to Priam outside the shelter of Achilles. Compare Athena's revelation to Odysseus. How are they similar? How do they differ?

   To explore this topic, examine another theophany such as that of Athena to Odysseus in *Odyssey* 13. Look for commonalities between that passage and the one showing Hermes revealing himself to Priam. Speculate about the meanings of those commonalities, either as an aspect of Homer's poetic technique or as a facet of our understanding of Greek religion. What sort of gods are these?

3. **Agamemnon's woman, Antilochos's mare:** At the beginning of the *Iliad* we see the traffic in women rather suddenly become the focal point of a disastrous conflict between Achilles and

Agamemnon. Briseis is herself the focus of a strand of a poetic tradition that has been largely obscured by time, though recently analyzed and celebrated by Casey Dué in *Homeric Variations on a Lament by Briseis* (Rowman & Littlefield, 2002). Toward the poem's end, in the funeral games for Patroclus in book XXIII, an irony surfaces when Antilochos speaks to Achilles using language similar to Agamemnon's from the first books of the poem—except that Antilochos is not referring to a woman: "But *the mare* I will not give up, and the man who wants her / must fight me for her with his hands." What do you make of this? Is Antilochos risking a joke here? Is Homer? What are the various meanings you can impute to this?

History and Context

Sample Topics:

1. **Burial customs:** To what degree are the burials of Patroclus and Hector probably appropriate to the Bronze Age, during which the Trojan War took place? To what degree are they probably appropriate to the Iron Age, during which Homer composed his poems?

To answer this question you need an orientation to the burial customs, and indeed to the general civilization, of Bronze Age Greece. One approach is to read a few books from various decades and various levels of popular versus scholarly interest. The books will disagree with each other in interesting ways that illuminate the field of this subject. I recommend M.I. Finley, *The World of Odysseus*; the *Cambridge Companion to the Aegean Bronze Age* by Cynthia W. Shelmerdine; and *Archaic Greece: The Age of Experiment* by Anthony M. Snodgrass.

Philosophy and Ideas

Sample Topics:

1. **Failure to protect:** Where does protection *succeed* in the *Iliad?*

There are many occurrences of the simile of the mother cow lowing over her calf to protect it, but the healthy calf stands for a dead warrior corpse, not a live man. The gods protect Hector both ways: after his death they keep harm away from his corpse despite Achilles' mad efforts to violate it, but first, they prolong his life and give him glory. A theophany [*theo* = god; *phany* = appearance] occurs between the lord Apollo and Hector. Consider the language of that sublime scene, for instance, "such an avenger am I," says Apollo to Hector. Compare the use of the same correlative adjective in "such an escort," which describes Hermes, whom Zeus sends in the guise of a Greek soldier (a Myrmidon, one of Achilles' men) to accompany King Priam through the sleeping Greek camp. Notice Homer using this formula for Hermes ("such an escort") three times in close succession: Zeus to Iris, Iris to Priam, and Priam to Hermes, the god whose many roles include that of the *psychopomp*, the one who leads the procession of the dead from this world into the next. As escort here in book XXIV, he is leading Priam into death not by present violence but by liberation into the end state that will soon stop Priam's pain. This begins with Hermes giving Priam relief about the fate of his son's corpse, followed by the revelation of Hermes' true identity and in turn by the meeting with Achilles, which hints at acceptance and renunciation.

The end of the *Iliad* is a tragic scene in a tragic world of scarcity and loss, bereavement and degradation, where Priam says "I have had to do what no mortal has done, I have kissed the hands that killed my children." Yet amid this grief, there is a scene of divine care and, more importantly, human majesty and peace. It occurs beyond grief and violence, apart from the community and yet embedded in it, where Achilles and Priam marvel at each other silently and, as if from opposite ends of everything (the Trojan War, the human lifespan, the scale of power) seem to give each other permission to eat together despite their grief for Patroclus and Hector respectively. That is a spectacle of the tragic consciousness that the narrative has achieved in the audience by this point. Because this resolution has been achieved, with the humanity of Achilles restored and Priam pulled back from the brink, now the funeral of Hector can proceed—which is to say, the poem can end and, beyond that, Priam and Achilles alike can die.

2. **Ethics and responsibility:** Discuss Achilles' use of the term *friend* or *dear one* (translating *philos*) in his speech to Lykaon prior to murdering him, and his use of the term in the meeting with Priam in Achilles' own tent? Seth Schein has written that the *Iliad* "is as much about Achilles's [love] as it is about his [wrath]." How would you pursue that idea, gathering support for it from the poem? Discuss Homer's decision to make this the second time Lykaon has been the helpless suppliant of Achilles. What does that artistic choice provide the poet?

Writing this essay involves comparing Achilles' response to Lykaon on the two occasions. If that comparison should happen to lead your mind on toward other comparisons, follow it. These can become the framework of an eventual argument. When Achilles throws Lykaon to the fishes, remember Talthybios the henchman of Agamemnon throwing a throat-slit pig into the water. What were the circumstances on that occasion? Now ask yourself what arises when you compare these similar circumstances to yet another juxtaposition in the text: Priam bringing the bodies of the oath-sacrificed lambs back to Troy in a wagon in book III and Priam bringing the body of Hector back to Troy in a wagon in book XXIV. What is suggested by comparing Priam bringing home the corpse of his son at one end of the poem and, at the other end, Chryses bringing home his daughter?

Form and Genre
Sample Topics:
1. **The catalog of nymphs:** Oral poetry has lists that are conventionally called catalogs. Some written poems make use of the catalog form by inheriting it from Homer; others avoid it because a written list can be tedious. In Homer's world of personal presence and live performance, though, the list was one more trance-inducing technique for keeping the language going without advancing the plot; in effect, a brake pedal for the poem's progress through its own narrative. After the death of Patroclus there is a mourning song, or threnody, sung by a group of sea nymphs with iconic names. Lattimore has wisely chosen to leave

them untranslated so that the original language in all its beauty can be enjoyed. Still, try reading a translation that renders the names of the nymphs: for example, Wave Receiver, the Bringer, the Powerful. Can you infer anything from these names?

As often with Homer, this portion of the *Iliad* is rich in meta-poetic moments, which is to say, moments when the poem seems to comment upon itself or its own structure. At book XIV, lines 264 and 274, the poet seems to comment on his own pacing. The *Iliad* is a grand structure that is populated by smaller structures. It also contains many loving depictions of structures in other artistic genres and crafts, lavishing on the details of those objects—Pandaros's bow, Odysseus's boat, Nestor's cup, and so on—the sort of zeal normally reserved for subjects. Why? Is there any self-reference in lines like these?

2. **"[F]astened it all in order . . ." book XXIV, 274:** Write an essay developing the idea that Homer is commenting on the construction of the *Iliad* in passages such as this one in which the poet is explicitly discussing the construction of some tangible object, while perhaps implicitly commenting on the poem at the same time.

Such a paper can build on the etymology of the word for chariot, *harma*, from which we get the term *harmony*. The reason is that chariots, like music, must be assembled so that all the parts are in the precisely correct relationships to one another. That, in turn, explains the political and erotic senses of the term "harmony." Since the semantic field of this term's application spans many domains, it is apt for this role as a self-referencing tool in Homer's hands. Look up *technê* using the Perseus search engine, or an index in the form of a reference book called a concordance. It will tell you all the occurrences of a given word in the works of an author, in this case *technê* and Homer. When you come to passages in the epics in which Homer explains the precise physical way in which something is done or made, consider the possibility that he may also be commenting upon his own artifice. Build an essay on the results by interpreting what you find. The arts are united by *technê*, comprising both dactylic hexameter poetry on the one hand, and all the other arts and crafts and trades on the other.

"Well then, / will you not get my wagon ready *and be quick about it,* / and put all these things on it, *so we can get on with our journey?*" XXIV, 263–65. This is spoken by Priam just after the lavish description of the ransom he has assembled for Hector's body. This line jump-starts both the mule wagon and the poem itself.

3. **Hector's death and Troy's:** When the parents of Hector learn that he is dead, the Homeric narrator describes the agony of their behavior with this curious line: "It was most like what would have happened, if all lowering / Ilion had been burning top to bottom in fire." Why?

This topic relates to the notion that the poet has assembled the *Iliad* from pre-existing materials on the subject of the Trojan War and that an earlier epic would naturally have focused on the consummation of the fighting: the sack of Troy itself. Our poet, Homer, has chosen to exclude this most obvious subject, focusing instead on the human relationships among the principals, especially conflict in those relationships. Instead of a poem about victorious united Greeks destroying a Trojan city, we see conflict within the Greek army, between Achilles and Agamemnon; instead of catastrophe (the graphic and lurid survey of a burning Troy, with its raped women and murdered infants), we get the chronic agonizing dread that precedes it. In the line quoted above, Homer is pointing toward this distinction, as if to contrast himself with his predecessors. What is it that he wants to establish?

Language, Symbols, and Imagery
Sample Topic:
1. **Andromache's headdress:** When Andromache sees Hector's corpse she faints. As she falls, she throws away the headdress veil from her marriage to Hector. Why? What links this object to Troy itself?

To address the full implications of this suggested topic, you need to unpack the implications of a Greek idiom: To remove the headdress of a woman and to sack a city are expressed with the same phrase. In exploring this strange equivalence, you might consider the legendary, non-Homeric material about the Palladium, a giant statue of Athena that kept Troy safe until it was removed. There is some kind of link in the ancient mind between the structural integrity of a city and the sexual integrity of women. The most obvious link is that conquered women were subject to sexual violence, but the Palladium story goes beyond that; Athena is a virgin goddess with the power to defend Troy. Angry with Paris, she attacks it instead. Where does Helen fit into all this?

Bibliography for "*Iliad* XVIII–XXIV: The Greater Wrath and Priam's Mission"

Edwards, Mark W. *Homer: Poet of the* Iliad. Baltimore: The Johns Hopkins UP, 1990.

Finley, M. I. *The World of Odysseus.* New York: Meridian Books, 1959.

Hall, John. *A History of the Archaic Greek World: ca. 1200–479 BCE.* Malden, Mass.: Wiley-Blackwell, 2006.

Heiden, Bruce. *Homer's Cosmic Fabrication: Choice and Design in the* Iliad (A.P.A., American Classical Studies 52). New York/Oxford: Oxford UP, 2008.

Nagy, Gregory. *Greek Mythology and Poetics* (Myth & Poetics Series). Ithaca, NY: Cornell UP, 1992.

Shelmerdine, Cynthia W. *The Cambridge Companion to the Aegean Bronze Age.* Cambridge: Cambridge UP, 2008.

Snodgrass, Anthony M. *Archaic Greece: The Age of Experiment.* Berkeley: U of California P, 1981.

Whitman, Cedric. *Homer and the Heroic Tradition.* New York: W. W. Norton and Company, 1965.

ODYSSEY 1–4:

The Telemachy

READING TO WRITE

THE *ODYSSEY* is the second of the two great Homeric epics. Where the *Iliad* depicts a heroic society whose highest value is successful violence, the *Odyssey* seems to search for a better, more sustainable ideal for male behavior. Part of the search for such a change is a new emphasis on the power of women and part is a shift of focus away from the old method of force and toward a new approach based on cleverness and deception. Odysseus was featured in the *Iliad* and remains in the *Odyssey*, a hero of both force *(biê)* and cleverness *(mêtis)*. But in the first of the two epics he was an important minor character; the *Odyssey* is his story, so Odysseus's more cerebral approach to problem-solving is itself magnified as a cultural value in this poem. Greek literature is highly conscious of that shift, since the myths deal with it in a variety of ways. The story of Ajax, which survives in a drama by Sophocles, is essentially the story of a man of force who lacks the subtlety and self-knowledge necessary to cope with loss—and it is Odysseus to whom he loses.

The German poet Johann Wolfgang von Goethe once remarked that the world of the *Iliad* is Hell. Reading its horrors of bereavement, humiliation, and gore, we may well be ready to welcome any movement away from those conditions toward peace and rational thought. Yet the shift comes at a price, as Sophocles is rather bitterly aware. In his *Ajax* as in his *Philoctetes,* the great tragedian gives us an Odysseus we cannot easily love. With cleverness comes deceit, manipulation, and treachery, qualities that Achilles finds repugnant. Yet as the strongest man in the world, perhaps Achilles can better afford to hold cleverness in contempt than others can. Sophocles the conservative is writing hundreds of years after Homer; if he shares the Achillean values of the *Iliad*, he does so with nostalgia and a yearning for what has been lost. Conversely, the late Homer of the *Odyssey* seems somewhat enamored of Odysseus and his scheming mind, as if the survival of that hero stood for the survival of the human community in general. Had the *Iliad* been the last word on the social development of humanity, we might have fought one another to extinction long ago. The heroic men of force were overwhelmed by force in their turn, but Odysseus survived. At the ending of the *Odyssey*, we are shown the dire possibility of endless violence in a cycle of retribution among feuding families. The poem shows us that possibility because it wants us properly to value the solution that comes from Athena. The *Odyssey* seems to contain its Iliadic climax—the violent slaughter of 108 young suitors and several of their female concubines—in both senses of that term: it contains it in that it provides a space for it, but more importantly it contains the violence just as a vessel contains corrosive liquid, or a cage contains a dangerous animal.

Among the first stories we are told in the *Odyssey* is that of the homecoming *(nostos)* of Agamemnon. Having led a vast armada to victory over a mightily fortified citadel full of wealth, and having personally distinguished himself in battle, Agamemnon was murdered in a domestic ambush by his wife and her lover Aigisthos. Those murderers were then murdered in turn by Agamemnon's avenging son, Orestes. Zeus himself tells this story, adducing it as an example of the way mortals undo themselves even while blaming the gods: Aigisthos was warned (by Hermes) not to kill the king and not to woo his wife, but he did both anyhow and soon perished. This message is consistent with the greater distance between mankind and the gods in the *Odyssey*, as compared with the *Iliad* (where the gods often fight alongside human beings on the battlefield at Troy). But it also suggests the failure of Agamemnon to think through the risks of his return, whereas Odysseus is exceedingly careful to come home in disguise and to properly time the revelation of his identity. The recourse to disguise is essentially Odyssean, and it matches the practice of his patron goddess, Athene.

TOPICS AND STRATEGIES

This section of the chapter will discuss various possible topics for essays and general approaches to those topics. Be aware that the following suggestions offer potential starting points, not some kind of master key to the perfect essay. Use this material to prompt your own thinking. Every topic discussed here could encompass a wide variety of papers.

Themes

Sample Topics:

1. **Inspiration:** Why does Homer begin the *Odyssey* with an invocation to the Muse?

The simplest answer is that this is a convention of ancient epic poetry, and that without such an invocation the poet would risk offending the gods, with potentially disastrous results. True and obvious, that answer is only the beginning of a more substantial response. Begin by asking what exactly the Muse provides to the poet. Compare the invocation at the start of the *Iliad,* and the other invocation to the Muses in *Iliad* II when the Catalogue of Ships is about to begin. You might go on to compare the approach to the Muse in the ancient poem *Theogony* ("Origin of the Gods") by Hesiod, Homer's near contemporary. Note that the Odyssey's first few lines (how many, exactly?) can't be attributed to the Muse, since they are addressed to her. This issue will emerge again in *Odyssey* book 8, when we meet the bard Demodocus. Note the implications of the strange construction "begin the story somewhere at least, for us, too": that the homecoming of Odysseus was already the subject of many poems now lost; that the poet thought of epic tradition as something that extends over many generations (which it clearly does); and that the starting point for the *Odyssey* is apparently a choice made by the goddess, not the poet—whereas the *Iliad* specifies its own starting point.

2. **Obscurity versus definition:** The mystery of Odysseus's whereabouts.

As Telemachus and Penelope grieve over Odysseus in the belief that he has perished, part of their pain concerns the obscurity surrounding his death. They explicitly state that a death in battle at Troy would have been far better than death at sea. A heroic death in the Trojan War would have resulted in a monument, turning his life into the fame-worthy fact of honorable death in daylight at the hands of such and such a warrior. Being "taken by the whirlwinds," on the contrary, costs a man his life without giving back the compensation of honor; on that account, it is especially terrible. In reality, Odysseus is alive and well, captive not to "savage men" (bestial, plural, male) but to Calypso (divine, unique, female). An essay on this issue would do well to include a reference to her name, which means "she who conceals." Take careful note of the poem's description of Calypso's island, Ogygia, "ringed about with trees at the navel of the ocean." What relationship can you make between this dread of obscurity and the need for disguise? Agamemnon stuck to the old ideal of fame and visible honor, came home in his own identity, and was promptly slaughtered. Consider our own culture's obsession with fame as you reflect on the homecomings of Agamemnon and Odysseus.

3. **Prophecy:** Why does Homer have the old warrior-prophet Halitherses state the plot of the poem explicitly in book 2?

Answering this question involves several different perspectives, each yielding a different type of answer. In terms of the narrative, the poet is supplying an end point (or, in Greek, a *telos*) toward which the action is continually moving. Since the telos is stated as prophecy, this gives us a new example of the impiety and rashness of the suitors as they mock and disregard it. For Telemachus, the prophecy of Halitherses can be added to the *theophany* (divine visitation) of Athena in book 1; both are new resources of hope on which he continues to build. It is also of some intrinsic interest to note that there are people on Ithaca who are not surprised by the course of events and who fully expect Odysseus to return. You might also bring in a reference to the passage, late in the poem, when the disguised Odysseus tells Penelope that Odysseus will return soon. That gives you two different characters making the same prediction on completely different grounds. Though Halitherses is speaking supernaturally and Odysseus is not, the hero's prediction is the more remarkable one because it is already true, and because he himself embodies its fulfillment. This belongs with a consideration of Eurymachos's reply to Halitherses.

Character

In the *Iliad,* the only character that thoroughly represents bad behavior is Thersites. Paris (alias Alexander) and Helen are both execrable for their violation of Menelaus's rights and of the rules of the guest-host relationship. Yet both Paris and Helen recoup their value with self-effacing remarks; also, Paris contributes to the fighting and will eventually, outside the textual parameters of the *Iliad* (but within its narrative awareness), kill the greatest of Greek warriors, Achilles himself. Helen's value gets established when the Trojan elders affirm it, and again when she mourns for Hector. We might have contempt for Agamemnon at the *Iliad*'s beginning, but by the time his apology and his *aristeia* (heroism and warrior's prowess) are presented, the poem seems to have conferred on him at least its qualified approval. In the *Odyssey* it is a different story: the suitors are 108 rude, mostly undesirable, poorly socialized characters that gradually forfeit more and more of our esteem until we are well ready for Odysseus and his son to do away with them. Their forte is depletion; they consume what does not belong to them and they produce nothing. Depending on your politics, you might associate the suitors with the undeserving rich or the undeserving poor; they represent the inequitable distribution of resources, an ancient problem that is always with us. That is why every reader can understand Telemachus's resentment of them, even that reader who is not a twenty-year-old male yearning for his famously heroic but absent father. What the suitors violate is decency, and they represent an order of things in which nothing matters except strength. In their defeat by Odysseus and just three other men (together with Athena and the approval of Zeus), we see the shift from an Iliadic world of force to an Odyssean world of cleverness and disguise.

Sample Topics:

1. **Odysseus's men:** According to the prologue of the poem (known as the "proem"), Odysseus was not responsible for the demise of his companions. He was "striving to save his soul and the homecoming of his companions; but he could not save them, for they perished of their own headlong recklessness. Children and fools, they ate the Oxen of the Sun and lost their day of homecoming." Does the rest of the poem bear out this claim?

This writing assignment asks you to assess and judge a particular narrative aspect of the poem, the guilt or innocence of Odysseus compared with that of his companions (in Greek, *hetairoi*). Notice that this question runs parallel to the simpler one about the Suitors and whether or not they deserve their fate. To answer the question, look closer at the passages that show Odysseus's men losing their lives. For example, 11 of the 12 ships are destroyed by the Lystragonians. Do you hold either Odysseus or the men responsible for this? The eating of the cattle of Helios (or "Oxen of the Sun") on the island of Thrinakia was clearly a mistake, but the men were on the verge of starvation. Now push further, by asking how they got into that condition. They were forced to stay on that island by a south wind sent by the gods, which blew for a whole month until the men had eaten all the provisions they had. Did anyone under Odysseus's command perish before the episode of the holy cattle? What about those whose brains were dashed out by the Cyclops? And whose idea was it to enter the cave of the Cyclops in the first place?

2. **Telemachus:** Does Telemachus grow up before his father comes home, or is it a process that only really starts when the disguised Odysseus meets his son?

The poem explicitly states in its first four books (the story of Telemachus, or Telemachiad) that the young man astonished his mother and her suitors alike with his sudden maturity. Yet this transformation is brought about by Athena's telling him about Odysseus, bringing the image of his father into his mind. The question is inviting you to read it as a false dichotomy, and then get out beyond that dichotomy by calling the growth of Telemachus a continual process. Its first phase occurs in Odysseus's absence, facilitated by something rather like literature—the evocative language of Athena as Mentor the Taphian, speaking to Telemachus of Odysseus's power and charisma. The second phase consists of the son's successful emulation of the father's two strengths: he keeps the secret of Odysseus's identity (which constitutes an example of *mêtis*, cleverness), and he fights effectively in the battle against the suitors (using *biê*, force).

3. **The goddess Athena:** We know from the *Iliad* that Athena has a close relationship with Odysseus, and in *Odyssey* 3 Nestor himself tells Telemachus that he knows of no other such relationship of open affection between a mortal and a god. Why then does it take ten years for Odysseus to return from Troy?

This essay topic concerns character, and yet character emerges over the course of the plot, so it will be necessary to speak of events and not mere personalities. Athena is clearly a greater presence in the *Odyssey* than any other god, even Poseidon, whose wrath is the cause of so much of Odysseus's wanderings. The most general answer is that polytheism provides a diversity of divine interests that can then compete for preeminence. If there is only one God, especially an omnipotent one, there can be no easy explanation for his failure to protect his devotees, since he has no powerful opponents. The *Odyssey* opens with a scene of divine politics, an Olympian council similar to those found in the *Iliad.* But just as Odysseus is absent from Ithaca (stuck on Ogygia with Calypso), Poseidon is absent from Olympus. This gives Athena the opportunity to intercede with Zeus for Odysseus, so that Hermes is sent to liberate the hero from Calypso's erotic captivity. The wrath of Poseidon afflicts Odysseus because he blinds Poseidon's monstrous child Polyphemus, and because the henchmen eat the cattle of Helios, who is also linked genealogically to Poseidon. But there is also a "Wrath of Athena," which seems to have affected the homecomings of the Achaeans, even that of Odysseus. Do you see evidence for this in the poem? Where? In terms of the temporal sequence, where does the wrath of Athena begin and end? Do you suppose there was a pre-Homeric strand of narrative that emphasized this wrath, whereas Homer has chosen to suppress it?

History and Context

We can assume that the two epics were composed, or put into their final form, by the same person. But in doing so we must not lose sight of the fact that these two poems depict different phases of the history of the Aegean region, phases that took many decades to transpire. The *Iliad* looks back to a definite historical event, albeit one whose exact position in history is a vexing enigma. We can be fairly confident that Homer was casting his mind some seven centuries into the past when he sang of the War at Troy. But the *Odyssey* is about what came next, in a temporally broad sense. True, the survivors of the war were still alive at the time of the narrative action of the *Odyssey*, and we have the nominal framework of a 10-year war followed by another decade of frustrated efforts at homecoming, but there seems to be much more than 20 years' worth of social change going on between the two poems. In the *Iliad* we find kings whose sway is unchallenged by any counter-vailing social force; the *Odyssey* shows a gap in the monarchy, during which a new class of boisterous nobles has arisen. Though we don't see any real new institutions emerging to make aristocracy a viable form of government, Homer seems to be a conservative voice who praises monarchy in a time when it was already on its way out, if not gone. During the Archaic period, after the dark ages but before the classical period of Athenian hegemony, the Greeks developed the city-state or *polis* (from which we get the term *Politics*, the title of Aristotle's great treatise on governance). This required overcoming the power of the kings, and it seems to have been groups of strong, charismatic aristocrats banding together who achieved this. You might be understandably reluctant to sympathize with such men after reading the *Odyssey*, where they are depicted as impious, bullying freeloaders. But remember to ask how Odysseus's household acquired so much wealth: by violently stealing it (with the exception of guest-gifts and trade). The *Odyssey* expresses mixed feelings about plunder; when Odysseus and his men make a raid on the Cicones, we are expected to admire their courage. When the suitors eat up Odysseus's household goods, we are to despise them for it. As far as expropriation goes, what the *polis* did was help to refine the business of piracy so that, in principle, only an official expedition of the state could get away with it.

Sample Topics:

1. **The Iron Age:** The decline of monarchy is not the only change compassed by the shift from the *Iliad* to the *Odyssey.* There is also an increased use of iron, as if the poet were moving away from the legendary Bronze Age and into what were, for him, modern times. Discuss the use of iron in the *Odyssey* and assess its significance. Include a reference to Telemachus's expression from *Odyssey* 4, "not even if he had a heart of iron."

To begin this writing assignment, use an electronic concordance like the Web site of the Perseus Project to search the poem for the word *iron.* That will help you to garner and sort the evidence for this increased use of iron. You will discover a proverb about iron in book 16, repeated at the beginning of book 19: "the mere sight of iron [weapons] stirs men up." There are plenty of other references to iron (Greek *sideros*), and yet the poem makes abundant reference to bronze, just as did the *Iliad.* It is as if the *Odyssey* depicts a transitional phase between the Bronze Age that ended in a widespread catastrophe around the probable time of the Trojan War circa 1200 B.C., and the onset of the Iron Age as the Greek world emerged from the dark ages that followed that catastrophe. Homer himself is thought to have been active in the Archaic period, when the dark ages were beginning to yield to a more dynamic order characterized by increases in trade, population, diversity of artistic activity, and complexity in the division of labor.

Note that the passage most explicitly concerned with iron metallurgy is the blinding of Polyphemus, where the hot wooden stake sizzles in the wet eye as a piece of iron sizzles on being plunged into water as part of the tempering process. This indicates the fascination of Homer and his audience for the rather magical properties unique to iron: It is dramatically hardened by the addition of carbon, turning it to steel (and such carbon is easily accrued in a primitive smelting furnace since the fuel, wood, is carbon-rich), and by the sudden cooling in water. But this could have been brought forward in any other episode with relative ease; it is important that it happens in the Cyclops story, since it forms yet another contrast between the technologies and practices of civilized life and the backwardness of the Cyclops. There is irony in the simile because the stake itself is a primitive wooden weapon, all that is available to Odysseus in the cave of Polyphemus.

2. **Women of power:** Consider the women of the *Iliad* and those of the *Odyssey*. Is there a shift in the latter to a greater sense of gender equity?

One of the patterns in the wanderings of Odysseus is a process whereby he gains access to a powerful female figure on whom his safety depends, and then wins her favor. This happens on Scheria, when Odysseus supplicates Arete and is assisted first by the Princess Nausikaa and next by her father, King Alkinoos. On Circe's island of Aiaia the powerful female is Circe herself, a magician who seems to be at least partly divine, and the enabling figure who helps him approach her is no less than the god Hermes. Finally in the Ithacan sequence it is his own wife Penelope who is the powerful female, and his helpers toward her include the goddess Athena and Eumaeus the swineherd. Though the *Iliad*, too, has its queens and royal women, there is far more space in the *Odyssey* for a kind of female power that is not strictly bound by the domestic sphere that Telemachus articulates in book 1 ("go and command your servants, and weave . . .").

Philosophy and Ideas

In the *Odyssey* we find a variety of cultural elements that were later developed into philosophical ideas. There is a potential contradiction in terms when we look for "philosophy and ideas" in a text that was composed before Plato was born, since he almost certainly invented the term *idea,* while the notion of philosophy seems to have been initially proposed by the pre-Socratic thinker Pythagoras. When we apply these terms to figures like Heraclitus, Parmenides, and the other so-called pre-Socratic philosophers, we mean that the subjects that Plato later explored as his main concerns—especially the true, the beautiful, and the good—are also at issue in the work of these earlier authors. If we are to do this, we should remember that what we discover in the Homeric text may or may not be rooted there; it may be our own invention. For example, there was for centuries a rich tradition of allegorical interpretation of Homer, which read the poems as coded philosophical treatises, as if Homer was really trying to write philosophy but could not because the genre had not yet been invented. The greatest exemplar of this allegorical ("other-speaking") tradition is Porphyry (A.D. 234–ca. A.D. 305). His famous treatise "On the Cave of the Nymphs" sounds like this, as he explicated *Odyssey* 13:

> Hence, since this narration is full of such obscurities it can neither be a fiction casually devised for the purpose of procuring delight, nor an exposition of a topical history; but something allegorical must be indicated in it by the poet who likewise mystically places an olive near the cave. All which particulars the ancients thought very laborious to investigate and unfold; and we, with their assistance, shall now endeavor to develop the secret meaning of the allegory. . . . That theologists therefore considered caverns as symbols of the world, and of mundane powers, is through this, manifest. And it has been already observed by us, that they also considered a cave as a symbol of the intelligible essence; being impelled to do so by different and not the same conceptions. For they were of opinion that a cave is a symbol of the sensible world because caverns are dark, stony, and humid; and they asserted that the world is a thing of this kind, through the matter of which it consists, and through its repercussive and flowing nature.

Porphyry goes on for some time in this vein, correlating the features of the cavern with those of unborn souls and the process by which he imagines those souls acquiring bodies. This technique is certainly ingenious, and it tells us a great deal about the reverence for Homer that persisted through antiquity and into modern times. But from the point of view of modern literary criticism—which you are being asked to write in the courses you take—such allegorical reading is an interpretive disaster. It brings its own interests and obsessions and dumps them onto the text, then claims to have discovered them there. Although his purposes went beyond the interpreting of the poem (and that is the problem), we can agree with Porphyry that the cave of the nymphs on Ithaca is a kind of womb and assert (as he does not) that when the Phaeacians deposit the sleeping Odysseus in that cave, his awakening from it amounts to a kind of rebirth. Doing so does not require us to say, with Porphyry, that the reason Homer says the nymphs weave purple garments in that cave is because this stands for the weaving of new baby bodies for unborn souls.

In Plato's *Symposium,* Socrates advises his hearers against excessive indulgence in eating and drinking (and though Socrates drinks his fellow symposium participants under the table, he does not get drunk). Similarly in Plato's *Phaedo,* Socrates explains that ghosts are the lingering souls of gluttons and hedonists whose overinvestment in material pleasures of the body (food, sex, possessions) is responsible for their condition (the accreted materiality of their spirits both prevents them from reaching the next world, and makes them visible in this one). So when philosophy emerges, it takes an interest in conduct and character, forming that branch of philosophy we call ethics, and one of its chief concerns is moderation.

Sample Topics:

1. ***Sophrosune* or "temperance":** Is temperance the most essential characteristic of Odysseus in the *Odyssey?*

An important ideal of conduct in the *Odyssey* is what we might call temperance, or moderation in the taking of pleasures and the consuming of resources. The Greek for this is *sophrosune,* from *so* ("save") *phro* ("heart, life") and the noun suffix *sune,* equivalent to the English suffix "-ness." *Sophrosune* is the quality of saving one's own life, keeping one's heart intact, displaying prudence. It is more rare than we might tend to assume. Aigisthos lacked it (*Odyssey* 1, line 34), because the gods directly told him not to kill Agamemnon and not to woo his wife, but he did so anyhow and lost his life. Agamemnon lacked it (no surprise to readers of the *Iliad*) because he came home openly and was promptly cut down. Like the suitors (and this analogy will come up again and again), Odysseus's crew of young soldier-sailors is described (*Odyssey* 1, line 7) with the term *atasthaliesin*, "headlong recklessness."

This ideal of *sophrosune* represents an embrace of the value of limits. While the ancient Greek obsession with plunder and heroic city sacking is hardly an inspiration toward sustainable living, there is an admirable element in the *Odyssey* and subsequent Greek literature that praises the limits within which safety alone is possible. Where does this respect for limits appear in the first four books of the poem?

The essay topic proposes that you make a case for or against the idea that *sophrosune* is the most important characteristic of the Odyssean hero. To develop this topic, go through the poem looking at the various deaths that befall people. You may be struck by how many are triggered by a lack of self-control, either in speech (Ajax, son of Oileus) or in excessive eating and drinking (Elpenor, Eurylochos, Antinoos, for example). It is perhaps somewhat striking that this epic should so elevate a characteristic that is essentially negative (not in the popular sense of the term, as in "bad," which it is not, but in its real meaning: that it negates or subtracts something, namely impulsive indulgence). Strength and skill with the spear meant the most in the *Iliad*, and lack of restraint was an important but minor theme—recall Pandaros and his bow, for example. But in the *Odyssey* there is an Iliadic episode at the end, apart from which we find nine years of frustration and setbacks. These are caused by episode after episode of recklessness, a trait mentioned twice in the first 35 lines of the poem.

2. Revenge: Is Odysseus's revenge justified?

Since it is only of interest whether the revenge is justified in terms of the values inherent in the poem, rather than some alien, external, or superimposed values, we need to "interpret Homer from Homer," as scholars say, and look for signs of the

Odyssey's own judgment on the matter of the revenge. When we do, we find the poet taking pains to make clear that Odysseus is not culpable for the extreme violence of his revenge because, on various grounds that you may be asked to investigate, the Suitors deserve it. To build an account of this in the service of an essay, look to the moments when the Suitors do unusually bad things—such as throwing an ox hoof at the disguised Odysseus or plotting to kill Telemachus. Then note the reactions to their behavior from people we have already been encouraged to trust—not the least of these is the goddess Athena herself, but also Nestor and Menelaus. As the examples mount up, it begins to seem as if we have in Homer a coherent ethic of behavior condemning the Suitors. And yet all this is bracketed by two episodes of the old Iliadic warrior ethic: the raid on the innocent Cicones just after the sack of Troy, and at the other extreme, the wholesale slaughter of the Suitors, rather than their imprisonment or indentured servitude. For the raid on the Cicones, we can perhaps exonerate Odysseus (or at least contain the implications of the raid for his character) by calling it an old incident, so close to the *Iliad* as to participate in its old rapacity. The destruction of the suitors is more complicated, but one aspect of the containment process is surely the intervention of Athena at the very end of the poem. But we are getting ahead of ourselves. What is of interest here is the way the opening four books are already setting up the suitors as the deserving victims of Odysseus's fury.

One of the means for doing so is analogy, the implied similarities between the suitors and Aigisthos as men who wooed the wife of an absent great man, and between Orestes and Telemachus as avenging sons. Conversely, the same passages imply the contrast between Clytemnestra the disloyal adulteress and Penelope the loyal wife; and between Agamemnon the rash, impulsive hero and Odysseus the sly contriver. What about book 4? What other woman appears in that book (about Telemachus's journey to Sparta) who might be implicitly compared to Penelope? And who first proposes the idea of a slaughter of the suitors?

Form and Genre

Like the *Iliad*, the *Odyssey* is characterized by a variety of stereotyped events known in the critical literature as "type scenes." Among these is the hospitality scene, which exemplifies an ancient Greek ethic of hospitality called *xenia*, or "guest-host relationship." Its requirements are these: feed your guest; don't ask his identity until after he has eaten; let him leave when he chooses, not when you choose; send him off with a gift. You'll find these conventions used as a gauge of the merit of several different characters, including the Suitors, Telemachus, Nestor, Menelaus, the Cyclops, Calypso, and Eumaeus, to name a few. For an essay on hospitality, ask yourself why this institution was so important in the ancient world and which features of more modern societies were absent in the eighth century B.C. so that these rules were essential. Next, go through the poem looking for type scenes of hospitality and compare the various hosts in the degree to which each of them fulfills or violates these rules. Notice that the Cyclops not only violates every single one of them, he also inverts them, eating guests instead of feeding them. Calypso, by contrast, is a wonderful host in all but the business of letting the guest leave at a time of his own choosing.

Sample Topics:

1. *Theoxeny:* This term refers to stock scenes in which a god comes in disguise to the home of a mortal in order to test the host's conduct. You may recognize its two elements, *theos*, "god" and *xenos*, "guest."

The *Odyssey* opens with such a story, when the disguised Athena visits Odysseus's home as a test of hospitality that Telemachus passes and the Suitors fail. What are some other moments of theoxeny, or apparent theoxeny, in the *Odyssey?* To answer that question, look at the incidents in which someone unknown arrives at a house and is received. Sometimes the theoxenic situation arises without the visit of an actual god, as when the disguised Odysseus makes someone observe that the Suitors would do well to show courtesy since the stranger *might* be a god. Do any biblical parallels come to mind? How far do those parallels extend, and what do they suggest?

2. *In medias res:* Why does the *Odyssey* begin "in the middle of things"? We do not even meet Odysseus until book 5. What are the implications of such narrative and structural choices?

This aspect is one of the most striking characteristics of the *Odyssey;* we hear plenty *about* Odysseus through the first four books (indeed, he is always the central subject in one way or another), but not until book 5 do we actually see him. The writing assignment is asking you to generate an explanation for this, so begin by observing your own experience of reading the poem. Were you waiting eagerly for Odysseus to appear? Could it be that by delaying the hero's arrival on center stage, Homer is giving us, too, a taste of Odysseus's absence and the yearning for him that has taken hold of his family and friends? When you finally see Odysseus, weeping on the beach of Calypso's island, are you delighted finally to reach him?

Bibliography for "*Odyssey* 1– 4: The Telemachy"

Bloom, Harold. *Homer's* Odyssey. Modern Critical Interpretations. New York: Chelsea House, 1988.

Brann, Eva. *Homeric Moments: Clues to Delight in Reading the Odyssey and the* Iliad. Philadelphia: Paul Dry Books, 1992.

Heubeck, Alfred, and Stephanie West. *A Commentary on Homer's Odyssey, Volume I: Introduction and Books I–VIII.* Oxford: Clarendon P, 1988.

Hexter, Ralph. *A Guide to the Odyssey: A Commentary on the English Translation of Robert Fitzgerald.* New York: Vintage, 1993.

Louden, Bruce. *The Odyssey: Structure, Narration, and Meaning.* Baltimore: The Johns Hopkins UP, 1999.

ODYSSEY 5:

Calypso and 6–8: The Phaeacians

READING TO WRITE

SUPPOSE WE follow the highly useful example of Bruce Louden in his 2001 book *The* Odyssey: *Structure, Narration, and Meaning*. There, the poem is seen as consisting of three great "sequences," rather like the three "movements" of the *Iliad* mapped out by Oliver Taplin in his *Homeric Soundings: The Shaping of the* Iliad. The *Odyssey* contains a sequence at Ithaca, split into the two parts of the Telemachiad (1–4) and the poem's second half (13–14); a Scherian sequence when Odysseus is among the Phaeacians, split into the part before (6–8) and the brief part after (13) Odysseus narrates his own story of his wanderings, centered on the story of Circe's island of Aiaia, which itself forms the Aiaian sequence (9–12). Notice that this forms what scholars call a ring composition, as the story forms concentric circles like the rings signifying the growth of a tree. Notice also that viewing the poem this way leaves out book 5, an important anomaly in this reading of the *Odyssey's* structure. You can write a compelling essay about book 5 in a variety of ways. It is the scene of Odysseus's longest stasis, encompassing seven years of the hero's life. Except for his journey on the high seas, which immediately follows it, it is also the point of his greatest isolation.

Here are the first 20 lines of *Odyssey 5* in the translation of Ian Johnston:

As Dawn stirred from her bed beside lord Tithonus,
bringing light to eternal gods and mortal men,
the gods were sitting in assembly, among them
high-thundering Zeus, whose power is supreme.
Athena was reminding them of all the stories
of Odysseus's troubles—she was concerned for him
as he passed his days in nymph Calypso's home.
"Father Zeus and you other blessed gods
who live forever, let no sceptred king
be prudent, kind, or gentle from now on,
or think about his fate. Let him instead
always be cruel and treat men viciously,
since no one now has any memory
of lord Odysseus, who ruled his people
and was a gentle father. Now he lies
suffering extreme distress on that island
where nymph Calypso lives. She keeps him there
by force, and he's unable to sail off
and get back to his native land—he lacks
a ship with oars and has no companions
to send him out across the sea's broad back.
And now some men are setting out to kill
the son he loves, as he sails home. The boy
has gone to gather news about his father,
off to sacred Pylos and holy Sparta."

The book opens with a reference to Eos, the goddess of the dawn; that is common enough in Homeric poetry. But as Louden points out, and as a search engine like Perseus will tell you, this is the only time in the *Odyssey* when we are told of her mortal lover, Tithonus. He was given the gift of immortality, but without eternal youth; his fate was to spend eternity as an enfeebled old man. The reference to this union between a goddess and a mortal is appropriate to a book about the goddess Calypso and her mortal lover Odysseus—especially since she will soon make a list of such pairings, to which the mention of Eos/Tithonus is parallel. The fact that Tithonus was debilitated by his immortality, however, is important for a full understanding of the *Odyssey* overall. For a suggestion about why this is so, see the following topic suggestion about death.

TOPICS AND STRATEGIES

This section of the chapter will discuss various possible topics for essays and general approaches to those topics. Be aware that the material below is only a place to start from, not some kind of master key to the perfect essay. Use this material to prompt your own thinking. Every topic discussed here could encompass a wide variety of papers.

Themes

Sample Topics:

1. **Nature versus culture:** What is the relationship between nature and culture in the *Odyssey?*

Often in this epic a stranger will ask his new host what kind of men he has reached, savage or civilized. Yet as we see in book 5, danger is not always located beneath the human community of hospitality; Calypso is a goddess, yet she has violated *xenia* for years by keeping Odysseus at her home against his will. Their business on Ogygia is natural; it is an expression of their sexuality. What releases him is culture: on the one hand, a chain of messages from Athena to Zeus to Hermes to Calypso to Odysseus; on the other, the construction, by labor and tools and artifice, of a raft with a rudder and sail. Opposed to that raft of art and human knowledge is the primal force of Poseidon's savage storm. In book 9, Poseidon is again the sponsor of savage nature, this time in the form of his offspring the Cyclops, whose savagery is all the more intense for its admixture of civilization—when a lion devours a man it does no evil, but the Cyclops is a speaking subject who makes cheese, herds sheep, and devours his human guests. Indeed the story of Odysseus can be thought of as the triumph of Athena (and by extension, her father Zeus) and civilization over Poseidon and nature.

When the hero is first washed onto the shore of the Phaeacians, he has been stripped of every outward sign of civilization. The simile that here compares Odysseus to a lion is
appropriate. Yet the thicket in which he sleeps is said to be
made of "two bushes growing from the same place, one wild,
one domestic." This may be symbolic of his own nature, or
of his adaptability to diverse environments. It also looks forward to the revelation about Odysseus's bed, with its olive tree
bedpost still rooted in the earth (by contrast to the wandering Odysseus himself). Another implication, albeit perhaps
somewhat farfetched, is that this is a spot that used to be an
orchard and has been left to grow wild again—a common situation for the Homeric audience. Since olives do not tend to
thrive without cultivation, this strange thicket is an apt site
for Odysseus's rebirth into civilization after the raw savagery
of the stormy sea. The bed of Odysseus and the handles of the
axes in the archery contest at the poem's climax are further
examples of the association between the protagonist and olive
wood.

2. **Supplication and prayer:** What role is played by supplication in
this part of the *Odyssey?*

The *Iliad* naturally has to do with war, and this imposes a
degree of uniformity on the various incidents of supplication
that arise in it. In the *Odyssey*, the situations and locations are
much more diverse. In the section of the poem we are considering now, there are two important supplications by Odysseus: in book 5, he begs a river at Scheria for mercy as he tries
to reach dry land without drowning. This might be said to
contrast with Achilles' fight with the river Skamander in the
Trojan plain. This can be paired with the next supplication,
in book 7, when Odysseus begs Arete for an "escort," that is,
a ship, to take him home. This forms a nice contrast with the
first supplication, which was about getting out of the water
and onto the land; this one is about getting out of the land
and onto the water. Note also that his prayer for Queen Arete

in this passage sounds like the opposite of what is occurring inside Odysseus's own halls: He hopes she will be able to pass on her possessions, undiminished, to her heirs, whereas his own possessions are being consumed by the suitors every day.

   3. Politics: What purpose might be served by the double scene of Athena's intercession?

Like the *Iliad*, the *Odyssey* gives us some scenes of Olympian politics that are somewhere between public life and family dynamics. Parallel to these are scenes of human politics such as the unsuccessful assembly called by Telemachus in book 2. But notice the way the scene of Athena pleading with Zeus for Odysseus seems to be repeated, occurring in one form at the opening of the poem and in a somewhat different form at the opening of book 5.

   To answer this question, ask yourself what effect the scene has on you. Like Athena's appearance to Odysseus on Ithaca in book 13, it may add to your impression that his piety is one element of his extraordinary ability to survive. Next, consider the grounds on which Athena appeals to Zeus for Odysseus's release: he has been a wise and kind king. Part of the point is that Zeus, as king of the gods, must be the sponsor of kingship in general, and if good kings are unrewarded, the institution of kingship may founder (as indeed it did, in the historical world outside the poem). This concern in book 5 with the quality of Odysseus's kingship fits with Athena's role at the end of the poem, which is to save the royal dynasty of Odysseus by preventing the vengeance of the suitor's relatives from escalating into the kind of permanent feud that would destabilize the entire society.

   Another approach to the same question would be to look for differences between the first "divine council" (it does not really seem quite so formal as that label implies) and the second one. What has changed in the meanwhile, to exacerbate the injustice of Odysseus's predicament? Who is now in danger who was not in such danger beforehand, and if he is blameless (that is, undeserving of the danger), where is the evidence for that? Until now, Odysseus has had for his patron Athena, a younger goddess, and for his opponent Poseidon, an older god. But this second council brings him the approval of a god of Poseidon's generation, which confers a cosmic authority not only on his resistance to Poseidon's outraged will but also to his bloody revenge at the poem's end.

4. **Structure:** As pointed out by J. B. Hainsworth in *A Commentary on Homer's Odyssey: Volume I,* the layout of *Odyssey* 5 is roughly: "council—journey—report—reaction."

Is this similar to book IX of the *Iliad?* Where else in Homer do you see this structure?

5. **Death:** Compare the situations of Menelaus at home in Sparta with Odysseus captive on Ogygia.

Among the Near Eastern and deeply ancient materials to which the *Odyssey* has been compared is the Akkadian-Sumerian epic of *Gilgamesh.* You need not undertake a full-blown compare and contrast essay to notice that *Gilgamesh* is largely concerned with mankind's yearning for an impossible immortality (if you are not familiar with the poem, you can easily obtain a summary by entering the terms "Gilgamesh summary" into a search engine). But in *Odyssey* 4, we see the fabulously wealthy Menelaus, married to the most beautiful woman in the world, granted a deathless existence on the Isles of the Blessed because he is Zeus's son in law. Yet Menelaus does not seem especially happy. Similarly, *Odyssey* 5 shows us the divine nymph Calypso offering Odysseus an immortality that he refuses (recall Odysseus's resistance to Helen's wiles at Troy, recounted in book 4). This resonates with the example of Tithonus mentioned at the book's opening, yet even if Calypso were to include eternal youth in the offer, Odysseus would still remain hidden—the meaning of Calypso's name—from the human community that is the source of meaning in life.

At the opening of book 5, quoted above, Athena reminds
Zeus that while Odysseus is stuck with Calypso, the suitors
are plotting to kill Telemachus—just as Aigisthos murdered
Agamemnon during Menelaus's protracted absence. Menelaus is living somewhat unhappily with a woman who is practically a goddess, but that divine beauty has brought much more
trouble than joy; Odysseus is with a true goddess and spends
his time weeping on the beach. To write an essay comparing
the two, trace the implications of these similarities and differences. Consider the scene where Menelaus is advised by
a divine female how to wrestle with her father Proteus. To
what helper of Odysseus's would you compare her? To Ino? To
Athena?

Character

In the *Iliad* there is hardly any opportunity to observe a city at peace;
all we see of one is the static and flat depiction on Achilles' shield. In
the *Odyssey*, we begin with the semipeaceful state of affairs on Ithaca,
which is like war because of the ongoing pillage and the prevailing sense
of occupation or siege, but remains peaceful because no blood is spilled
until Odysseus's return. Among the Phaeacians, however, we see people
living what seems like a fairly stable and happy life. When Nausicaa goes
out to wash the clothes by the river, we see the washing pits, which may
remind us of the washing pits the Trojan women used to use, before the
war came.

Sample Topics:

1. **Calypso:** Does she deceive Odysseus?

To develop an approach to this topic, look closely at the speech
of Hermes to Calypso and then at the way Calypso carries out
his instructions. She swears a great oath and keeps it. Yet she
also keeps trying to persuade him, even after Hermes has con-
veyed Zeus's demands. Whose idea was it that Calypso should
give up Odysseus? When she speaks to Odysseus, does she
admit that she is acting under compulsion?

2. **Odysseus's choice:** Compare the choice of Odysseus (remain with Calypso and enjoy an immortality of experience or return home to Penelope and grow old with her until death) and the choice of Achilles (remain at Troy and achieve a short life with an immortality of fame or return home to Peleus and grow old until death).

Writing on this subject requires that you ask yourself several additional questions. Each hero is obligated by one of his choices to perpetrate a massacre, but for which one is the massacre part of a homecoming, and for which one is the massacre the opposite of a homecoming? One of the heroes chooses between a normal human lifespan and a much shorter one; the other chooses between a normal human lifespan and an indefinitely long one. The hero who chooses immortality chooses an immortality of mere fame, which he later rejects in *Odyssey* 10, while the hero who gives up immortality rejects the immortality of experience. Yet this opportunity to be alive forever is exactly what most Europeans have been praying for over the course of the past 2,000 years. What might it suggest about Homeric culture that Odysseus simply does not want it?

3. **Nausicaa:** Give examples of Nausicaa's rhetorical sophistication. How does she communicate with her father Alcinous? How does she manage her side of the confrontation with Odysseus near the seashore? How does she interact with her mother? How does Odysseus manage his side of these interactions?

Examine the things Nausicaa says, and consider the ways she shapes her choice of words to suit the person to whom she is speaking. Consider Odysseus's initial speech to Nausicaa, how he de-eroticizes their encounter by supplicating her from a distance, and by praising her beauty with a comparison to a young tree. Look at Odysseus's supplication of Queen Arete. Does he lie to her in defense of Nausicaa? Where and how? Why?

4. **Zeus:** Consider Zeus at the outset of book 5 of the *Odyssey*. Is Athena reminding him of the position he took in book 1, or is it only Homer reminding the audience?

This topic raises the possibility that the poet wants the nature of Zeus's rulership to remain ambiguous. As in the *Iliad*, Zeus provides the *telos* or desired outcome of the story, delegating to other gods the functions of bringing us closer to that telos and keeping us from reaching it too quickly. This should remind you of Odysseus getting closer and closer to Ithaca, but not so quickly as to preempt (the first half of) the poem. In this regard, consider Poseidon as the principle of the poem's continuation that defers the ending, and Athena as its principle of progress that approaches the ending.

5. **Which god?:** On at least two occasions in book 5, two characters differ in their accounts of the origin of a storm. Hermes says the storm that harried the Achaeans after the Trojan War came from Athena, but Calypso attributes it to Zeus. Odysseus on his raft is near despair with the thought that the storm he endures is from Zeus, but the rescuing nymph Ino tells him it comes from Poseidon. What is the significance of this kind of ambiguity?

Hermes' attribution of the post-Trojan storm to Athena seems to be the mark of an older poetic tradition that Homer is revising. The most full treatment of this idea is an excellent book by Jenny Strauss Clay, *The Wrath of Athena: Gods and Men in the* Odyssey. Generally, the ambiguity is similar to that which arises when an omen occurs (often in the form of bird flight) and mortals disagree over its interpretation. Remember also the opening lines of the *Iliad*, which ask the crucial question, "which god was it . . . ?" What is common to both Zeus-sent storms?

6. **Demodocus's song:** Consider the song of Demodocus about the adultery of Aphrodite and Ares, which they committed in

the absence of her husband, Hephaestus. What parallels arise between that story and the situation of Odysseus? What do these parallels imply?

One ready implication is that Demodocus has figured out the identity of the mysterious stranger at the Phaeacian court and has chosen to sing this particular song as a subtle way of informing Odysseus that he knows who he is. That would be ironic, since Demodocus is blind, yet he has perceived what others have missed (the same situation occurs later when Odysseus's blind old dog, Argus, detects him). In the course of telling his own tale in book 9, Odysseus calls the blindness of Polyphemus "unseemly"; could that be a slight directed at Demodocus, in retaliation for this subtle jibe? Look at the simile that occurs when the stake is driven into the Cyclops's eye: it compares Odysseus to an ironworking smith, which is Hephaestus's occupation and identity. Another, rather different parallel arises if we remember the old correspondence between Aphrodite, the adulteress in Demodocus's story, and Helen, the adulteress in the *Iliad*.

Philosophy and Ideas

As in the *Iliad*, the idea of transience is central to the *Odyssey*. While we might expect hedonism to accompany this focus on the brevity of life ("eat, drink, and be merry," says Isaiah 22:13, "for tomorrow we die"), the *Odyssey* is just as adamant about moderation and impulse control as it is about transience. In the *Iliad*, people coped with the fact that life is short by throwing themselves into gory warfare and making it even shorter. They strove for an immortality of fame that would serve as a substitute for the immortality of experience that only gods can have (with a few exceptions, as Menelaus learns in the *Odyssey*). In the *Odyssey*, the coping mechanism is much different, as though Iliadic *kleos*—war fame—had been discredited somehow. Odysseus copes with mortality by accepting it; this acceptance is most evident in his refusal of Calypso's offer, but also in his refusal of Nausicaa and, he claims, Circe. Odysseus survives because his cleverness and strength are coupled with piety, the successful effort to avoid hubris. That term denotes not just "excessive pride," but also taking too much; taking that to which one is not entitled; doing outrage; competing with the gods. Yet the *Odyssey* never really solves the ethical problem surrounding heroic pillage: if the Suitors are to be executed for consuming what does not belong to them, why is Odysseus to be excused for stealing the livestock of the Cicones? One could claim that the Cicones were allies of the Trojans, so their property is fair game for the Greeks even after the war has ended.

Sample Topics:

1. **Transience:** Compare the fate of Odysseus's raft and the Acheans's wall and ditch in *Iliad* XII.

You might start your essay with the observation that both of these human structures are destroyed by Poseidon. The raft is built by Odysseus alone, for lack of "oarsmen and companions"; the wall and ditch are built by many Greeks, for lack of one man, Achilles. The raft is a means for moving Odysseus (and the poem) forward; the wall and ditch are meant to stop the forward motion of the Trojans. What other parallels can you find?

2. **Desire:** What patterns of desire and gender do you perceive in the *Odyssey?*

In the first four books of the poem, we witnessed Penelope pursued by suitors whom she does not want. Now we see Odysseus captive to Calypso, whom he does not want, and though he is subtly wooed by Nausicaa, he does not want her either. There seems to be more frustrated desire in the world of the *Odyssey* than there is consummated mutuality. Note also that in the *Iliad*, where women were chattel, male desire was common while female desire seemed represented only by Helen, who left Menelaus for Paris (yet she tried to refuse him, too, telling Aphrodite "go to him yourself!"). In the *Odyssey* we learn that when Helen's affair with Paris was over, she took a second Trojan husband, Deiphobos. We also see Odysseus pursued by Calypso, Nausicaa, and, according to him, Circe.

In Clytemnestra, we have a paradigm of the lustful adulteress, in contrast to steadfast Penelope.

3. **Honesty:** Describe Odysseus's use of deception in his sojourn on Scheria. Is he honest or dishonest with them? Why?

Scheria is the country of the Phaeacians, a people who are dependent on Poseidon for their life and livelihood. Odysseus learns fairly early that their amazing nautical prowess comes as a gift from Poseidon; their ruling dynasty is itself descended from Poseidon; and their central marketplace bears a shrine to Poseidon. Yet Odysseus has landed there as a helpless refugee from Poseidon's wrath. All he has with which to advance his interests is his cleverness, his ability to hatch wily deceptions, and yet he tells the truth. The truth he tells, indeed, is a confession of the offense against Poseidon that has reduced him to helplessness: the blinding of Polyphemus and the boast of his own identity that allowed the Cyclops to curse him by name. This ran the risk of forfeiting the Phaeacians' esteem, but it seems to magnify it instead. As you look for the reasons that might help explain this surprising outcome, consider the daily life of the Phaeacians and of Alcinous in particular. What is missing from it? Is something missing from their life that Odysseus might represent and that might also explain Nausicaa's response to him?

Form and Genre

In the *Iliad* there is remarkably little poetry within the framework of the epic poetry that drives the tale. We are shown splendid artifacts like the shield of Achilles, but the only example of song comes when Achilles is singing to his lyre when the three ambassadors visit him in book IX. The *Odyssey*, on the other hand, is rich in this phenomenon, as if it is trying to think through questions about what poetry is and what it can do. No fewer than three human singers take the place of the Muse who narrates the poem: Demodocus, the bard among the Phaeacians; Phemios, who sings for the suitors under compulsion; and Odysseus himself, who performs for the Phaeacians the long narrative of his adventures in the Aiaian sequence from book 9 to book 12. One might also claim that the proem (the first few lines of the *Odyssey*) is sung by a distinct singer, since it invokes the Muse and therefore cannot be her own utterance.

Sample Topics:

1. **Ekphrasis:** This term refers to poetry that is about another work of art. What are the advantages of this technique in the *Odyssey?*

This writing assignment can be approached by looking for differences between the embedded song and the expectations that might be outside of it. For instance, when Demodocus is singing about the Trojan Horse at Odysseus's request, does he sing the story in a way that honors Odysseus, or does he minimize Odysseus's role? When Odysseus is singing his wanderings, he says at the outset that Circe, too, wanted him for her husband, but is there any evidence for this in the narrative itself? It has even been suggested that the entire song of Odysseus's wanderings is a fiction designed by the hero to deflect responsibility for the deaths of his crew away from himself and onto them.

2. **Ring composition:** What examples of ring composition can you find in the first eight books of the *Odyssey?* Remember, ring composition is the practice of arranging recurrent elements in the poem so that they resemble the concentric rings of a tree stump.

Look for resemblances between the effort of Telemachus to get off the island of Ithaca and the effort of Odysseus to get off the island of Ogygia. Then look for resemblances between the approach of Telemachus to Nestor and then to Menelaus, and the approach of Odysseus to Nausicaa and then to Arete. How do these various elements and narrative threads interrelate?

Language, Symbols, and Imagery

There are roughly three times as many similes in the *Iliad* as there are in the *Odyssey*. It could be claimed that this makes them more striking in the *Odyssey*, being more rare. Book 5 contains the simile of the sick father who becomes well, to the relief and delight of his children.

Sample Topics:

1. Similes/the cure of the father: Why is this simile so well chosen? How does it fit and reflect the contextual world of the poem?

Clearly, you will want to mention the ways that the simile fits what it describes (which you can see by paying attention to the context). But then you should consider any contrasts between the tenor (what is being brought up in imagery) and the vehicle (what is at hand, being described). For instance, a wave that scatters the timbers of Odysseus's raft is compared to a wind blasting a heap of dry husks; there is ironic contrast between the wet (with which he must contend for days) and the dry (which he craves). A few lines later, Odysseus bestrides one timber "as if he were riding a horse," which could only happen on the firm land he desperately wants. It may be worth mentioning that even this simile remains captive to Poseidon's enmity, since he is the god not only of oceans and earthquakes, but also of horses.

2. Similes/the Trojan woman: Why this simile?

Begin with the context. When Odysseus hears the bard Demodocus sing the tale of the sack of Troy, in which he himself joined Menelaus to retrieve Helen from Deiphobos's quarters, we are told that as Odysseus sits at the table of the Phaeacians listening, he weeps like a captive woman who lies prostrate on her dying husband who has fought to save his children from death and his wife from slavery, even as her enemies jab her in the back with spears to get her to move along into a life of misery and servitude. This brilliant and harrowing piece of poetry raises several problems. Demodocus's poem is about a triumph of Odysseus, the success of his Trojan Horse scheme and the accomplishment of the initial purpose of the war: getting Helen back. More importantly, Odysseus and the Achaeans were the besieging aggressors against Troy; they inflicted a soul-destroying grief and bereavement on Priam, Hecuba, and Andromache, which the *Iliad* depicts with the same terrible pathos as this simile. There is even a non-Homeric tradition (found in Proclus's summary of the lost poem *Sack of Ilium*) that it was Odysseus himself who murdered the infant Astyanax. Indeed the *Odyssey* consistently refers to Odysseus as "much suffering" and more unfortunate than any other man. Yet he suffers none of the shattering losses that afflict Achilles or Priam, or any of the other Iliadic characters who lose their children or parents or partners. Odysseus does not seem to have been especially attached to his Ithacan companions, about whom we hear nothing in the *Iliad* and little more in the *Odyssey*. It is as if the poem, like Odysseus's very name, were aiming for a suggestive confusion about the difference between causing pain and suffering it. The simile of the Trojan captive woman is shocking in its attempt to blur that distinction, to transfer our pity from the victim of violence to the perpetrator by conflating the two figures in a simile. We are told that only Alcinous was able to notice Odysseus's tears, and yet a woman in the situation described in the simile—especially in a Mediterranean culture—would likely be hysterically keening with a loud wail (like Sophocles' Antigone, for example) that would be difficult to miss. As you consider this issue, recall that the simile comes not from Odysseus but from the Muse herself.

Note also that there is a pattern whereby the phrases that the *Iliad* used to describe the direct experience of pain are used in the *Odyssey* to describe aesthetic response to a poetic account of pain. Look for examples wherever a character in the *Odyssey* becomes a temporary narrator—especially Demodocus, Phemios, Odysseus, and Eumaeus.

Bibliography for "*Odyssey* 5: Calypso and 6–8: The Phaeacians"

Ahl, Frederick, and Hanna Roisman. *The* Odyssey *Re-Formed.* Ithaca, NY: Cornell University Press, 1996.

Clay, Jenny Strauss. *The Wrath of Athena: Gods and Men in The* Odyssey. NJ: Princeton University Press, 1987.

Heubeck, Alfred, and Stephanie West. *Commentary on Homer's* Odyssey (Volume I, Introduction and Books I–VIII). Oxford University Press, 1988.

Kirk, G. S. *Myth: Its Meaning and Function in Ancient and Other Cultures* (Sather Classical Lectures, Volume 40). Berkeley: University of California Press, 1970.

Louden, Bruce. *The* Odyssey: *Structure, Narration, and Meaning.* Baltimore: The Johns Hopkins University Press, 1999.

ODYSSEY 9–12:

The Wanderings

READING TO WRITE

ONE OVERARCHING theme of the *Odyssey* is the struggle with or con-frontation of the *Iliad*. As we have already seen, this second epic represents an effort to overcome its predecessor, partly by suggesting that the ideal of heroism celebrated in the *Iliad* has outlived its useful-ness. On multiple occasions in the *Odyssey*, newcomers or their hosts pose some form of the question, "Are you civilized men who respect the gods, or are you pirates bringing pain?" Yet the Greek army in the *Iliad* endured ten years of warfare precisely by raiding the nearby towns until they managed to raid Troy itself. Cattle rustling was a celebrated occu-pation among the Bronze Age Indo-Europeans, for example in the Irish epic *Tain*, or "Cattle-Raid." A major difference between the expropriation of the household goods of the Cicones by Odysseus and the expropria-tion of Odysseus's household goods by the suitors is that Odysseus faced armed opponents and the risks of combat, whereas the suitors simply ate the king's animals while he was gone. Yet by this criterion, Odysseus's attack with the bow would make the suitors justified—yet they are not, and of course he kills them. In short, there is little rational justification for much of Odysseus's behavior in the *Odyssey*. In the *Iliad*, his actions were defined by the Greek war effort; in the *Odyssey*, he is simply an adventurer in pursuit of his own advantage, irrespective of the cost to those who help him or to those for whom he is responsible. One cannot even claim that coming home as soon as possible is his top priority, since he suggests to Alcinous that he would stay on at Scheria for another full year if it meant a greater quantity of parting gifts—and this happens after he has been to the underworld and learned of the sorrowful yearning for his return that afflicts his wife and his father. Another important theme in this as in other sections of Homer's *Odyssey* is excess, especially excessive consumption of wine.

TOPICS AND STRATEGIES

This section of the chapter will discuss various possible topics for essays and general approaches to those topics. Be aware that the material below is only a place to start from, not some kind of master key to the perfect essay. Use this material to prompt your own thinking. Every topic discussed here could encompass a wide variety of papers.

Themes

The desire for experience is one important theme of the *Odyssey;* another is the excessive desire for wine and food. This raises the question whether the desire for experience, too, can be excessive, as the Cyclops episode seems to suggest and as Dante asserted almost 2,000 years later in canto XXVI of the *Inferno.*

Sample Topics:

1. **Motive:** What motivates Odysseus?

One traditional answer is that Odysseus is motivated by a lust for life, a thirst for experience. Defenders of this view often point to the proem, with its thematic line "he knew the minds and towns of many men," as if that were also his primary goal (Dante takes this to be Odysseus's defining motive as he depicts him in *Inferno* canto XXVI). He does seem to have been motivated by sheer curiosity in his encounter with the Cyclops, and yet that episode quickly turns from a mission of exploration to an acquisitive raid for sheep and cheeses, and then into a disastrous bid for Iliadic warrior fame. One might also point to the first *nekuia* or "journey to the underworld" in *Odyssey* 11 as a mission of knowledge. He goes to consult Teiresias about how to get home, yet (as Ahl and Roisman point out in their book, *The* Odyssey *Re-Formed*) that piece of information ought to have been available directly from Circe, who knows the past and the future, so the point of going down anyhow might have been to learn from the experience. This episode, too, has an element of fame seeking: by making a *nekuia*, Odysseus joins the tiny group of heroes who have successfully done so, among them Heracles, whom he meets. His appearance as an archer suggests a comparison to Odysseus.

More importantly, the *nekuia* shows us the Iliadic heroes Agamemnon, Achilles, and Ajax reduced to insubstantial phantoms, while Odysseus still lives and breathes. Achilles explains that he would rather be alive as a dirt-poor sharecropper than reigning as king over all the dead. What does that suggest about Achilles' famous choice of a short life with heroic warrior fame instead of a long life without it? This passage of the *Odyssey* has often been read as a damning verdict on the Iliadic ideal of heroism. What happens next is that Odysseus spells out to Achilles the bloody slaughter perpetrated by Achilles' son Neoptolemus, whereupon Achilles goes away utterly delighted. Like his great opponent Hector in the *Iliad*, he bestows on his son the same heroic ideal that brought his own life to a tragic, early, and violent close. The wording of those lines seems to confer special emphasis on the large number of people Neoptolemus killed, which is perhaps surprising since he was also preeminent for the high rank of those he killed and captured. Among the many victims of Achilles' son, Odysseus mentions by name only Eurypylos, whereas tradition maintains (right down to Shakespeare's *Hamlet*, which tells the story using Neoptolemus's other name, Pyrrhus) that Neoptolemus killed the Trojan king Priam himself and carried off Hector's widow Andromache as his concubine (a story found in, for example, Euripides' drama *The Trojan Women*). The emphasis on quantity is striking, and it may suggest that the social cost of Iliadic heroism is too high. Again, all of this is narrated not by the Muse herself nor by Demodocus but by Odysseus.

2. Xenia ("hospitality"): Is Odysseus a good guest?

Among the Phaeacians, Odysseus is careful not to compete against Laodamas, the son of his host Alcinous, when the games are under way. He also eventually tells them his real name, as is proper for a guest. Still, he wheedles as much booty out of the Phaeacians as he can. He also accepts the offer of a convoy even after learning of the prophecy that one day Poseidon (the very god who he knows is angry with him) will destroy a Phaeacian ship and ring the whole place about with an isolating mountain in anger over their conveying "someone" over the sea. As Ahl and Roisman write, "The most terrifyingly consistent feature of Odysseus in the *Odyssey* is his ability to bring death and destruction, not life and new hope, upon everything he is associated with" (129).

As for the Cyclops, it was a strange or bold *xenia* for Odysseus and his men to enter the cave of their host before he got home (presumptuous, intrusive, hubristic behavior that suggests or mirrors that of the suitors) and begin eating his cheeses and sacrificing his animals, expecting to get a guest gift in addition to what they had already stolen. It is the savagery of the Cyclops's behavior—his brutal eating of three pairs of men, and his hubristic contempt for Zeus Xenias who presides over hospitality—that shocks us out of our awareness of this problem. Odysseus is more frank about the sheer imprudence of his confrontation with the Cyclops—it is the one time when his companions were right and he was wrong—but he is more interested in celebrating the cleverness with which he overcame Polyphemus than lamenting the foolishness (let alone the injustice) of his approach and of his disastrously boastful retreat. As if mirroring the Cyclops's hubris about Zeus near the beginning of the episode, Odysseus speaks hubristically of Poseidon near its end: "not even the Earthshaker will be able to heal your eye . . ."

3. **Excessive eating and drinking:** Is wine a weapon in the *Odyssey?*

Another way to think of hubris is as "asking for trouble." The Cyclops does this not only by drinking too much wine but by drinking it full strength. Elsewhere we are told that this wine was to be mixed in a ratio of one part wine to 20 parts water. We also learn from Odysseus where he got the wine. It was not stolen outright from the Cicones; rather, Odysseus was given it as a gift by Maro, a Ciconian priest of Apollo, as a gesture of appreciation for sparing his life. Yet the result was that Odysseus's men got drunk, ignored their commander's plea for an immediate departure, and stayed long enough to be seriously assaulted by the Cicones and their allies. Odysseus says he lost "six men per ship," which is a somewhat euphemistic way of saying that because he accepted the gift of the wine, seventy-two of his men were killed. The mistake certainly was not sparing the lives of Apollo's priest and his family—the plague in *Iliad* book I was surely a memorable lesson against threatening Apollo's priests and their families—but accepting the wine. Had he spared Maro and refused the wine, he would have been empty-handed with regard to that particular family (though there was plenty of livestock stolen from other Cicones), rather like Agamemnon after he had to return Chryses's daughter without any ransom; this could have been achieved without the harm that Agamemnon incurred in the form of the plague, and that Odysseus incurred in the form of the drunken crew and the counterattack. Odysseus then uses the wine as a weapon against the Cyclops, much as Maro had used it against him. Now he offends not Apollo but Poseidon.

4. **Drugs and pain:** What is their value for Homer?

So far we have seen drugs functioning almost exclusively as painkillers (the Greek-derived term is *analgesic*, which you may have seen on your aspirin bottle). There was Helen's powerful analgesic, so potent that under its influence you could witness the slaughter of your own family and not shed a tear. This bears comparison with Penelope's request that the bard Phemios stop singing the painful song about the Trojan War, which in turn raises the comparison between Telemachus's contrary request that he continue, and Odysseus's request to Demodocus that he sing a song of the Trojan War, which then brings him to tears. There was Circe's drug, also dropped into wine like Helen's, which played a role in the transformation of Odysseus's men into pigs (though her magic wand did the rest). Hermes provided Odysseus with a counterdrug, the root of Moly, whose flower is visible to men but whose dark root is familiar to the gods. Its action seems to be purely prophylactic and inhibitive; it doesn't do anything but prevent Circe's drugs and magic from working. Then there is the "white food" of the lotus, which caused those who ate it to forget all about their yearned-for homecoming. If drugs in the *Odyssey* are mainly used to prevent pain, evaluating them will require an evaluation of pain. There is much to suggest that the *Odyssey* bears a profoundly counterintuitive argument in favor of both pain and death as sources of meaning in human life.

Calypso, like the Phaeacians, dwells far from human society in a divine realm where labor and its attendant pains are unnecessary. Yet Odysseus rejects the opportunity to remain in each of those apparently blissful places, and he finds Calypso's company miserable (at least after an initial period of enjoyment). The Phaeacians themselves seem naïve about the world, cowardly about the Cyclopes, and effete in their customary entertainments. Nausicaa does not want any of her Phaeacian suitors and jumps at what she thinks might be the chance to wed someone from outside. Menelaus and Helen dwell in a palace of incomparable wealth, living at ease almost as the gods do, yet they are obviously unhappy, even on the day of a double wedding of their children. Menelaus learned from Proteus that he will not die in Argos, but will go to the Elysian plain for an afterlife of ease, yet this does little to cheer him. All this suggests that both death and pain are seen by Homer as valuable limits to mortal life, without which there is the risk of a jaded complacency. The gods experience occasional pain, as when Diomedes wounds Aphrodite in the *Iliad*, but they cannot die. Therefore they cannot sacrifice themselves for anything more valuable than their own lives, nor can they really choose among competing courses of action (one possible definition of free will), since there will always be time for them to pursue neglected alternatives in the future. When Demodocus sings the song of the adultery of Ares and Aphrodite, we hear of the pain of cuckolded Hephaestus, but the other gods simply laugh at the situation. By contrast, adultery among mortals leads to the Trojan War and the slaughter of thousands; the deaths of Agamemnon, Aigisthos, and Clytemnestra; and the wiping out of Penelope's hundred and eight suitors. Nothing seems to matter among the gods, except insofar as it intersects with the world of mortals, where resources and opportunities have a scarcity that makes them urgent and meaningful.

Character

As you assess Odysseus's character, remain aware that the account of his wanderings in books 9 through 12 is Odysseus's own. He is presenting himself and his conduct in the best light possible, and the major burden of that task is to account for how he became the only Greek commander to return from Troy without a single surviving companion. Alcinous explicitly asks Odysseus to tell him about the men under his command who died at Troy, and the hero simply avoids the question.

Sample Topics:

1. **Elpenor:** What is the significance of this character?

> Neither heroic in battle nor clever in scheming, Elpenor is a surprising figure in being one of the few named members of Odysseus's crew despite his limitations. Yet if Odysseus's rhetorical goal includes self-aggrandizement, as it seems to, then perhaps Elpenor is not such a strange choice for special mention: in comparison to him, Odysseus seems positively godlike. Elpenor may also be part of the effort to upstage or critique the *Iliad*, since he insists on a heroic funeral rather like the rites of Patroclus (albeit on a somewhat smaller scale), complete with burning and a burial mound. He did little to deserve such a tribute, yet Odysseus carries it out. While this

may raise Odysseus in our esteem, it also inflates the currency of such heroic rites, since we now have at least one instance in which they do not really correspond to the kind of heroism they claim to represent. Besides these, Elpenor has at least two other functions. First, his is the only accidental death in the poem, and it is caused by excessive drinking. So he is a figure of excess, the same failing that afflicts the men who eat Hyperion's cattle and who open Aeolus's bag of winds. As the least heroic of Odysseus's men, he has been compared (by Bruce Louden) to Leodes among the Suitors. Second, his death occurs just before the first journey to the underworld, and he is the first shade Odysseus encounters upon reaching it. Therefore Elpenor is the innermost ring in a ring composition that surrounds and encircles this episode.

2. **Nobody:** What is the signification of the dual manifestations and multiple connotations of the term in the *Odyssey?*

The ruse of Odysseus's name in the episode of the Cyclops is an area that demands at least a little familiarity with the Greek. First, note that there are two equivalent forms of "nobody" in the poem, *ou-tis* and *mê-tis,* where *ou* and *mê* are negations and *tis* means "somebody." You might think the occurrence of "nobody" in two different forms would defeat the effort to present it as a proper name, but somehow it doesn't; perhaps we can attribute this to the dimness of the Cyclops. The benefit of the *Mê-tis* variant, which arises for grammatical reasons, is that it forms a homophone with a word you have already seen: *mêtis* as cleverness, as in the common epithet *polymêtis Odysseus,* "Odysseus of the many devices." Since the ploy of the paradoxical anonymity in the Cyclops's cave is the consummate piece of *mêtis* in the entire poem—unassisted by any god, unlike many of Odysseus's other achievements—the whole episode amounts to a striking piece of *mêtis* on the part of the poet.

Look at the Cyclops's response to Odysseus's eventual self-disclosure. Polyphemus reveals his knowledge of a prophecy that one day he would be blinded by a person named Odysseus, but that he is surprised that it turned out to be someone so puny, a nonentity, "a Nobody." So the usage in that incident amounts to a third form of the name that is not one. An interesting issue for an essay is the interplay between fame (an Iliadic value) and anonymity (an Odyssean tactic). When he finally reveals his name to the Cyclops, the result is not only fame but a disastrous curse that would not have been possible otherwise. Among the Phaeacians, Odysseus delays the disclosure of his name as he did among the Cyclopes, but when he reveals it he claims "my fame reaches to heaven." The entire second half of the poem is about Odysseus's prudent, tactical delay in revealing his identity, having learned the lesson of Agamemnon's death. Perhaps the question is whether anonymity is just a new tactic for achieving fame at the right time, or a new value that replaces fame. Achilles in the underworld seems to have no use for his glory whatsoever—and yet he rejoices to learn that his son has achieved something similar.

3. Agamemnon: Explain Odysseus's depiction of his dead rival.

The descriptions of Agamemnon, Ajax, and Achilles are Odysseus's substitute for what his host Alcinous has actually requested, namely a description of Ithacan casualties in the Trojan War. The reason he cannot provide that is because, as far as we can tell, none of them died in the war and all of them died during the journey home, when prudent leadership would presumably have had a much better chance at saving them than during combat with the Trojan soldiers. But Agamemnon's own contingent was wiped out by Aigisthos and his men shortly after they returned to Mycenae, so Odysseus is not the only one who failed to keep his soldiers alive (although Agamemnon succeeded in getting his men to their homeland, whereas Odysseus did not). Agamemnon's description of the slaughter in his halls sounds somewhat like the eventual slaughter of the Suitors in the halls of Odysseus, so there is a contrast in Odysseus's favor: Agamemnon came home with a contingent of soldiers but was killed along with them, whereas Odysseus will come home alone and triumph over 108 young men.

Remember that Odysseus is telling all this to his Phaeacian hosts. Look at what he has Agamemnon say about him, and then look at the words he attributes to his own men during the Aeolus episode. He recounts what they supposedly said about him when he was asleep, which he could not have known.

4. Ajax: How does Odysseus present Ajax?

A paper on this topic should make reference to *Iliad* IX, since it is the other major Homeric depiction of the relations between Odysseus and Ajax. The famous contest over the arms of Achilles does not appear in the *Iliad* itself. In this passage Odysseus appears to apologize, but Ajax turns away and will not forgive him. Two points to note are Odysseus's sudden loss of interest, and his claim that when Ajax killed himself "there was no one to blame but Zeus." This means both that nobody blamed Ajax, and that nobody blamed Odysseus (whose victory drove Ajax to despair) or Athena (who judged the contest).

Philosophy and Ideas

Knowledge is important in the *Iliad*, in that Achilles learns too late of Patroclus's disobedience and death; Diomedes is gifted by Athena with the temporary ability to see through the disguises of the gods, a gift that could have saved the life of Hector. But in the *Odyssey* knowledge seems even more important because the range of problems that arise is so much broader than those of straightforward warfare.

Sample Topics:

1. Knowledge: What information does Odysseus withhold from his men?

Almost every time some of Odysseus's followers are killed, there is some crucial information that Odysseus already possessed, but chose to withhold from them. This is easy to miss, but once noticed, it is shocking enough to make one wonder (as the critics Ahl and Roisman do) whether the hero decided at some point that returning alone might be safer than returning with a contingent of followers as did Agamemnon. After all, he would have to account for their presence and their identities; they might be easily recognized; and he could hardly hope to keep them all silent as they dispersed to their various Ithacan homes. Agamemnon's example shows both that disguise is necessary, and that it is impossible in the company of a homecoming squadron. Consider, then, the episodes of Scylla and Charybdis, the Oxen of the Sun, and Aeolus, looking for information that the hero conceals from his men to their eventual detriment.

2. **Blindness:** Discuss the theme of blindness in the *Odyssey*, noting its relationship to concealment.

The term *concealment* is a clue that implies an interest in Calypso, whose name means "she who conceals." Where else in the *Odyssey* is there a form of concealment that also prevents the concealed from perceiving what lies outside? On Ogygia, Odysseus can neither see the world of "men and towns" nor be perceived by it; hence the remarks by Telemachus about how obscure Odysseus's image has become, "taken by the whirlwinds." But there is also the moment at the table of the Phaeacians when Odysseus "conceals" himself inside his cloak as he weeps over the Trojan War. Polyphemus is blinded by Odysseus, who then further conceals himself by hiding under the belly of the great black ram—which is reminiscent of his concealing himself *inside* the belly of that other beast, the Trojan Horse. You might contrast those two incidents with the transformation of some of Odysseus's men into animals on Circe's estate. Blindness, meanwhile, also pertains to Teiresias, whom Odysseus consults in book 11, and to Demodocus the bard. If you can coordinate the relationships among those figures, you will have the makings of a good paper. Bear in mind that blindness does not have to stand for the same thing in all cases; you might find a way to differentiate between a good blindness (that is compensated for in some meaningful way) and a bad (that represents mere uncompensated loss).

3. **Abandonment:** Examine *Odyssey* 11, lines 321–25. Why is there no mention of Theseus's abandonment of Ariadne?

To write an essay on such a narrow question will require some expansion. To do this, ask yourself what features of the passage at hand are shared by other, perhaps nearby, passages. Ariadne was famously abandoned by Theseus after she had showed him the way out of the Minotaur's labyrinth. Odysseus is doing the narrating at this point, and he leaves this out. Who might Odysseus be said to have abandoned, after receiving her help? Certainly Calypso, Circe, and Nausicaa fit this pattern. But it was his original family to which he was originally committed, and he left them all behind—though tradition says he went to the Trojan War involuntarily, under compulsion. Ariadne was killed by Artemis, while the hero's mother Anticleia says she was not killed by the arrows of Artemis but died from yearning for the absent Odysseus.

Form and Genre

As a student writing an essay about the *Odyssey,* you may be somewhat hampered by two possible gaps in your knowledge: not knowing Greek and not being familiar with the vast terrain of interlocking and competing stories that constitute Greek mythology. The first gap can be dealt with in part by reading literary criticism such as the books named in this book's bibliography, since those provide transliterations and definitions of key terms like *xenia* ("hospitality, guest-host relationship"), *mêtis* ("cleverness, deception, guile, technology, the practical arts"), and *biê* ("strength, force"). The second can be addressed in the same way, since many such books (for instance Jenny Strauss Clay, *The Wrath of Athena: Gods and Men in the* Odyssey) are rich in this kind of material. But the better and more ambitious solutions are of course learning ancient Greek, which you can do either at a local school or university or by attending an intensive summer program, such as the Latin-Greek Institute in New York City, and reading extensively in the literature of the ancient world.

The *Odyssey* is an epic poem, and its entire existence is situated in the shadow of its great predecessor, the *Iliad*. Both poems appear to draw upon an older, common stock of mythical traditions, and it is not always clear what is an innovation and what is an inheritance. Still, in the *Odyssey* we can detect a rich tension between the two poems, not only in their differing ideals of heroism as discussed above but also in the competition among their heroes.

1. **The songs of Demodocus:** What does the first song of Demodocus imply about the relationship between the *Odyssey* and the *Iliad?*

   To tackle this topic, notice that the song deals with a quarrel between "the best of the Achaeans." In the *Iliad*, of course, that quarrel is between Achilles and Agamemnon, not Achilles and Odysseus. How does this square with the rest of the performances of Demodocus? Are they, too, flattering to Odysseus, detracting to him, or both?

2. **Odysseus as narrator:** What does Odysseus's activity as narrator imply about the rest of the poem?

   As you address this question, bear in mind that it potentially presents two divergent courses to consider and pursue. On the one hand, the gaps and deceptions in the narration of Odysseus imply that the rest of the poem may be more reliable, since it is free of his machinations. On the other hand, there is the opposite implication, that if these distortions can arise in the part of the poem narrated by Odysseus, they may well arise in the part narrated directly by the Muse. Perhaps some direction can be inferred from the fact that most of the outlandish features of the poem, the monsters and magic, seem to occur when the narrator is Odysseus himself.

Language, Symbols, and Imagery

Even without appealing to the original Greek, it is possible to consider some of the features of Homeric symbolism. The Aeolus episode, for example, seems loaded with implications, though not necessarily integrated into the narrative.

Sample Topics:

1. **The Aeolus episode:** What is the symbolism contained in this sequence, and what is its significance?

The striking thing about the household of Aeolus is that it is both divine and incestuous. His six daughters are married to his six sons, and nobody seems to have a problem with this state of affairs. Recall that Zeus and his wife Hera are also siblings, and it becomes clear that incest is somehow acceptable for the gods, though (as the Oedipus story makes clear, both in the *Odyssey* and in Sophocles' famous play) incest is the most grievous mental health disaster for human beings. It has been suggested that the children of Aeolus are to be identified with the points of the compass and the winds to which they correspond, with each spouse blowing in the opposite direction of its partner.

2. **Caves:** What is their significance in the *Odyssey?*

The question of caves can be broadened to treat of enclosures in general, which can often be understood as womblike spaces (as was mentioned in the discussion of the Cave of the Nymphs on Ithaca, which Proclus took to be a symbolic womb). But it is equally important to note that wombs are deeply ambivalent places of both shelter and imprisonment, nurturance and erasure. The harbor of the Lystragonians is an enclosure that gives safety from the waves of the sea, but it proves to be the most disastrous location in the whole poem, costing Odysseus more men than any other encounter. His own ship was saved by remaining outside the harbor; that is, by resisting the temptation of easy shelter. This matches Odysseus's personal action in the landing at Scheria (the land of the Phaeacians), where he endures additional hours in the water rather than make an earlier landfall that might have killed him.

Caves seem to shelter those who are subhuman and those who are superhuman—gods like Calypso and the Ithacan nymphs, and monsters like Polyphemus—both of whom can be associated with the human past, but not the present. The womb, of course, can be associated with the past of the human individual.

Compare and Contrast Essays

When you write a comparative essay, make a list of similarities and differences but be sure to move beyond that list into an argument that gives it structure. That way, the paper will amount to an interpretive reading of the text and not just an unorganized heap of its basic elements. As you build your list, look for patterns and their implications.

Sample Topics:

1. **Compare the Phaeacians and the Cyclopes:** What is their relationship?

We are told that the Phaeacians used to be neighbors of the Cyclopes, but that under Alcinous's father Nausithous, they moved far away because the Cyclopes had been harassing them. This makes for some odd implications, because Odysseus tells his Phaeacian hosts that the Cyclopes have no ships. How were they able to harass their neighbors, whom they could not reach? Odysseus also describes a fertile island full of goats and edible plants, which the Phaeacians apparently failed to exploit (Homer may have lived during an era of Greek expansion and colonization, when such a find would have been highly prized). Instead they moved to a place of great isolation, even though they appear to be concerned with achieving fame among the broader human race. Is Odysseus emphasizing this to embarrass his hosts?

We are also told that Poseidon is the divine ancestor of both the Cyclopes and the Phaeacians. Both enjoy an endless supply of food crops without any agricultural labor except for the harvest. To both Polyphemus and the Phaeacians, Odysseus says that he has no ship; to the former he is lying, while to the latter he is telling the truth. The Cyclops is a horrible host who eats his guests (though they are very bad guests); the Phaeacians are middling hosts, since when Odysseus supplicates Arete she remains silent and Alcinous does nothing until prompted by someone else. The Phaeacians live isolated from other people, as Polyphemus lives (according to Odysseus at the outset of book 9) isolated from the other Cyclopes.

2. **Compare Calypso and Circe:** How are they similar, and how are they different?

To answer this question, begin from the basics and look closely at the text. Both of these characters are divine female powers with an erotic interest in Odysseus. He overcomes each of them with divine help; in both cases, the god who assists him is the male Hermes. It is generally a female god who assists Odysseus against the male god Poseidon; these include Calypso (who saves his life), Circe (who directs him), Ino/Leucothea (who saves him from drowning by providing her magic veil), and Athena (who helps him again and again, though not always). Note the position of Hermes' assistance within the two narratives of Calypso and Circe. As you examine the text, look for repetitions that might constitute ironic contrasts or similarities.

3. **Compare Teiresias and Proteus:** Both characters are sources of information. How is it derived from each?

To develop an essay on this topic, examine the similarities and differences between the episode in *Odyssey* 4 where Menelaus is advised by the goddess Eidotheia how to get information from Proteus, and the later episode in which Odysseus is advised by the goddess Circe how to get information from the shade of the dead Theban prophet Teiresias.

Bibliography for "*Odyssey* 9–12: The Wanderings"

Clay, Jenny Strauss. *The Wrath of Athena: Gods and Men in the* Odyssey. Princeton, NJ: Princeton UP, 1987.

Crotty, Kevin. *The Poetics of Supplication: Homer's* Iliad *and* Odyssey. Ithaca: Cornell UP, 1994.

Dimock, George. *The Unity of the* Odyssey. Ann Arbor: U of Michigan P, 1989.

ODYSSEY 13–15:

The Return to Ithaca

READING TO WRITE

A s YOU approach the task of writing about this section of the *Odyssey*, the topics may not jump out at you with the same vividness as they did in the books discussing Odysseus's wanderings. It is relatively easy to find something to say about the episode of the Cyclopes, with their primitive culture and their horrible behavior toward Odysseus, along with the contrast between them and their carefree relatives, the refined Phaeacians. While the present books of the poem are perhaps more challenging subjects for academic commentary, they are also intriguing in their own right, as they bring us out of the world of the fantastic and into that of human affairs, where our own problems lie.

Here is an excerpt in the old translation of Butcher and Lang:

"Of Ithaca have I heard tell, even in broad Crete, far over the seas; and now have I come hither myself with these my goods. And I left as much again to my children, when I turned outlaw for the slaying of the dear son of Idomeneus, Orsilochus, swift of foot, who in wide Crete was the swiftest of all men that live by bread. Now he would have despoiled me of all that booty of Troy, for the which I had endured pain of heart, in passing through the wars of men, and the grievous waves of the sea, for this cause that I would not do a favour to his father, and make me his squire in the land of the Trojans, but commanded other fellowship of mine own. So I smote him with a bronze-shod spear as he came home from the field, lying in ambush for him by the wayside, with one of my companions. And dark midnight held the heavens, and no man marked us, but privily I took his life away. Now after I had slain him with the sharp spear, straightway I went to a ship and besought the lordly Phoenicians, and gave them spoil to their hearts' desire. I charged them to take me on board, and land me at Pylos or at goodly Elis where the Epeans bear rule. Howbeit of a truth, the might of the wind drove them out of their course, sore against their will, nor did they willfully play me false. Thence we were driven wandering, and came hither by night. And with much ado we rowed onward into harbor, nor took we any thought of supper, though we stood sore in need thereof, but even as we were we stepped ashore and all lay down. Then over me there came sweet slumber in my weariness, but they took forth my goods from the hollow ship, and set them by me where I myself lay upon the sands. Then they went on board, and departed for the fair-lying land of Sidon; while as for me I was left stricken at heart."

So spake he and the goddess, grey-eyed Athene, smiled, and caressed him with her hand; and straightway she changed to the semblance of a woman, fair and tall, and skilled in splendid handiwork.

What does Odysseus achieve with this particular elaborate lie? He warns the young shepherd that he is a dangerous man, one who not only refused to be subservient to so great a personage as the king of Crete, but who also would not put up with being robbed. Not only did the legend-arily corrupt Phoenicians not dare to try stealing from him, but the last person who did so paid with his life—though he was both a king's son and a fast runner, as this young shepherd appears to be. He also estab-lishes that he fought at Troy (which happens to be true), adding to his prestige and his possible threat. There is a partial analogy between Odys-seus's situation now, washed up alone on an unrecognized Ithaca, and his situation at the beginning of book 5, washed up alone on that other beach where he met Nausicaa. Though he was more vulnerable there, being naked and half starved, here he is encumbered by a material wealth that gives him a new and different kind of vulnerability.

TOPICS AND STRATEGIES

This section of the chapter will discuss various possible topics for essays and general approaches to those topics. Be aware that the material below is only a place to start from, not some kind of master key to the perfect essay. Use this material to prompt your own thinking. Every topic discussed here could encompass a wide variety of papers.

Themes

Far more than the *Iliad*, the *Odyssey* is dominated by what are called "recognition scenes," in which one character first comes to understand, and then comes to acknowledge, the true identity of another character. Indeed, Aristotle observed that in a sense the entire *Odyssey* is one long recognition scene. His term for this kind of scene is *anagnorisis*, and it plays an important role not only in the analysis of Homer but also of Greek tragedy (on which Aristotle wrote the seminal work, the *Poetics*) and therefore of Shakespearean tragedy and comedy as well. Anagnorisis is especially important in the second half of the *Odyssey*, since Odysseus is in disguise and he reveals himself severally to many different persons at different times. As if to announce that theme, Homer begins the first half of the poem with a striking concentration of anagnorises packed closely together: the goddess Athena recognizes Odysseus despite his lie about his identity; Odysseus recognizes Athena when she reveals herself (a *theophany*); and Odysseus recognizes Ithaca when Athena both drops the transfiguring mist she had shed about the island and narrates a descriptive tour of the landmarks that convince the hero that he has really come home.

Sample Topics:

   1. Death and rebirth: How does book 13 symbolize Odysseus's death and rebirth?

> First, note that the whole episode of the Phaeacians has brought Odysseus from a deathlike sleep in the olive thicket as a naked and homeless beggar all the way up to the status of an honored guest of the queen, sent off with more treasure than he would have brought back from Troy. That was itself a sort of death, rebirth, and growth to social adulthood. Here the process begins again, but with important differences. Both are cases of landing on an unknown island and sleeping (like a corpse or a fetus), then working one's way up to full social

status. But the assistance of Athena was covert at Scheria, and here it quickly becomes overt. The band of difficult young men he faced there was just a few Phaeacian athletes, none of whom posed much of a threat; the Suitors are far worse. As you look for indications of the symbolic nature of Odysseus's sleep, note Homer's descriptions of it. You might also add a mention of the specifics surrounding Odysseus's first sleep inside his own palace, when Penelope tries to provide him with comfortable bedclothes and he insists on something more consistent with his beggar persona.

2. **Recognition and nonrecognition with Eumaeus:** What are the indications that Odysseus has already tried to reveal himself covertly to Eumaeus in books 14–18? What are the indications that Eumaeus already knows who he is?

Among your concerns for the writing of a paper on this issue would be the following: what inconsistencies arise in the accounts of himself that Odysseus gives within the hearing of Eumaeus? Does Odysseus say or noticeably assume anything about the swineherd that a truly alien stranger would not have known about? In what sense might it be in Eumaeus's best interest not to recognize Odysseus until later? Might he recognize him unconsciously but not consciously?

3. **Recognition between Athena and Odysseus:** What are the stages of this process?

First of all, note that this recognition does indeed happen in stages. Like the peculiarly gradual healing of the blind man by Jesus in chapter 8 of the book of Mark, this is a story of the clarification of a mortal's vision by the visit of a god. First Athena is in disguise, but so is the island itself. There is some cruel play in this, since it causes Odysseus considerable exasperation. Why does Athena do it?

Also, note that Athena is disguised as a young shepherd, "a feeder of sheep." There may or may not be any significance to this detail, but on Ithaca the cast of characters is to some degree defined by what kind of animal it is over which they preside. Penelope dreams herself the keeper of a great flock of fifty geese, the Suitors; Philoitios is the thoroughly loyal cowherd; Eumaeus, the ambivalent but generous swineherd; and Melanthius, the goatherd whose abuse of Odysseus results in a horrible mutilation and death.

Character

Odysseus reveals himself much more readily to people who have never met him than he does to his former intimates and acquaintances. The first to be told of his return is Telemachus, who never met him before. Neither had the cowherd, who gets more trust than the swineherd, who has entertained and hosted Odysseus and whom the hero knew for years. As you ask yourself why this might be, consider the inertia of the current social arrangements on the island and the uncertainty of the future. Consider also the implications for Odysseus's nature.

Sample Topics:

1. **Telemachus topic 1:** Why does he delay the process of letting Laertes know that he has himself come home from his expedition?

Here it will be necessary to look at the details of the passage and try to assess whether there is an element of callousness beyond what the circumstances require. Note also that on the spectrum of the human lifespan, Telemachus and his grandfather on opposite sides of Odysseus's position of mastery.

2. **Telemachus topic 2:** Why are the serving girls so afraid of Telemachus?

In the search for information on this subject, look also for indications about the poem's implicit approval or disapproval of the harsh side of Telemachus's character. Recall Odysseus's treatment of Thersites in the *Iliad.*

3. **Telemachus topic 3:** In keeping with these questions about the harsher aspects of Telemachus's character, ask yourself if there are any other implications in the poem that he might be more dangerous than he seems.

Notice that the poem explicitly singles out one of the Suitors (a particularly likeable one, at that) for death at "the hands and spear of Telemachus," a phrase that occurs long before it is fulfilled. Also, there is the presence of Theoclymenos, an age-mate of Telemachus who is a fugitive because he has killed one of his own relatives. Rather than turn from him in horror, or send him to some sort of authority (as does the young Euthyphro in Plato's dialogue of that name), Telemachus offers him friendship and protection. Look up the meaning of Penelope's name, and then consider the bird omen that Theoclymenos interprets for Telemachus. Add that to the Orestes analogy— the story of Agamemnon's famous son who killed his own mother because she had killed her husband Agamemnon— and you have a vague but real hint that there is hidden in the character of Telemachus a faint, Hamlet-like threat against his mother.

4. **Eumaeus:** Describe Eumaeus's response to the disguised Odysseus.

The key to this assignment is to pick up on the complexity of Eumaeus's behavior. It is easy to assume that his welcome of the wandering beggar represents total acceptance, since it contrasts so sharply with the sheer awfulness of the goatherd Melanthios, for example. But in reality Eumaeus is quite cagey and tentative in his handling of the stranger. Over the course of several books, he engages in an elaborate pattern of half-measures and underperformance, including the refusal to permanently lend him his cloak; advising him to leave; warning Penelope about him; reluctantly and haltingly carrying out Penelope's instructions, and so on. Trace these and other indications of Eumaeus's ambivalence, and speculate about why he is so cautious and difficult. As you write, remember to weigh Eumaeus's motives, which include not only affection for his master and perhaps some (repressed?) resentment of his long absence, but also fear of loss and hope of gain. Naturally, these affect the timing of Eumaeus's choices. A similar calculus of decision pertains to Penelope.

Philosophy and Ideas

You may be asked to write a paper about the ethical dimensions of Homer's *Odyssey*. Such assignments often make use of the term *theodicy*, coined by the German Enlightenment philosopher Leibniz as the title of a book he published in 1710. It is formed from two Greek words, *theos* for "god" and *dikê* for "justice," to denote the difficult mystery of divine justice and the origin of evil. Writing such a paper demands some familiarity with this term, so it is worth at least a moment's attention. For Leibniz as for most monotheists, the existence of evil in the world (whether moral evil in human conduct or natural evil in the form of disasters and disease) poses a vexing theological problem, so long as one is committed to the premises that there is only one god and that this god is both all-powerful and all-good. Unless the evil of undeserved suffering is somehow a mere illusion, then one of those commitments must yield—since an omnipotent god would be capable of preventing evil if he wanted to, and if he were also all-benevolent, he would want to. There are only a handful of solutions to the problem, and the most common solution is to suppose that evil is indeed an illusion that arises from the limits of human knowledge. If we could see God's grand design whole, runs this argument, we would understand that both moral evil and natural evil ultimately increase the opportunities for good to arise, in the forms of forgiveness, rescue, healing, restitution, justice, and so on. This whole edifice is (or was) an important part of the humanities curriculum, and it still rises to the fore whenever texts like the book of Job or *Paradise Lost* are taught. But the term *theodicy* can also be useful in treating the issue of divine justice in the polytheistic world of Homeric epic and Greek tragedy, despite the differences in its application.

Sample Topics:

1. **Theodicy:** Does the *Odyssey* have one overarching idea of the way divine justice operates in the cosmos? If not, how does it manage the tensions arising among competing ideas of that justice?

The place to start building a response to this writing assignment is *Odyssey* 1, line 32, where Zeus complains about the human tendency to blame the gods for everything. By contrast, says the king of the gods, human beings actually incur their own suffering "by their own recklessness." He gives the example of Aigisthos as the paradigm of self-imposed disaster, which is especially appropriate not only because Aigisthos violated the norms of marriage (with adultery), social structure (with regicide), and hospitality (by killing his host), but also because Hermes explicitly warned Aigisthos not to assassinate Agamemnon and not to woo his wife Clytemnestra. One essay-writing strategy would involve going through the poem gathering up such warnings and setting them in parallel in your argument, using interpreted omens, prophecies, and oracles.

Against these, if you are persuaded that the poem supports it, you can set up a competing theodicy based on the claim that the gods do not in fact administer any systematic justice. On this view, the gods are indeed in control of the cosmos (within the constraints of fate), but their administration is capricious and irrational. Having spelled out these two competing theodicies of the *Odyssey*, you can then speculate about the degree to which this results in a mere impasse or is somehow resolved by the outcome of the poem.

2. **Truth:** Assess the strange stories Odysseus told the credulous Phaeacians. What suggests that those stories were true, and what suggests they were not?

There are indications in the remarks of King Alcinous that he suspected Odysseus was lying, yet those same remarks can be interpreted in the opposite way by refusing to take them ironi-cally. An Odysseus who had to account for his total failure to "save . . . the homecoming of his companions" might well invent a story of Lystragonian giants who ate the men of eleven ships, fifty men per ship in one quick orgy of cannibalism. Yet when the hero is at home in disguise, trying to exercise self-mastery and refrain from punishing the disloyal servant girls too soon, he calls upon the memory of the Cyclops. Surely he would not do so if that memory were a mere fiction. If Odysseus never blinded Polyphemus, why was Poseidon angry with him? It seems there are reasons to credit even the wildest of Odysseus's stories, and yet the more reasonable ones about Crete are in fact lies. All of this fits quite well with the atmosphere of innuendo, caution, and indirection during the period of Odysseus's disguise, since it forces the people around him to conceal the degree to which they suspect him of being the returned Odysseus. Consider and explain the ways in which it is in the hero's interest to delay their recognition and their acknowledgement, and the ways in which it is in the interest of Penelope, Eumaeus, and others to delay the same. Notice that the beings who are outside all of this deception and equivocation are the gods, above the human community, and the dogs, beneath it.

3. *Moira:* What is Odysseus's "portion"?

Writing about a work in translation is very different from writing about a work written in your native language. You cannot exert the same degree of pressure on the author's word choices, since they are really those of a translator who does the best he or she can to let the semantic nuances of the origi-nal text shine through. That is why books such as this one provide you with certain key terms of the original language in an effort to better equip you to pick up on those nuances and make use of them. One such term is *moira*. Sometimes translated as "fate," its literal meaning is simply "portion." That means that it arises both in abstract contexts, where characters are thinking or speaking about a person's lot in life, and in concrete contexts, such as the apportionment of meat at a feast. In a paper about the distribution of meat as an expression of social status, you can discuss the excellent portions with which Odysseus is fed at Scheria by Alcinous, and in Ithaca by both Eumaeus and Telemachus; the metamorphosis of Odysseus's men at the hands of Circe (who turns them not into lions or wolves like their predecessors, but into swine, making Odysseus into a bit of a swineherd); and the cannibalism of the Cyclops and the Lystragonians. All of that dimly parallels the larger issue of *moira* as destined outcome of a person, arising from a combination of fate, the gods, and one's own conduct. Aigisthos, for example, is said to suffer "beyond fate" because he ignored the explicit warning of the gods. One's portion of good things becomes bad if it becomes excessive, as is clear from the behavior of the suitors. A comparable term is *aisa;* its meaning is similar to *moira* and it, too, is often personified (and therefore written with a capital letter) as a goddess of human outcomes. It occurs, for example, in line 101 of *Odyssey* 16 (a line sometimes omitted as spurious), when the disguised Odysseus speaks of his own homecoming and says "there is still a portion of hope." One could claim that the context of a shared meal in the hut provides an undertone of meat apportionment in the scene.

4. The self: Is Odysseus one person, many persons, or none?

Writing for this assignment involves looking beyond the obvious sense in which the hero is of course one person. The reason to do so is not merely to produce an essay but because Homer has a certain usefulness for life, which the poem advertises with its repeated emphases on the multiplicity of Odysseus's mind—Odysseus of many plans, many thoughts, many turns, many devices; all those epithets beginning with the prefix *poly*—and its famous trick of the name No-Man or Nobody in the Cyclops episode. The *Odyssey* is also a repository of wisdom about issues of identity and mortality. Though it may or may not be clear to you from experience, there is a sense in which the management of a self in history can be somewhat confusing and even overwhelming. Remember the moment in your childhood when you first realized that the only reason you lived in your neighborhood was that it was the place your parents happened to find jobs? Or when you discovered that you identify with your ethnicity or country of origin solely because of an accident of birth, which could just as easily have been otherwise? Perhaps, like Odysseus, you have been to war, where you acquired a soldier identity that became a difficult burden after the war itself had ended for you.

Look closely at the *anagnorisis* ("recognition scene") between Telemachus and Odysseus in the swineherd's hut. Note the phrase "no other Odysseus will come." Remember that this includes the beautiful young Odysseus of roughly Telemachus's own age for whom Penelope has been weeping all these years: he is never coming back. Note also that when Telemachus suspects Odysseus is not his mortal father but a god, the hero's reply is *Ou tis toi theos eimi:* "I am not any god, however" or "I am not any god to you." The point is that the line begins with the form of "Nobody" that Odysseus gave to the Cyclops for a name that is not one. One might even construe an undertone of yet another construction, "to you I am the god Nobody." That would aptly express the way Telemachus has revered for his entire life a father who was not really a person but a fantasy based on hearsay and longing. This is an admittedly rather labored interpretation, but its purpose is to remind you of the richness of the text. In Telemachus's response, there is a play on Odysseus's name, as if to draw the identity of his father back in close, even while the general sense of Telemachus's speech is pushing it away: "You surely are not my father Odysseus, but some god / Enchants me, so that I may groan even more in my grieving *[oduromenos]*. That participle *oduromenos* is a form of one of the verbs from which the name of Odysseus has been derived.

5. **Two proems?:** Examine the opening of the second half of the *Odyssey*, and look for ways that it echoes the opening of the first half. Why does Homer do this?

The first step is of course to compare the opening of book 1 to the opening of book 13. But the matter turns out to be a bit more subtle, because although the proem has a corresponding passage at the beginning of book 13, it is not at the very beginning; it starts around line 88. Go over the parallel passages point by point, and note their similarities and differences. Next, consider their placement and the fact that this second "proem" occurs in the middle of the epic. Since the second half resembles the *Iliad*, at least in its conclusion with the battle in the hall, this is a significant reinstatement of the themes of wisdom and endurance, rather than sheer strength. It also resembles the proem of the *Odyssey* and differs from that of the *Iliad* in its anonymity. The name of Achilles, complete with patronymic, occurs in the very first line of the earlier epic; the *Odyssey*, by contrast, does not name its hero until line 21. In these proemlike lines of book 13, we hear of *andra*, "a man," with the word in the same initial position that it held in the epic's opening line, "who had suffered much in his heart in the time before . . ."

Language, Symbols, and Imagery

An important element of language use in the second half of the *Odyssey* is truth and lying, since Odysseus will have to engage in extensive deceptions and subtle negotiations as he moves through his estate, testing his people and the Suitors. In his encounter with Eumaeus we see very elaborate verbal acrobatics aimed at feeling out the degree of loyalty he can expect from the swineherd.

Sample Topics:

1. **Odysseus's various accounts of himself:** How do the identity stories that Odysseus tells to Eumaeus differ from those he tells to Athena on the beach, or to the suitors? What are the implications of the differences?

In writing an essay in response to this question, the key is to look for ways Odysseus shapes his stories to accommodate the particular hearer to whom he is speaking. Look for discrepancies among Odysseus's various autobiographies that may have been heard and perhaps noticed by others. Eumaeus, for example, can be expected to have noted the differing accounts of himself that he gave in the swineherd's hut and in the hall with the Suitors. What might Eumaeus be thinking as a result?

2. **Similes:** Comment on the similes in this portion of the *Odyssey*.

When Odysseus is trying to sleep, he tosses and turns like a roasting sausage. Does this connect with the roasting goat stomachs full of blood and fat, which were the prizes for the fight with Iros? Does Iros resemble such a stomach? In his beggar disguise, Odysseus often reduces himself to "the belly."

3. **Thigh imagery:** Comment on the significance of Odysseus's thighs.

The thigh is the site of the scar by which Odysseus is recognized by Eurycleia, Philoitios, and Eumaeus. It is also the body part that makes the Suitors suddenly realize they have underestimated the stranger, as he squares off with Iros and hikes up his own garments. It has also been suggested that the way Odysseus strung his bow was by trapping it between his thighs and using those muscles, stronger than arms, to bend the bow so that he could string it with his free hands.

4. **Odysseus's name:** What is the significance of the name "Odysseus"?

We learn how Odysseus got his name in the story of the boar hunt on Mt. Parnassus, which is related by the Muse when the old servant Eurycleia is bathing the stranger and recognizes him by the scar on his thigh. Since the scar came from that long-ago hunting expedition, we are treated to the digression of this story as a way of deferring the release of tension that the recognition occasions. There are several different verbs, including but not limited to *odunai* and *odusasthai,* which have been associated with the name of Odysseus. What these verbs have in common are elements of both anger and pain, pointed both backward toward the self and outward toward others, both mortal and divine. Insofar as the meaning of the name is "divine wrath," we have a somewhat striking parallel to the *Iliad,* whose first word is *mênis,* a term for rage that is used almost exclusively to refer to the anger of the gods, with the famous exception of Achilles, the wrathful mortal who briefly transcends human limitations in his savage fury. For further associations between Odysseus and the boar (the animal that gives him his identity-enhancing scar), recall the helmet of Odysseus in the Doloneia of the *Iliad.*

The hero is given his name by his grandfather Autolycus, a devotee of the thief god Hermes, who stole the cattle of Apollo at the age of three—and who assists Odysseus himself on at least two separate occasions. The followers of Odysseus perish for a similar crime at Thrinacria, while Odysseus, the one whose ancestral legacy fits with divine cattle rustling, refrains. It is perhaps remarkable that Autolycus named the new baby Odysseus "because I have been angry at many people," since this Autolycus was a famous thief and liar; one would expect him to be at least equally mindful of other people's anger toward him. The "Wrath of Athena" against Odysseus is the controversial subject of a wonderful book of that title by Jenny Strauss Clay; the wrath of Poseidon against him is not controversial at all.

In his book *The Unity of the* Odyssey, George Dimock derives the hero's name from a verb meaning "to will pain toward." As you gather the applications of this meaning, consider the strangeness of its selection for the central hero of Homeric epic. If Odysseus is "the man of wrath," how can he be so in the shadow of Achilles, whose wrath was so much more elemental, transcendent, and heroic? And how is it that Odysseus's other salient characteristics are cleverness and restraint, neither of which goes especially well with the heroic form of anger?

Compare and Contrast Essays
Sample Topics:

1. **Odysseus and the Cyclops versus Odysseus in the rest of the poem:** Compare Odysseus's behavior in the Cyclops episode with his behavior in the second half of the poem.

When Athena makes it clear to Odysseus that he has in fact returned to Ithaca, his response seems to show the same self-restraint and impulse control he showed in the cave of Polyphemus, when the temptation was to kill the Cyclops but the solution was to blind him instead. Had he killed his savage host, he would have remained trapped inside the cave by the immovable door stone. Here in Ithaca, the situation is almost opposite and yet it calls for the same inner disposition: impulse control, temporary repression of identity, and well-timed violence. Odysseus has the serving women shut the palace doors, just as the Cyclops had sealed off his cave. Odysseus was unambiguously the guest of Polyphemus, and not his host, yet *xenia* was disabled, by Odysseus's thieving and by the Cyclops's savagery. In Ithaca Odysseus is both guest (as wandering beggar) and host (since in reality it is his house), but *xenia* is just as absent since the Suitors are bad guests and Odysseus, like the Cyclops, kills his visitors.

2. **The *Odyssey* and the Bible:** Compare the theodicy of the *Odyssey* with that of the Bible.

You have probably noticed that in the *Odyssey*, characters sometimes expect or at least pray for principled behavior from the gods, especially Zeus, whereas at other times they strive to accept the evident lack of such behavior. Indeed, expressions of yearning for divine justice tend to be articulated in the grammar of the "optative" mood, used for wishes, while expressions of exasperation or acceptance in response to divine caprice

are generally in the indicative mood, used for factual statements. Is there such a dual theodicy in the Bible, as well? In
your search for biblical material that will speak to this issue,
consider the God of Genesis and Exodus, who makes explicit
contracts with his people. Now consider the God in the book
of Job, or in Genesis chapter 21, where he "tests" the obedience
of Abraham with the mental torture of a command to kill his
beloved only son, Isaac.

3. **Religion in the *Odyssey* and in Plato's *Euthyphro*:** Compare
   the religious outlook of the *Odyssey* with that of Plato's *Euthyphro*. Does Homer's poem stand up to Socrates' challenge?
   Might a better defense of Homeric religion be made than the
   one put forward by the young man named Euthyphro?

   To pursue this topic, your first step is of course to read the
   brief Platonic dialogue to which it refers. In the meantime,
   the heart of the matter is a pair of rather striking points that
   appear in it, points probably made by Socrates himself since
   Plato wrote this dialogue fairly early in his career. First, people are being naïve when they define justice as "the will of the
   gods," since different gods want different things. In the *Odyssey*, this is most clear in the tension between Athena and Poseidon (though that is not an example given in the *Euthyphro*).
   Second, even if we put aside this issue of conflict among the
   various gods, there remains another, even thornier problem,
   which Socrates poses in the form of a question that strikes
   like a thunderbolt: "Is the Holy holy because the gods love
   it, or do the gods love it because it is holy?" Here the word
   "Holy" stands for piety as well as sacredness. The question is
   an either/or. Must it be so?

   If you read it as an either/or, you inherit a key element of
   what historians and classicists call the Socratic enlightenment: each alternative presents an unsettling problem. If the
   holy (for example, the entire range of practices and attitudes
   that a culture regards as pious, especially "right conduct") is
   only holy because the gods love it, then it has no inherent holi-

ness of its own; if the gods happen to love or choose or command something repugnant (such as human sacrifice), human
beings would have no choice but to obey and to try to share
the gods' opinion. On the other hand, if the reason the gods
love what they love is because it does indeed possess its own
intrinsic holiness, then why do we need the gods? Why not
simply engage in right conduct for its own sake, bypassing the
supernatural altogether? Are the gods simply lords of force
and compulsion, mere bullies like the Cyclops? Read the brief
dialogue by Plato in the light of Homeric epic in general and
the *Odyssey* in particular, and try to come up with arguments
in defense of Olympian religion. You might also benefit from
reading *Greek Religion* by Walter Burkert (Wiley, 1991) and
*Did the Greeks Believe in Their Myths?: An Essay on the Consti-
tutive Imagination* by Paul Veyne (Oxford UP, 1988).

Bibliography for "*Odyssey* 13–15: The Return to Ithaca"

Allen, R.E. (trans). *The Dialogues of Plato, Volume 1: Euthyphro, Apology, Crito,
Meno, Gorgias, Menexenus.* New Haven: Yale University Press, 1985.

Burkert, Walter. *Greek Religion.* Hoboken: Wiley, 1991.

Clay, Jenny Strauss. *The Wrath of Athena: Gods and Men in The* Odyssey. Princeton, NJ: Princeton UP, 1987.

Dimock, George. *The Unity of the* Odyssey. Ann Arbor: U of Michigan P, 1989.

Veyne, Paul. *Did the Greeks Believe in Their Myths?: An Essay on the Constitutive
Imagination.* Oxford: Oxford UP, 1988.

ODYSSEY 16–24:

The Final Books

READING TO WRITE

THE CLOSING books of the *Odyssey* rival the pivotal "wanderings" (books 9–11) in their intrinsic interest, since they contain the climax and denouement of the entire epic. Readers of Virgil will recall that the *Aeneid* contains a wandering half, followed by an Iliadic half full of combat; this is loosely modeled on the way Homer's *Odyssey* contains a brief burst of war poetry toward its conclusion. There are, however, several distinctly un-Iliadic aspects of the fighting in Odysseus's palace. For one thing, the conflict pits four men against 108, a perversely uneven fight; and yet, these four are aided by the goddess Athena, while the suitors, for all their manpower, are unarmed for the majority of the fight and quite defenseless. They are also drunk and taken by surprise; they do not expect to be attacked at all, nor do they expect Odysseus to return, nor Telemachus to be suddenly brave enough and strong enough to resist them. The suitors, and perhaps other people as well, seem surprised by Penelope's contest of the bow. Some readers have supposed that she and Odysseus planned it together, since otherwise it is hard to see how he would have managed to carry out his revenge against so many, yet there is no clear indication of such advance collaboration in the poem. On the other hand, it is readily plausible that Penelope has recognized the identity of the disguised beggar and is proposing just this particular contest in order to hand the victory to her husband. The idea comes from Athena, who can be seen as an independent divine agent as well as an aspect of

212

the mind of Penelope, who has overheard the remarks in the hall that immediately precede her proposal.

Here is a passage from the beginning of *Odyssey* 21, in the Victorian translation of 1900 by Samuel Butler. Note that Butler uses the Roman name Minerva for the goddess Athena and the Latin form of Odysseus's name, which is "Ulysses."

> Minerva now put it in Penelope's mind to make the suitors try their skill with the bow and with the iron axes, in contest among themselves, as a means of bringing about their destruction. She went upstairs and got the store-room key, which was made of bronze and had a handle of ivory; she then went with her maidens into the store-room at the end of the house, where her husband's treasures of gold, bronze, and wrought iron were kept, and where was also his bow, and the quiver full of deadly arrows that had been given him by a friend whom he had met in Lacedaemon— Iphitus the son of Eurytus.

The passage continues, about 15 lines later:

> This bow, then, given him by Iphitus, had not been taken with him by Ulysses when he sailed for Troy; he had used it so long as he had been at home, but had left it behind as having been a keepsake from a valued friend.

Look closely at the first sentence, with its phrase "a means of bringing about their destruction." If the contest is to be only among the suitors themselves, how is it to lead to their destruction? Could it be that the destructive part is Athena's intention, while Penelope actually intends to choose a husband based on an archery competition? It seems unlikely, and yet we have heard Penelope describe a dream in which she was sad because an eagle, the returning Odysseus, came and slaughtered all of the domesticated geese that Penelope referred to as her own and that she associated with the suitors.

That dream was interpreted by Odysseus twice, since he did so first inside the dream (a rare instance of a dream that comes with its own interpreter) and then from outside, as the disguised beggar. Penelope's response is that some dreams come from a gate of ivory and are false, while others come from a gate of horn and are true. This simple dichotomy contrasts with the complex layering of truth and deception that characterizes Odysseus, Penelope, and Athena, not to mention the Homeric Muse herself. Here at the beginning of *Odyssey* 21, we learn that the handle of the key to the storeroom is made of ivory, a detail that might have no significance or that might suggest that the storeroom has hitherto been a place of old imaginings locked away, like the private fantasy world of Penelope's dreams and longings. It contains the bow of Odysseus's, which, like Penelope, was left behind when he went to Troy and has not been touched by him since. However, like the gate from which true dreams issue, including Penelope's dream of the slaughtered suitors/geese, the bow itself is made partly of horn. If the figure of the dual gates can be extended further, we might even suppose that since horn represents the truth, Odysseus in his physical strength is uniquely able to bend the bow of horn just as Odysseus in his cleverness is uniquely able to bend the truth.

TOPICS AND STRATEGIES

This section of the chapter presents various possible topics for essays and general approaches to those topics. Be aware that the suggested topics represent points of departure, not some kind of master key to the perfect essay. Use this material to prompt your own thinking. Every topic discussed here could encompass a wide variety of papers.

Themes

Key themes in the closing sections of Homer's *Odyssey* include interpersonal recognition, disguise and deception, adaptation and improvisation, divine justice, revenge, hospitality and its violation, marriage, identity, and violence. In other words, Homer is engaged in a sustained exploration of the fundamental concerns of his society throughout this epic poem, and the climax (together with its strange aftermath) brings these issues into focus in beautiful and terrifying ways. In Shakespeare's *Hamlet,* the young hero has a painful epiphany when he discovers that "one may smile, and smile, and be a villain"—that is, people who appear to be good can turn out to be secretly evil. In the

Odyssey, it is the protagonist and not the villain who is the figure of disguise, and the appalling discovery is not disguise but its opposite, a comfortable naiveté: the suitors can smile and smile and be utterly doomed. Their slaughter is scary precisely because they failed to heed the prophecies, omens, and outright warnings that they would be killed if they persisted in their easy indulgence of appetite and grandiose fantasy. While Odysseus was out in the world, learning to accept his humanity and mortality through suffering and seeking, they were at his home, indoors and at ease, living without effort like the gods (or like their favorites, the Phaeacians, whose life of ease is also eventually stopped). One of the gods' oft-repeated and defining characteristics is that they live "at ease." As George Dimock has emphasized, the Suitors' central flaw is their contempt for the reality of their position. Already in the *Iliad,* Homer sang the potential horrors of the delusions that mislead us, as in Agamemnon's captivity to Atê, the goddess of mental blindness and "ruin," and in Achilles' similar captivity to his own smoldering anger. Dolon thought he would carry off the horses of Achilles; Hector thought Apollo was Deiphobos; Pandaros thought he would win glory by breaking the truce. Here in the later poem, person after person has been told some prophecy of a man named Odysseus who will eventually arrive and cause pain, but none of them recognizes that the new arrival is he. Which is more frightening: the monsters like Scylla (gigantic and bizarre man eaters), which nobody has ever seen, or the disastrous experience of the 108 suitors, whose all too familiar complacency destroys them? Remember that "one barrel of oil provides the latent energy of up to 25,000 hours of human labor, or 12.5 years working 40 hour weeks." Our consumerist culture is itself based on a fantasy of inexhaustible abundance and ease, like the ambrosia of Olympus, the groves of the Phaeacians, or the household of Odysseus viewed from the perspective of the freeloading suitors. Their demise is a fable for our times.

Sample Topics:

1. **Change of purpose:** How does Odysseus deploy the technique of adapting to difficulty by using things for purposes different from their apparent purpose?

This assignment is unusually general, so you have the freedom to range over the whole poem looking for examples. Then the task will be to link them all and sift out some sort of claim about Odysseus's character. The most important tool in the poem is Odysseus's bow, which was formerly used for hunting and which he did *not* bring to Troy for use as a weapon of war. He tells the Phaeacians that he was an excellent archer at Troy, though we never see him shoot an arrow in the *Iliad*—worse, he claims that only Philoctetes was a better archer. That, too, was probably a lie, since it makes no exception for Teukros, the greatest of Greek archers at Troy (and who, in turn, was bested in the archery contest in *Iliad* XXIII by Meriones, also unmentioned here). Penelope turns the hunting bow into an instrument for the contest of the suitors, but as soon as Odysseus has fulfilled that use of the bow, he makes it into the homicidal weapon it had not yet been for him. In Polyphemus's cave, Odysseus converts the post into a lance; in his shipwreck, he converts the mast into a floatation device; in building his bed, he converts the olive tree into a bedpost still rooted in the earth; the Trojan Horse appears to be a religious offering but is in fact a sort of personnel carrier; and so on. Look at the prophecy of Teiresias for another striking example of an object whose purpose changes.

2. **Revenge:** Is the death of the Suitors really necessary?

Pursuing this topic requires attention to several different areas. First, there are the terms of the marriage contest. Does Penelope consent to marry the beggar if he prevails, or does she refuse that possibility in advance, and what effect does that have on the situation? Then there are the remarks of Agamemnon in the first and second underworld scenes, where the poet seems to be working to convince the audience that the suitors richly deserve their slaughter. Consider Odysseus's warning to Amphinomus, the failed supplication of Leodes, and the successful supplication of the bard Phemios. Another approach would be to compare the excessive feasting and hubris of the suitors with that of Odysseus's men, who are condemned by the Muse in the proem ("they died by their own recklessness, children and fools") and ultimately cornered by the gods and inadequately (if at all) protected by Odysseus. Enraging the hundred noble families of Ithaca, Same, and Doulichion makes the job of Odysseus's restored kingship much harder, and it only becomes possible because of Athena's intervention. But what might the job of renewed kingship have been like if Odysseus had permitted the Suitors to disperse, instead of killing them all?

3. **Recognition:** Why does Odysseus test Laertes?

This portion of the *Odyssey* presents a difficult puzzle, since there is no threat present that might provide an obvious rationale for Odysseus's disguise. Nor can the point be simply to find out whether Laertes still loves his son and actively grieves for him, since the old man's living situation and his demeanor are enough to show how he feels. What is going on here? Is Odysseus being sadistic? If so, what might be the origin of that trait? Is he using the lie and the disguise to manage his own otherwise overwhelming feelings at the reunion? If so, why does he insult his father before revealing himself? Autolycus the famous thief, liar, and oath-breaker is the grandfather of Odysseus, the one who named him (as we have seen, derivations of the name include the meanings "man of pain" and "divine wrath"). To which side of the hero's family does he belong: the mother's or the father's?

Character

Sample Topics:

1. **Penelope:** Describe the pattern of power struggle between Penelope and the disguised Odysseus.

As you gather material for this essay, pay attention to the way the characters address one another. "Zeus-born son of Laertes, resourceful Odysseus" has a much different set of associations than does "strange man." Similarly, it is one thing to call

Penelope the "wife of Odysseus," another to address her as the "mother of Telemachus." To support that claim, you might turn to book 5 and take note of Calypso's shift of tone once the departure of Odysseus has changed from a worrisome possibility in her mind to an inevitable reality. What does she call him beforehand, and what after?

2. **Eumaeus:** When does the allegiance of the swineherd shift decisively toward Odysseus, and why?

Eumaeus is cautious almost to the end and throws his lot in with the hero only when it becomes clear to him that he has more to gain and less to lose by doing so than by hanging back any longer. Proving that will require attention to the subtle ways in which he disobeys instructions or reinterprets them, makes promises he does not keep, sends out cues of recognition and doubt, and bargains for the personal gains to which he feels entitled.

3. **Iros:** What is the significance of the fight with the beggar Iros?

When writing on this subject, points to consider include the way the fight changes the Suitors' perceptions of the beggar; Odysseus's decision about whether to kill Iros with one blow or merely knock him out; the possible ironic echo of the moment in the *Iliad* where Odysseus is isolated and has to choose whether to stay and fight against a multitude or try to retreat; and the parallel with the Phaeacian situation where hostile words were exchanged instead of blows, with the similar result that Odysseus grew in status.

Philosophy and Ideas

Sample Topics:

1. **Marriage and *homophrosune*:** Compare the marriage of Odysseus and Penelope to the ideal of *homophrosune* ("like-mind-

edness"), which Odysseus described to Nausicaa as the ideal quality of marriage.

Like any question about marriage, this one calls for a balance between the real and the ideal. The "like-mindedness" that Odysseus praises both is and is not what he and Penelope seem to have on their hands. They are both clever schemers, both masters of manipulation, delay, and improvisation, but in what ways does this similarity separate them rather than unite them? Recall that Odysseus's speech about ideal marriage is spoken in a distant magic kingdom where the palace is guarded by living metal dogs; the crops grow all year round without cultivation; and the ships steer themselves by reading the thoughts of the passengers. From such a position it is easy to praise marriage and envision its perfections, since the real tasks of an enduring relationship lie utterly elsewhere, in Ithaca.

2. **Responsibility:** Does Odysseus manipulate the suitors into treating him even more badly than they might have otherwise done? In John Milton's epic poem, *Paradise Lost,* God goes to some trouble in order to "render man inexcusable" so that he can be sure Adam and Eve deserve the punishment he has in store for them. Might there be a hint of that dynamic here in the *Odyssey?*

Writing this essay requires going over the interactions of Odysseus with the Suitors in the final books of the *Odyssey* and seeking out the hero's subtle provocations of his competitors. You might also compare this to Odysseus's dealings with the other two parallel bands of boisterous young men, the Phaeacian athletes and his own Ithacan soldiers journeying home from Troy.

3. **Time:** The action of the *Odyssey* spans some 40 consecutive days, yet its narrative covers the 10 years of Odysseus's return

from the Trojan War. What are the implicit ideas about time in this epic, and how do they differ from or resemble those in the *Iliad?*

Writing this essay will require a broad knowledge of the poem to address a broad idea. One place to look for insights about Homeric notions of time and humanity's temporal situation is in the scenes where stories are being told internal to the poem, such as Eumaeus's hut and the hall of the Phaeacian king Alcinous. The "endless nights" there resemble the boundlessness of time in the episode of the Sirens, where there is nothing but memory of the past, and of the Lotus Eaters, where there is nothing but the oblivion of a narcotized present. Consider Calypso, too, since she offered a liberation from time while also consuming the largest quantity of Odysseus's limited lifespan—seven years, almost as long as the decade of the Trojan War itself.

Form and Genre

Sample Topics:

1. **Structure and authenticity:** Some scholars reject the final book of the *Odyssey* as a late addition to an older poem. What evidence can you gather in support of this hypothesis? What evidence challenges the scholars' contention?

Without access to the original, much of the significance of this question and the means of addressing it remain out of reach. Yet it is not an uncommon question. So, unless you receive such a writing assignment in a course offered by a classics department, your professor is asking you to use the English translation of the poem to search for the sort of clues that can be seen there. Ask yourself about the style of the 24th book, and the kind of world order it suggests. Here, Athena pacifies the grieving and furious relatives of the slain Suitors in a kind of psychic magic comparable to mass hypnosis. Is this the same Athena we knew in the earlier books? If she has become a different kind of goddess, does that necessarily mean that there is a different poet at work in this tale of sudden reconciliation? Next, consider what the poem would be like if it were to end at an earlier point, such as the close of book 23. Does such a truncated *Odyssey* seem more "Homeric," somehow more homogeneous in tone or worldview? What aspects of the poem change when you remove book 24? With the "Second Nekuia," we are reminded that the suitors still exist though their lives are over with. The omission of book 24 would remove that reminder though the Homeric idea of the afterlife established in book 11 would remain. What is the effect of exhibiting the dead shades of the defeated Suitors?

2. **Pacing:** Describe the way Homer speeds up or slows down the flow of the poem at those points where he believes a change of pace will optimize the effect on the audience.

Assignments like this one focus on the craft of the poet, and because you are likely reading the poem in translation it will not be possible to cite examples from the words themselves (doing so involves a branch of literary criticism called "prosody"). A famous line in Milton's *Paradise Lost* shows technical mastery in slowing down: "with sweet reluctant amorous delay . . ." If you were reading that line in translation rather than in the English original, you might miss the subtle sensuality of the word "reluctant" as it activates the tongue, but you would still be able to notice the "delay" caused by the piling up of those three adjectives before we finally get the noun at the end. Word order in Greek is often quite different from that of even the best English translations, but you can still see Homer's handling of the poem's changing speed in the way he introduces digressions; stops to dwell on a particular image, simile, or situation; or sums up a long process by various techniques of compression. For example, there are 108 Suitors, but how many of them are we actually shown trying to string the bow?

Language, Symbols, and Imagery

Sample Topics:

1. **Language:** "There is a land called Crete." Describe the "Cretan tales" Odysseus tells while in disguise. What effect do they create for the character and for the poem?

The strongest theme to consider, in pursuing this topic, is probably the artful manner in which Homer conflates truth and lies, the facts of the Muse and the fictions of Odysseus. By blending and layering truth and falsehood, the poet is able to compromise the boundary between them and bring people to a greater acceptance of the limits of human knowledge. Again and again, there are ironic exchanges between truth and falsehood: Eumaeus believes all of Odysseus's lies but disbelieves the truth he tells in swearing that Odysseus will return. Even that is a kind of conflation: since Odysseus is already home, it isn't quite true to say that he will return very soon.

This question asks about the false stories Odysseus tells in the poem's second half as he fabricates an alternative identity as part of his disguise. There are three such tales, told respectively to Athena in her disguise as a young shepherd, to Eumaeus in his hut, and to Penelope. All involve some connection to Idomeneus, the Cretan king whose two outstanding characteristics are his age—gray haired and older than all other heroes fighting at Troy except for Nestor, yet still able to execute an *aristeia* (a surge of destructive force) in battle— and his feat of returning home without losing a single soldier. Both of these characteristics are, of course, relevant to Odysseus's homecoming; time of life is relevant because he is no longer the young hunter his people remember, and because his disguise makes him even older than he has really become. There is an obvious contrast between Idomeneus's success at "striving to save . . . the homecoming of his companions" and Odysseus's utter failure to do so.

As you prepare to write on the Cretan tales, note the language in which they are articulated. When Odysseus tells Penelope his story, he speaks as if she has never heard of the gigantic and famous island of Crete. Is it likely that she is so ignorant? Look for the evidence that she probably knows plenty about the place, and then ask yourself what this might imply about Odysseus's tone in the exchange. If he is being sarcastic, to what sarcasm of hers might he be responding? Is he emphasizing a contrast between her homebound loyalty and the travels of faithless Helen?

2. **Bird imagery:** Make a survey of bird imagery in the *Odyssey* and speculate about the way Homer uses this class of animals to make the world intelligible.

Several kinds of animal are loaded with significance in the Homeric poems, but birds are especially important because they have a "mantic" function; that is, their flight is one of the ways people derived what they regarded as divine knowledge of human affairs. This business of divination by the interpreting of bird flight is technically known as *ornithomancy.* Birds (presumably buzzards and vultures) also eat the corpses of men who lack friends capable of burying or burning them before the birds can defile them. As a start, use a concordance or a search engine to look for occurrences of the goose, the swallow, the eagle, and the vulture. What characteristics of each bird make it suitable for the purposes to which it is put by the poet?

3. **Ship imagery:** What is a ship, and what is not? Consider the transformations and the similes by which Homer both invokes and explores the idea of the ship.

Ships are important to the Homeric audience, who saw the waning of the dark ages and the reemergence of seafaring, trade, and colonization; the fantasy of the Phaeacians is a testament to this passion. But ships were also dear to the earlier Bronze Age people whom the poem claims to represent; indeed, it now appears that the Achaeans, especially Agamemnon's Mycenaeans, may have been among the population known as "the Sea Peoples" who attacked Egypt in the 12th century B.C. The Trojan War itself was a decade of siege warfare on land, yet it began with a huge nautical expedition and ended with the sea voyage home. During the decade of fighting, the Greeks dwelt "by the ships," whose enormous hulks were a looming silent presence that at one point became the scene of the fighting, including the striking image of Ajax on board a beached ship fighting off the Trojans with a giant pike designed for fighting at sea. He was on a ship on land instead of water, plying a pike instead of an oar, going nowhere fast. In the *Odyssey*, ships are emblematic of both human ingenuity and human helplessness before the wrath of the elemental god Poseidon. What object or objects begin as ships (or other nautical paraphernalia) and turn into something else, either literally or metaphorically? What begins as something else and becomes a ship?

Compare and Contrast Essays

Sample Topic:

1. **The journeys to the Underworld:** Compare the first *nekuia* ("journey to the underworld") with the second.

Writing this essay requires attention to the figure of Agamemnon, and the way he is made to confront the Suitors. Like him, they were killed in a house with their minds not on battle but on domestic pleasures of food and wine. But in their role as wooers of a hero's wedded wife, they correspond not to Agamemnon but to his killer, the hubristic Aigisthos. You might also note the repetition of the praise of Penelope and the different effect it has this time around, since we have seen her pass the tests Odysseus has set her.

Bibliography and Online Resources for "*Odyssey* 16–24: The Final Books"

Dimock, George. *The Unity of the Odyssey.* Ann Arbor: U of Michigan P, 1989.

Hagens, Nate. "A Closer Look at Oil Futures." September 4, 2006. http://www.theoildrum.com/story/2006/9/2/171333/1102

Scott, John A. "Dogs in Homer." *The Classical Weekly*, vol. 41, no. 15 (May 3, 1948), pp. 226–28.

INDEX